FRANCIS THOMPSON

BY PAUL VAN K. THOMSON

Why I Am a Catholic

FRANCIS THOMPSON

From a painting by John Lavalle in the Boston College Library

FRANCIS THOMPSON

A CRITICAL BIOGRAPHY

BY

Paul van Kuykendall Thomson

THOMAS NELSON & SONS

Edinburgh   **NEW YORK**   *Toronto*

Nihil Obstat:

> Rev. John F. Cox, Ph.D.
> Censor Librorum

Imprimatur:

> ✠ Russell J. McVinney, D.D., LL.D.
> Bishop of Providence
> Providence, February 2, 1961

Library of Congress Catalog Card Number: 61-7864

MANUFACTURED IN THE UNITED STATES OF AMERICA

To

Terence L. Connolly, S.J.
Priest, Scholar, and Honored Friend

PREFACE

Had he written nothing else but "The Hound of Heaven" and "The Kingdom of God," Francis Joseph Thompson (1859-1907) would probably still be the most well known representative of the late Victorian revival of creative literary activity among English Catholics. The appeal of these two poems has been universal. Just a few years ago the phrase "many-splendoured thing," which is taken from "The Kingdom of God," appeared as part of the title of a popular novel that was made into a film, and millions who had never heard of Francis Thompson were either singing or listening to a melodious, if somewhat insipid, tin-pan alley production called "Love Is a Many-Splendored Thing." But "The Kingdom of God" continues to be read for itself, and it shows every sign of surviving long after the novel, the film, and the sentimental ballad have been forgotten. As for "The Hound of Heaven," it has its enthusiastic admirers all over the world and is known in an astonishing variety of translations and various separate English editions.

The world in which Thompson lived and died ended with the First World War, and the very word *Victorian* became a synonym for *old-fashioned*. Yet our age, which has been so much changed in its outlook by the immense accomplishments of the science of physics, is but the day after yesterday to the

Victorian world, which was itself so altered by the discoveries of biology and geology, as well as by those of an earlier physics and chemistry. If in our own time Communism is a marching giant, in 1848 it already had become significant enough for the authors of *The Communist Manifesto* to write, with some measure of accuracy: "A spectre is haunting Europe—the spectre of Communism."

Much that torments and confuses us, as well as a great deal which gives us reason to have hope for the future, was coming to birth during the last half of the nineteenth century, when the England of Francis Thompson was the financial, industrial, and imperial leader of the world. Many thoughtful men then felt, with Matthew Arnold, that they were indeed between two worlds: one dead, the other—which is our world—struggling to be born.

Those whose lives moved into the 1860's often felt themselves to be moving into a decade of disturbing change, and they were no less concerned with the pace of unpredictable, fundamental transition than we. Beneath much of the apparent smugness and complacency of late Victorian life there was a deep undercurrent of doubt and a sense of grave uncertainty. By the last decade of the century, which was the period of Thompson's greatest poetic productivity, many read the portentous signs of the coming of world conflict, and the widespread revival of religious activity in England—not only among Catholics but also among Anglicans and other Protestants—was in part an evidence of an alarmed search for an island of assurance in the rising sea of troubled events and amazing discoveries.

Thompson, as his life abundantly demonstrates, had more than enough personal difficulties with which to contend, but they were in some respects not only the general difficulties of the times but also the particular problems which any artist faces in finding his place and function in the modern world. Much of what he wrote bears the indelible mark of his own era; much of it looks back to the earlier Romantics and beyond them to the metaphysical poets of the seventeenth century. But both in his poetry and in his criticism one also has glimpses of techniques and ideas which are contemporary with our own days.

As many a critic of Victorian society saw, the wealth of England's industry, like her vast political power, tended to move in the direction of polarization. There was a concentration of abundance at one end of the social scale. Thompson, during most of his adult life, lived, for a variety of reasons, where scarcity was the rule. When he died, he left almost no material possessions, but in his room there were disorderly piles of manuscripts and notebooks, which Wilfrid Meynell, his friend, guardian, and literary executor, retrieved.

These literally constituted the poet's entire estate, and they provide invaluable sources for the study of his mind and work. They also pose a number of problems. Some of the material is written in ink in a firm, clear copybook hand. However, much of it was jotted down in pencil and is quite obscure. Moreover, the systematic care which a professional librarian might have given to the conglomerate collection was largely lacking while it remained in Meynell's possession. This, coupled with his generous habit of giving bits and pieces away to visitors who had admired Thompson's poetry, did nothing to improve the initial disorder.

During the years since 1907, Thompson's notebooks and manuscripts have been somewhat dispersed, but the greater part of them is now in the Thompson-Patmore Collection of the library of Boston College. There they have been carefully catalogued and handsomely housed. My own study of these materials lies back of this brief attempt to present at least some of the many aspects of the life and mind of Francis Thompson. None of my work would have been possible without the generous help and encouragement of the Rev. Terence L. Connolly, S.J., who as librarian, scholar, and curator of the Thompson-Patmore Collection has made it the outstanding instrument of research which it has become.

I am therefore deeply grateful to Father Connolly, as well as to his able assistant, Miss Martha Dubay for her always gracious and willing help in obtaining the materials which I needed. My grateful appreciation must likewise go to many others: the Very Rev. Kevin Harrison, O.F.M., Cap., for allowing me to study and photograph the manuscript of Thompson's essay "In Darkest England"; to Professors George Kumler Anderson and Charles Horace Philbrick, II of Brown University, for the invaluable guidance which they have given to me; and to the Very Rev. Robert J. Slavin, O.P., President of Providence College, for his encouragement and support. Without the help of my wife in the preparation of the manuscript, this book would never have reached the publishers. I can only say that I am as thankful to her as I am to Francis Thompson for all that he has taught me of the nature of poetry and its enduring worth to modern men.

Paul van K. Thomson
Providence College

CONTENTS

FRANCIS THOMPSON

CHAPTER ONE

MARIONETTE THEATRE

I

Thomas De Quincey died in 1859, the year that Francis Thompson was born. Reading his *The Confessions of an English Opium-Eater* twenty years later, Thompson was to recognize in its author a fellow explorer of the vagrant world of dreams. With the spirit of that romantic wanderer who had known Wordsworth, Lamb, and Coleridge, he would feel a compulsive sympathy, and he was to retrace much of De Quincey's tortured way through the libraries, the streets, and the lower depths of Manchester and London. In time he would have his full share of knowledge of the drug which, as De Quincey characteristically described it, "buildest upon the bosom of darkness, out of the fantastic imagery of the brain, cities and temples, beyond the art of Phidias and Praxiteles."

Like De Quincey, too, Thompson was to show a remarkable lack of concern for dates and hours. He has been quoted as saying that he could never recall the precise year of his birth, and it seems appropriate that there should be a slight confusion about the exact day. Everard Meynell, in a biography that was first published in 1913, says that Thompson was born on December 16, 1859. That is also the date which appears on a bronze plaque that was placed to the right of the entrance of his birthplace at 7 Winckley Street in Preston, Lancashire. This plaque, which was erected by public subscription in 1926, contradicts the inscription on a worn stone tablet that was put over the door in 1910:

FRANCIS JOSEPH THOMPSON
WAS BORN IN THIS HOUSE
DEC. 18, 1859.

Nearly a mile away is the Jesuit church of St. Ignatius, where Thompson was taken by his godparents, Joseph and Mary Brown, to be baptized before he was a week old. Father Terence L. Connolly, S.J., a devoted and scholarly authority, reports that the baptismal record is in agreement with the stone tablet and concludes that December 18th is presumably correct. Some doubt as to the accuracy of the church record is, however, suggested by the fact that the entry not only misspells Thompson's name as Thomson but also gives his mother's maiden name as Moreton when it was actually Morton.[1]

In an article published in May, 1890, Thompson mentioned the way in which the intellectual and literary life of Victorian Catholicism was enriched when "the great flood of the Oxford Movement burst its Anglican banks" and brought with it such men as Newman, Frederick Faber, and Aubrey de Vere.[2] Elsewhere, speaking of the so-called Catholic literary revival, he said, "All of us who write are indirectly the children of the Oxford Movement."[3] In his own case, this was the literal truth, for his mother, Mary Turner Morton, and his father, Dr. Charles Thompson, had both rebelled against the Establishment and fallen in love with Catholicism before they met and fell in love with each other.

A preoccupation with religious questions surrounded the life of the undistinguished house on Winckley Street. The plain brick building, with its three narrow stories and its flat roof, presented a face of shut-in anonymity to the world—as did the other houses in the row of which it was a part. But within burned strange new fires of an old faith. In 1859 Darwin published his *On the Origin of Species,* and Meredith set the English novel on a new psychological quest with *The Ordeal of Richard Feverel.* Both of these events, occurring in the year of his birth, were to have their future influences upon Thompson's world and work, but his mind was first fed with the fruits of the romantic generations that had immediately preceded him—and above all with the religious romanticism of the Tractarians and those who had, in a sense, rejected the accepted values of the present in favor of an older tradition.

Lancashire, a northwest maritime county that faces the Irish Sea, had, like the other counties of the north of England, some lingering memories of an earlier period of resistance to the Reformation, but the industrial city of Manchester, where Thompson's mother was born in 1822, had little about it to recall the far-distant Catholic past. Her father, Joseph Morton, at first a bank clerk and later the manager of the Manchester Assurance Co., seems to have shared the general middle-class distaste for Roman Catholicism. Consequently, when Mary Morton decided to adopt that religion in 1854, she was alienated from her family. Like the conscientious Protestant parent described by Newman in a lecture in 1851, Joseph Morton might well have written to his daughter:

> There is just one thing I cannot stand, and that is Popery; and this is the very thing you have gone and taken up. You have exercised your right of personal judgement; I do not quarrel with you for this; you are old enough to judge for yourself; but I too have sacred duties, which are the unavoidable result of your conduct.... My affection for you is as strong as ever it was, but you have placed yourself under influences hostile to your father's roof and your own home, and you must take the consequences.[4]

Mary Morton took the consequences. At first she responded to that revival of interest in the religious life which had already been displayed by some of the Tractarians within the established church. She became a novice in the Catholic community of the Sisters of the Holy Child Jesus, but she found that she did not have such a vocation and remained only a short time. It is possible that her health may have had something to do with this decision. There was a history of early deaths in her family and her own constitution was not robust.

In any case, she took the position of a governess with a family near Manchester, after the manner of so many heroines of the novels of the age. There were, in fact, few other opportunities for respectable employment open to a young woman of her background.

Before she had become a Catholic she had been engaged to the son of a Chelsea family that had been sympathetic to her interest in the Church. But her fiancé had died and it appeared that she would never marry. When, however, she met Dr. Charles Thompson, who was a young house surgeon in the Homeopathic Dispensary in Manchester, their mutual devotion to Catholicism formed the basis for a friendship, and the attraction they felt for one another developed into a love that led to their marriage in 1857.

Charles Thompson's whole family had become involved in the currents of religious change associated with the Oxford Movement and the growing number of prominent converts to Rome. His father was Robert Thompson of Oakham, Rutland, but the family lived for a time in Bath. Of the nine children born to Robert Thompson and his wife, eight lived to adulthood. Of these, five eventually became converts to Catholicism, together with their parents. Two of Charles's brothers were clergymen in the Church of England. One of them, the Reverend Henry Thompson, was educated at Magdalen Hall,

Oxford, and appears to have remained content with the Anglican Church, which he served at Kirk Hammerton and in Greatham. The other clerical brother, Edward Healy Thompson, having served for a time as a curate, left the Establishment and became a Catholic layman. Charles's sisters, Anne and Charlotte, not only became Catholics but nuns as well, and his brother John, who was employed by the Bank of England, also was converted to Catholicism.

Both John and Edward Thompson seem to have had some interest in creative writing, but they displayed little talent for it. Edward, who wrote some articles and a number of sonnets of very poor quality, later denounced Francis Thompson's "Dream Tryst" as "erotic poetry" and had little sympathy for his nephew's devotion to literature. John Thompson managed to produce a rather dreary little volume called *Vision of Liberty and Other Poems,* which quickly earned a richly deserved obscurity. As for Dr. Charles Thompson himself, the poet told Wilfrid Blunt in August, 1907, that neither of his parents had much understanding or appreciation of "literary things."

Thompson's parents were never really settled in Preston, where his father had begun private practice; in the course of seven years there they had four different addresses. But it was in Preston that their children were born. The first was a son, who lived only a day. Francis, the second child, was born when his mother was thirty-seven, but she also bore three daughters: Mary, who was usually called Polly, born in 1861; Helen Mary, who was born in 1862 and lived only two years; and Margaret, known to the family as Maggie, born in 1864.

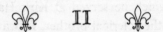

The family life became more settled when the Thompsons moved to Ashton-under-Lyne, a suburb of Manchester, in 1864. There, at 226 Stamford Street in another plain, red brick house with a flat roof, Francis Thompson lived his strange boyhood years. As converts to Catholicism, his parents were, in that period, virtually cut off from all social contacts with families of their own class and background. Young Francis virtually had no playmates other than his sisters. In Preston, which in medieval times was called Prestune—the priests' town—the family had made the acquaintance of Father John Carroll, who had charge of the chapel of St. Peter in Stalybridge. He was to be a lifelong friend and a figure of some prominence in Catholic circles, for he was finally made Bishop of Shrewsbury in 1893. He and other priests of the district were almost the only social callers at the house on Stamford Street.

Another close friend was Canon George Richardson, the parish priest of St. Mary's Church, Wellington Road, in Ashton-under-Lyne. His brother was to marry Francis Thompson's sister Margaret, and Dr. Thompson, seven years after his wife's death, was to marry Canon Richardson's sister Anne.

These events, and Mary's becoming Mother Austin of the Religious of the Presentation, lay far in the future as Francis Thompson played at cricket with his little sisters on the church grounds of the mission at Stalybridge or sat curled up with a book in a corner of the staircase at home. His passion for cricket, like his passion for poetry, began early and never left him. Frail, slope-shouldered, sometimes hesitating in his walk, Francis Thompson's delicately featured face and gentle voice would fill with sheer delight when he spoke of the great names of English poetry or the scores and stars of his country's national game. Tales of battle also stirred his frail being when he was a child, and to the last days of his life he never lost his enthusiasm for military adventure and the martial pomp of the Empire, under whose Queen-Empress he was a subject.

It was, of course, evident from the beginning that he would never win glory on the cricket field or become a dashing figure in a crack British regiment. But he dreamed of these things often, just as he re-enacted in his imagination the daring episodes of the novels of Scott, which he loved, or wept with intense pleasure over the magic beauty of the poetry of Shakespeare, whose plays he began to make a part of himself when he was no more than seven or eight years old.

Shy, silent, often playing quietly alone in a world that was isolated from the common experience of other children, Francis Thompson early experienced real anguish in the act of trying to communicate with those around him. Years later, in the prose manuscript called *Out of the House of Bondage*, he was to write:

> To impart themselves, to be understood—that is the final travail of all men; except some noble few who would yet more gladly receive and understand. To attain both is the most soaring of human ambitions: to attain either the most seldom-compassed of human experiences. The very means by which we prepare its fulfilment prepare the frustration. We move, all of us, under disguises, the rending of which would leave life intolerable, the presence of which makes life a doubt.

Frequently as a child he felt that he never wanted to grow up and assume the freedom and the responsibility of an adult world. When he was five, his parents took him for an excursion to Colwyn Bay on the Irish Sea. The family often went there during his childhood, as well as to such places as Holyhead and New Brighton. And he felt delight and security at such times, with the little isolated family group on the beach, where he and his sisters wrote cricket scores in the sand or watched the play of light on the crest of the waves at sundown.

In his poetry, as in his notebooks and essays, he often speaks of childhood with a romantic glow that recalls Wordsworth's pictures of it. Yet, perhaps influenced by his later personal tragedy, he also condemned the idea that childhood is the happiest time of life and spoke of its fears and cruelties. Most significant is the passage in one of the many notebooks that were found among his papers after his death, in which he says that there is both terror and desolation in the child's first realization that one can lose one's mother, and a sense of utter helplessness in being for the first time without her. His attachment to his mother was profound, and it seems quite probable that even as a small child he did experience real terror and a sense of tragedy to come whenever she was not near him, just as he felt happy and secure in her presence.

Until he was eleven, Francis Thompson knew nothing of the world of schoolboys. Except for two months during which he attended the school of the Sisters of The Cross and Passion in preparation for his first Holy Communion, he was educated privately at home. He was allowed to read almost at will such of his father's books as interested him, as well as many of the books from the local public library. He dwelt upon Coleridge's "Rime of the Ancient Mariner" and "Christabel"; he continued to plow zestfully through the Waverley novels; and the ballads of Macaulay set his feet to marching. He read, too, in the library of Father Carroll, and it seems that he probably expected to become a priest from the time that he began to think about his future as an adult.

Knowing how great an attachment he had for his mother, one can imagine that this pious woman, who had sought a religious vocation for herself, often hoped that it might be fulfilled in her son and strongly influenced him in that direction. Moreover, apart from his father, there were no educated men in the orbit of his experience as a child other than priests. His imagination, on the other hand, was peopled with chivalric figures out of the novels of Scott, and his nerves tingled to Macaulay's imagined trumpets.

He often combined military and religious images in his inner vision of his own future, and whispered his dreams to the marionettes and the dolls, which as he later wrote, he managed to wring from his sisters "by eloquence and fine diplomacy."

In an essay on dolls called "The Fourth Order of Humanity" Thompson said, with something of the wistful humor that marks some of his prose: "In the beginning of things came man, sequent to him woman; on woman followed the child, and on the child the doll. It is a climax of development; and the crown of these is the doll." [5] He never felt any of "the youthful male's contempt for these short-lived parasites of the nursery," and he recalled how as a boy he had fallen in love with a doll. She was crowned with fairness, and he "bowed before the fourteen inches of her skirt," seeing in her a heroine out of Shakespeare. And in her company he was content.

He was content, too, when he could baffle his sisters with simple tricks of magic or entertain them with a little marionette theatre whose tiny actors played out the creations of his imagination and answered the directions of his will as he made them perform a scene from *Julius Caesar* or some other Shakespearean play. Everard Meynell, in fact, notes that when Thompson died there was found among his few belongings a cardboard marionette theatre which had provided him with "amusement and occupation till the end of his life."

III

If Coleridge, Shakespeare, Macaulay, and Scott furnished the favorite reading and the food for his boyish imagination, it was nonetheless with Shelley that Francis Thompson probably identified himself in reacting to his first real contact with the world of school, far from those who had loved and protected him in the safe confines of his own family.

Father John Carroll had studied for the priesthood at the College of St. Cuthbert, or Ushaw College, near Durham, and it was there that Francis Thompson was sent when he was eleven. Beginning the fall term in September, 1870, he remained at Ushaw for seven years.

Readers of Thompson's well-known essay on Shelley [6] may well find in the description of the persecution which "overclouded" Shelley's schooldays some of Thompson's own remembrance of that "petty malignant annoyance recurring hour by hour, day by day, month by month," which is "the most terrible weapon that boys have against their fellow boy." Certainly the timid eleven-year-old—who was, according to an eyewitness, teased and frightened by other boys on his first trip to Ushaw, while a bag of jam tarts got crushed in his pocket—must have been very unhappy. And Everard Meynell quotes a passage from one of the notebooks, which, when all allowances have been made for possible morbid exaggeration, must present something of the truth of Thompson's early school experience:

> Fresh from my tender home, and my circle of just-judging friends, these malignant school-mates who danced round me with mocking evil distortion of laughter . . . were to me devilish apparitions of a hate now first known.

... And as such they live in my memory, testimonies to
the murky aboriginal demon in man.[7]

Yet, Ushaw was not dedicated to the rough, hearty spirit
that supposedly marked the Victorian public schoolboy destined to serve the causes of the Empire. Many among its students and faculty would have relished the following description
of the hearty Anglo-Saxon type which appears in Thompson's
Commonplace Book, now in the Boston College Library:

> Your Englishman takes off his coat and goes into a dis-
> cussion (in print) head down; shoves, scuffles, kicks,
> rolls under ... and scrambles out, with a cheerful confi-
> dence ... that he has "had a go for it" and held his own.
> Vain to point out that he was never near the ball. That is
> a matter he cannot understand and cares nothing for ...
> and he is ready to renew battle with all comers accord-
> ingly.

Of course, Ushaw did not always provide him with the privacy he longed for. Nor did he find there the kind of friendship which he might have discovered in Henry Patmore, the
son of the poet and essayist, a fellow Ushaw boy who displayed
a love for poetry as intense as his own. But the evidence of his
school contemporaries gives strong support to the idea that a
parallel between Thompson's years at Ushaw and Shelley's
time at Eton is hardly accurate.

His classmate, Father Adam Wilkinson, for example, recalled that "Tommy" was well liked, a good handball player,
and known for his shy good humor. If he was sometimes sur-
prised by a cricket ball coming at him, he nonetheless loved
typical schoolboy adventures and organized a small band of
"pirates" who had a secret hiding place in an old wall. He was
known, too, for his love of history and stories of battles, as
well as for his skill at rhetoric. He wrote speeches for the
school debating group, but he was too shy to read them and

asked others to do it for him. Like many another of his age, he loved to compose satirical portraits of his classmates and teachers.

Ushaw was founded and developed in the classical Catholic tradition of those English scholars and students who had lived and worked at Douai, exiled by the religious revolt of the sixteenth century. Redolent with the memories of the Catholic martyrs of Tudor times, it was especially marked by a deep devotion to the Virgin Mary. During his years there, Thompson walked with his fellow students in the daily procession in her honor that was a feature of the school's devotional life during the month of May. And kneeling before the white statue of Our Lady of Ushaw he joined with the others, from young boys to venerable priests, in the singing of the *Magnificat*. In this ceremony, as in his daily participation in the Liturgy, Thompson's imagination received impressions that were stored in his memory and shaped the imagery of his greatest poetry.

In the Early English Gothic buildings of the junior house or seminary at Ushaw, Thompson followed the four-year course that led him to a three-year college program of "high figures, grammar, and syntax." He was trained in the full tradition of Christian humanism and taught to compose poetry both in Greek and in Latin. French was the modern foreign language, and he did well in it, but for mathematics his fervent imagination had no taste and he early displayed his inability to approach problems with the method of science.

Even as a schoolboy he felt a distrust for the analytical treatment of man and the universe. To him it seemed to be like nothing so much as the hopeless activity of a tiny creature working around the periphery of a spider's web, and becoming increasingly lost in the hopeless task of trying to unravel it, thread by thread.

In the library at Ushaw he found something far more to his liking—an excellent collection of the poets of the seventeenth century; and he would exclaim over Crashaw or Donne with the most intense feeling of excitement. With his exquisite ear alert to every suggestion of sound and accent, he would read poetry as it must and should be read—aloud. Sometimes, stirred by his reading, he would lose his silence and his shyness and, standing in a favorite spot before a great open hearth, he would talk in such a flood of words that it seemed nothing could stop him.

He had a fondness not only for reading aloud but for copying down passages of poetry that especially moved him with their beauty or their power. His own juvenile creations in his *Ushaw College Notebook* and his *Notebook of Early Poems* show that what seems to have fascinated him in his first love for poetry was the scope which it gave to his restless imagination—his inner marionette theatre—as well as its peculiar power to give vividness and a sense of immediacy to otherwise vague, transitory sensations and emotions.

These youthful works often remind one of Thompson's own, quite inaccurate, description of Keats as a poet possessed of the "roaming luxuriant sweetness of a child's fancy"—a child "who had broken into the store-closet of literary preserves." [8] In many instances the tone is as sentimental as the imagery is luxuriant, and typical is a poem called "Child Faerie," which gives a highly colored picture of a "fay-maiden," who may well have come out of *A Midsummer Night's Dream,* as she falls asleep in the blossom of a golden king cup.[9] Sometimes, too, it is possible to mark the influence of Coleridge, as in the fragment called "Amore," [10] where the theme of the demon lover is evoked. The following passage is typical:

> So she came at length, white-stoled and sapphire-sashed,
> To a violet dell of moonlight water-washed;

To a moonlight dell of violet, sole-sequestered as an islet,
To a tranced dell of violet, water-washed.

At school it was thought that Francis Thompson would quite possibly be a poet of some excellence, and there were many who thought that he would also be a priest. The medal of the Virgin which he had worn from early boyhood, and was to wear at his death, was more than a token of formal religious practice; it was, beyond doubt, the symbol of a deep interior faith that was nourished, sustained, and matured by the chapel devotions at which "Tommy" was regular and faithful during his Ushaw years. As he knelt before the Host upraised in the service of Benediction and sang the great hymns written so long before by St. Thomas Aquinas, Thompson surely envisioned himself often as one standing before the altar vested for Mass.

Yet something of the spiritual problems of "The Hound of Heaven" and "To the Dead Cardinal of Westminster" must have come into being at Ushaw. A great master of the Catholic spiritual life, as well as a qualified psychiatrist, Dom Thomas Moore, remarks that what he calls Thompson's "shut-up type of reaction"—his deep, continuous introversion—gives evidence of a schizophrenic tendency in him. This, Dom Moore suggests, could well have arisen from an early conflict in Thompson's mind between the pleasures of the imagination and the demands of his conscience, his parents, and his environment generally.[11]

In the *Ushaw College Notebook* there is a prose fragment of boyish composition called "Low Figures," which exemplifies this very condition. Written when he was about fourteen and presented in a highly imitative style that recalls the "Gothic" atmosphere of a tale by Edgar Allan Poe, "Low Figures" describes a nobleman who is permitted to see certain important scenes of his life reproduced in a magic mirror. He watches himself learning his prayers from his mother, again he sees himself, as a child of ten, rejected as a weakling by his father when he asks to be permitted to join in a hunting party. Finally, he sees a scene which is so terrible that he cannot describe it.

In his interior world Thompson may be said to have had a marionette theatre—or a magic mirror—in which the figure of his mother was always the symbol of a secure place of retreat and his own role was that of one rejected by a virile world of male responsibility to such a degree that he was overwhelmed by a horrifying feeling of inadequacy and a deep sense of guilty failure to be all that was expected of him.

It is certain that his confessor concluded that it would be best for Francis Thompson if he did not go on to the priesthood, and it is clear from the letter which announced his dismissal that in spite of his obedience and his excellence in many of his studies, the authorities at Ushaw found in 1877 that "nervous timidity" and "a natural indolence" gave sufficient evidence for them to conclude that it was not "the holy will of God" that he should be a priest.

Silent, and apparently indifferent to his future, Francis Thompson came home. Having approached the sanctuary with that awkward, sometimes distracted, way of walking which was to carry him far away to the streets of Manchester and London, he had been rejected.

 IV

Manchester was as ugly as Ushaw had been beautiful. For the wide, open country and the lovely college campus, Thompson exchanged the cluttered streets, the grimy buildings of the great textile mills, and the dreary corridors of Owens College, where he went, passively and without complaint, to study medicine.

Having completed the entrance examinations successfully in July, 1877, he was duly enrolled as a medical student in the college which later became a part of Manchester University. He was probably the most unlikely candidate for a medical degree ever to enter there, but he left his mark in a way that more competent students could not, and the presence of the poet was memorialized years later by a stone tablet, carved on the walls of one of the corridors by no less an artist than Eric Gill.

It seems quite clear from what he later told Wilfrid Blunt that Thompson was in no sense placed in the position of having to agree to a stern paternal insistence that, having failed to become a priest, he should follow Dr. Thompson's professional example. On the contrary, it appears to have been his mother's wish that since her son could not serve at the altar of God, he should choose "the next best thing" and serve God's afflicted creatures. Closing the world out, turning more completely inward, he accepted this idea with the same docility that his teachers at Ushaw had observed and praised. All the horror he felt for the very sight of wounds and blood, all the dislike he had for the scientific dissection of both man and the universe, all his compulsion to create beauty and to seek the one in the many—he never revealed to his family.

Yet, Thompson was never an antiscientific obscurantist. It is true that in his ode "The Nineteenth Century" he remarked that the world had "crowned" science "beyond its due." But in the same poem he praised the work of Sir Humphrey Davy, the chemist, and the great Michael Faraday, who formulated the laws of electrolysis. He likewise paid tribute to the advance of biology in the following passage:

> And theirs the greatest gift, who drew to light
> By their sciential might,
> The secret ladder, wherethrough all things climb
> Upward from the primeval slime.
> Nor less we praise
> Him that with burnished tube betrays
> The multitudinous diminutive
> Recessed in virtual night
> Below the surface-seas of sight. (ll. 82-90)

As several commentators on his poetry have remarked, Thompson's poetic diction is sometimes colored by the scientific idiom one might expect to find in the work of one who was once a medical student. Moreover, in his notebooks there are entries which show that he had a certain scientific curiosity. In *The Large Commonplace Book,* for example, he noted that the scales of a butterfly are inserted by rudimentary points, which leave tiny holes, "like pin-rows," when they drop out. In the same notebook there are notes on biological mutation and on the theory of the evolution of the equilateral triangle from a point. Elsewhere, he refers to the study of the powers of perception in animals and notes that red rays of sunlight are said to be the only effective ones in plant assimilation. Among his private papers there are, in addition, a number of notes on the causes of such natural phenomena as waterspouts, cloudbursts, the terrigenous deposits left by icebergs, and the coming of cyclones.

He did, of course, rebel against what seemed to him to be the exclusive materialism of much nineteenth-century science, just as he rebelled against the complacent, brutal, unimaginative commercialism of the age. Manchester, the city to which he travelled by train each day during his years as a medical student, was a perfect example of the products of this Philistinism. Many times in his pathetic journeys there he must have

thought the same question he asked in an article on Bliss Car-
man in 1904: "We are minded to ask, is there freedom for
thinker and artist in the modern Western state, gripped by the
dollar and the driving-wheel?" [12] In the same vein, but with
the irony of which he was often capable, he wrote in one of
his notebooks:

> All which really matters is not what you take out of
> your heart, but what you put into your pocket. And
> blessed are they which live in these days, and are en-
> lightened to understand these truths which you under-
> stand! A blessing we devoutly trust to be spared. [13]

Such thoughts as these were never revealed at home, where
he gave the impression of studying medicine at a time when he
was frequently writing and vainly sending his poems to maga-
zines that did not accept them. Of course, Manchester, the city
of industry and commerce, had its respectable share of muse-
ums, libraries, galleries, and concerts, and these were the places
that Thompson visited. They were his consolation and retreat
when he was supposed to be present for lectures on anatomy
or hours in the dissecting room. Coming home late from a con-
cert or a visit with a musician, it was difficult for him to get
up in the morning, and he frequently left for his train with his
shoe laces untied and his clothing in some disarray.

His frail health, too, began to break under the pressures
within and the disorder of his habits. In 1879 he suffered his
first long illness—which was probably tuberculosis. Feverish,
he lay in bed for days, and it may have been then that he first
became acquainted with laudanum. The soothing powers of
this tincture of opium in alcohol presented him with a new
place of refuge far more private than the corner of the staircase he had sought as a boy. And his mother, as her last gift,
presented him with a copy of De Quincey's *Confessions*. As he

had once identified himself with Shelley, so now he entered the strange and terrible world of De Quincey.

He recovered his health sufficiently to continue the charade of his medical studies in Manchester, where the taking of opium among the brutalized and depressed textile workers had become a common means of escape from the blessings of industrialism. By the end of 1880 the habit was on him, and it seems likely that he sold some of his medical books and instruments to obtain the drug which, like the power of music, provided him with release from the torments he would not reveal to his father, who began to suspect him of alcoholism.

His mother died on December 19, 1880, and Francis Thompson, at the age of twenty-one, felt utterly isolated. In later years he expressed his feelings in "This Is My Beloved":

> Son of the womb of her,
> Loved till doom of her,
> Thought of the brain of her,
>   Heart of her side,
> She joyed and grieved in him,
> Hoped, believed in him:
> God grew fain of her,
>   And she died.
>
> Died, and horribly
> Saw the mystery,
> Saw the grime of it—
>   That hid soul;
> Saw the slime of it,
>   Saw it whole.
> O mother, mother, for all the sweet John saith,
> O mother, was not this the Second Death? [14]

Having already failed his medical examinations in London, in the grip of the opium habit, his sense of guilt was enormous. The double life he lived in silence was to him a betrayal of all the hopes of the one woman he had loved more than he knew himself. The stomach disorders that were to plague him all the rest of his life had already begun to torment him, but these physical pains did not compare with the misery of the remorse of his conscience, trained to sensitivity as it had been during his seminary years. His sister Mary, who was closest to him after his mother's death, could not help, for he talked to no one of his innermost thoughts. But years later, as Mother Austin, she came to believe, with good reason, that he took laudanum in that time of his desolation more to quiet his conscience than to relieve the pain of his body.

In 1882 he went to Glasgow to take his medical examinations for the second time. But he failed again, and returned to Manchester for two more years, where his absence from classes finally produced a report to his father. Dr. Thompson then decided that it was futile for his son to continue and found him a job with a manufacturer of surgical instruments. This lasted exactly two weeks. There was no place for Francis Thompson in the world of the utilitarians. He became, of all things, an itinerant salesman for an encyclopedia. In two months he had read every word of it and had not sold a single volume.

Only the army, it appeared, remained. Unlike Coleridge, however, he never was permitted to cut a ridiculous figure as a soldier. Thompson, who had dreamed so much of military heroism in his boyhood, was measured by the not-very-particular medical examiners of the Queen; he was marched and drilled with other potential privates; and he was sent home as physically unfit. There was no room for him in the building of the Empire. Like the cassock, the red coat was not to cover his frailty.

CHAPTER TWO

CITY OF DREADFUL NIGHT

In his typically paradoxical fashion, G. K. Chesterton wrote that the shortest way of describing the Victorian age is to say that Francis Thompson stood outside of it. Whether or not one can accept this comment completely, it is true that Thompson was, from the beginning, an outsider—in the most profound sense of the word. Moreover, he was the child of those who had chosen to become outsiders to the whole world of the Establishment. At Ushaw it had seemed for a time that in the life of the priesthood, with its bonds of fraternal affection, he might find his place and the fulfillment of his deepest attachments. The discovery that he had no vocation left him with a truly clerical solitariness that was never to be mitigated by the common priestly life of a rectory or a religious community. Thus, well before the time that he acquired the habit of taking laudanum in his illness, he had become acquainted with a very present sense of isolation that could never find relief in the one sanctuary where the temporal demands of his age were at least of secondary importance. As Father Terence Connolly says, the sense of being "a spoiled priest" made "the very fronting of existence a torture to him." [1]

At Ushaw, too, he had become acquainted with the "fierce Bacchante" of poetic creativity.[2] Years later, in an unpublished poem called "An Allegory of Poetic Composition," he devel-

oped the theme that "the poet to himself is wed." As a schoolboy he was already conscious of the inner storm and stress of
creative expression. Among the poems in his *Ushaw College
Notebook,* there is, for example, a juvenile lyric, "Song of the
Neglected Poet," in which he imagines a poet addressing his
own soul and saying that all the interior struggle which goes
with the creative process is well worth the cost.

This interior struggle, was, even in boyhood, one aspect of
his isolation. Frequently, he experienced immense difficulty in
really communicating with even the most sympathetic of lis-
teners. As he once wrote to Alice Meynell, ". . . when we *can*
communicate ourselves by words, it may often become a sensible effort to a sensitive person through the mere dead weight
of language, the gross actualities of speech." [3] For him, the
"veritable spirit" of every human being was a feminine *Bona
Dea,* and speech was something masculine, which could never
penetrate the innermost mysteries of the soul.

Consequently, he was an outsider in most conversations.
Unlike Oliver Wendell Holmes, Thompson found talk "stub-
bornly unplastic," like wrought iron. [4] In a manuscript called
Out of the House of Bondage he remarked that as soon as the
limner takes a piece of red earth in his hands to work it, that
piece of earth imposes its "edict on his shaping brain." So
from infancy, the sovereign spirit within us is "given in tutelage
to this unworked compost of clay," which is the body, and the
"muddy accents of the human tongue" inhibit true communication.

This theme recurs in his poetry, but nowhere more strikingly than in the lines from "House of Bondage":

> The spirit's ark sealed with a little clay
>   Was old ere Memphis grew a memory;
> The hand pontifical to break away
>   That seal what shall surrender? Not the sea

> Which did englut great Egypt and his war,
> Nor all the desert-drownèd sepulchres.
>
> (II, ll. 1-6)

From the time that he returned home from Ushaw, Thompson was literally an outsider even in the circle of his family, whose greatest hopes for him were disappointed when they learned that he could never be a priest. At Ushaw it had seemed that the creative drive which filled his notebooks with verse held promise that even if he were not ordained, he might find his life in poetry. But his parents, who had little comprehension of what he felt, were, in spite of their many attempts at kindly understanding, not likely to have appreciated any painful attempt he might have made to explain his need to write. Nor did the failure of his poems to find a publisher seem to indicate that he was going to receive recognition elsewhere.

While his mother lived, his attachment to her held him, but after her death his breaking with the little world of Ashton-under-Lyne became inevitable. It merely awaited an occasion. On Sunday, November 8, 1885, Dr. Thompson was at home alone with his son. Mary was away for the weekend. In the midst of the silence of the Victorian Sabbath, there was little evidence in the streets of either life or conflict. The plain brick placidity of the house was a decorous cover for a quarrel that arose between the two ordinarily quiet men, who confronted each other with a frankness that was unaccustomed between them. Perhaps, they simply met another impasse as the questions of Francis' future and of his past failures were finally brought into the open. Quite possibly, the long-suffering doctor suspected his son of tampering with his supplies of laudanum and accused him of having done so.

In any event, the day ended in bitterness, and during the night, Francis Thompson, having almost reached the age of twenty-five, left home without career or definite purpose before him. The next day, Mary found a note saying that he planned to go to London. He had, in fact, left the world of middle-class respectability. The role of the outsider had become his life.

II

In a review of De Quincey's *Confessions,* which Thompson did for the *Academy* in April, 1899, appears the following: "It is not only the turbulent who break bounds and scandalise decorous authority: the timorous, ill-understood child of genius, who cannot fit into the pigeonhole made for him is ofttimes driven into that revolt not native to him." [5] Revolt against family obligations was not more "native" to Thompson than revolt against the moral code of his religion. Yet, he left his father's house secretly in the night and for some years let the dark magic of laudanum have its way.

He was, of course, in revolt against the vulgar, self-confident, matter-of-fact mentality of which Manchester was both the product and the symbol. He stood wholeheartedly with Carlyle against the spirit of the Utilitarians, and the doctrines of Rossetti and the Pre-Raphaelite Brethren had made an early and lasting impression upon him. To the practical readers of the *Westminster Review,* poetry appeared to be but a trifling thing, and although this journal represented an extreme bias, its essential Philistinism was typical of the feeling of a significant number of people, which did not decline as the nineteenth century progressed. Those whom Carlyle had called the "Millocracy" increasingly set the tone of the times, as Thompson observed in "Sidereal Musings," an unpublished series of lightly ironical comments based on the various constellations:

> The Scales are there, let none admire,
> For the same reason as the Lyre.
> Justice and Poesy in the sky
> Are set this truth to signify——
> That heaven may find in them some worth,
> But there's no use for them on earth.

The utilitarian frame of mind, against which Thompson felt a deep sense of revulsion and frustration, was affected by Evangelical religious influences and was often sententiously moral. This resulted in what Thompson described as "the typical 19th century social stigma on artists (in the wide sense of the word)." [6] There was something suspicious about imaginative creativity in the minds of the "Millocracy," a feeling which Thompson caricatured in one of his notebooks:

> Depend on it, Sir, there is something wrong with a man when he can't use the straight-forward language of honest Englishmen, of plain, honest Englishmen, Sir! There's something underhand about the fellow; or he's not safe, he's a crank, a genius, something repugnant to honest English good sense, Sir! [7]

Nor did English Catholics generally exhibit a very different point of view. In the draft of his well-known essay on Shelley, Thompson remarked that he had found a "Calvinistic" spirit among many of his fellow Catholics, which would not permit poetry to enter the precincts of the Church "unless she come to them in sackcloth."

Far more vehement than this, however, is an extended section in his notes [8] in which he lamented the indifference of ecclesiastics to the work of men of creative genius. Artists, he admitted, frequently prove to be more sensitive to the attractions of sensual beauty than other men, and they are likewise often more susceptible to sensory pleasures, "both lawful and unlawful." These characteristics, however, do not, he insisted, absolve churchmen from making an effort to appreciate and aid "these creatures of glorious natural gifts."

This passage ends in a climax of passionate rhetoric, which —although it was written many years later—echoes something of what Thompson must have felt as he left his family and wandered out into the night. Catholics, he said, had not only failed to compete with Satan for the souls of many great modern artists, but, worse than that, they had appeared to scorn and distrust those whose creative gifts God's adversary seemed to honor and welcome: "By how much to him they are precious, to you they are vile, yet ye marvel that the wits of the world are against you. Fools! It is because of your folly!" [9]

As Thompson declined to judge "so unhappy a being" as Shelley,[10] so one is inclined to feel that Thompson's own moral failures at least call for an equally charitable understanding. As he himself remarked, in the arts it is often true that, "The harvest waves richest over the battlefields of the soul; . . . the heart, like the earth, smells sweetest after the rain." [11]

The night into which he walked in November, 1885, seemed interminable. He went, at first, to Manchester, his slope-shouldered figure burdened with little more than his books, most of which he was forced to sell in order to sustain his life and feed the hunger of his addiction.

In Manchester, the city of De Quincey, there was for Thompson a retreat from the universal ugliness, not only in laudanum but also in a public art gallery where a plaster cast of the Vatican Melpomene had been on display for a number of years. Standing in silence before her enigmatic beauty, he would "meditate and worship the baffling mysteries of her meaning." [12] Longing to create a lasting beauty in his poetry, he saw in this "goddess," whose name he did not then know, the symbol of that tormenting and consoling loveliness, of which Yeats was to write:

Bow down, archangels, in your dim abode:
Before you were, or any hearts to beat,
Weary and kind, one lingered by His seat;
He made the world to be a grassy road
Before her wandering feet.

She was beauty, but she was also the ancient muse of
tragedy, and it seems peculiarly fitting that Thompson should
have been attracted to her. When he left Manchester for
London, in a mood of gloomy foreboding and "in the desperate
spirit of an *enfant perdu*," most of his books were gone, but
he carried in his pocket two volumes that he would not
surrender—the tragic plays of Aeschylus and the poetry of
William Blake. With Aeschylus, he was to explore the mystery
of fate and freedom; with Blake, he was to protest the ugly
tyranny of the "dark, Satanic mills."

⚜   III   ⚜

His stay in Manchester was as brief as it was aimless. In the
end, he was compelled to write home for money to buy his
train ticket to London, where he arrived hesitant and alone.
It is reasonable to suppose that he hoped somehow to find a
publisher for his work, but his native shyness, his utter lack
of contact with the world of practical affairs, and his sense
of defeated isolation made the necessary effort all but impossible. What the world demanded, he felt unable to give.
Everard Meynell, who knew him more intimately than anyone
else who has attempted to describe his life, says that Thompson
"came to London than he might exist and no more." [13]

For him, the outsider, existence had become anguish. There
was always opium's promise of a way out, but in the taking
of it, Thompson knew nothing of that freedom from a sense

of guilt which surrounds the self-indulgence of an amoral
man. Even J. C. Reid—who sometimes treats Thompson as
if his life were little more than a case study in drug addiction
—admits that the poet's religious faith was the constant barrier
"that stood between him and complete surrender to self." [14]
Outcast, he nonetheless had a sensitive, clerically formed conscience, which lay bare to the searching inquisition of his
God. On the nights when he tried to sleep in the alleys of
Covent Garden's wholesale market, he may well have watched
the giant arrows of the hands of the clock on St. Paul's with
a tormenting sense of the judgment of his wasted years. Later
in his life he had many haunting memories of such a "night-
mare time," when

> Forlorn, and faint, and stark,
> I had endured through watches of the dark
>   The abashless inquisition of each star,
>   Yea, was the outcast mark
>   Of all those heavenly passers' scrutiny;
>   Stood bound and helplessly
> For Time to shoot his barbèd minutes at me;
>   (*Sister Songs,* I, ll. 277-283)

When he first came to London, however, he did not at once
become a vagrant. With his love of books and his faint hopes
of making some contact with a publisher, he managed to find
employment as a messenger for a bookseller. As with the
encyclopedia he had undertaken to sell, Thompson seems to
have spent more time reading the books he collected from
various publishing houses than he spent in delivering them
to their destination at the shop. Consequently, he did not
hold his job as a messenger very long.

It is not surprising that Thompson did not then look for
help from his uncle John Costall Thompson, who was employed
by the Bank of England and not disposed to look favorably on

what he called his nephew's "sort of Bohemian life." There could not have been any mutual understanding between them.

His father sent him an allowance of seven shillings a week at the address of a reading room in the Strand, but Thompson was irregular in collecting it. Having cut his ties with his father's world, he did not feel entitled to his father's money. When the payments were returned because of his failure to call for them, the last, thin link with security was broken.

But he did not embrace hunger and vagrancy with a romantic ideal of asceticism. His own words in the essay "Health and Holiness" are a true reflection of his experience and his mood:

> The pride of life is no more; to live is itself an ascetic exercise. . . . Man is his own mortification. Hamlet has increased and multiplied, and his seed fill the land. Would any Elsinore director have advised austerities for the Prince, or judged to the letter his self-accusings?—and to this complexion has many a one come. . . . Merely to front existence, for some, is a surrender of self, a choice of ineludibly rigorous abnegation.[15]

Learning to find the eleven pence a day which he needed to "front existence" in the urban jungle of nineteenth-century London's lowest levels of survival, left him little opportunity for a life of arty Bohemianism, such as his uncle imagined. He became a bootblack, a seller of newspapers and matches, a scarecrow figure that ran after cabs on the off-chance of a tip for lifting luggage or holding the horse's head while the passengers alighted. He competed with those who were adepts in the ways of the streets and the doss houses, and he seldom won.

Everard Meynell says that in all the time that he knew Thompson, he never heard the poet speak of the beauty of London. His memories of it were vivid recollections of wanderings from midnight to dawn through the Strand, Covent Garden, Trafalgar Square, parts of Piccadilly; he recalled sleeping on the Embankment, watching the shadows of Black-friars Bridge, and coming to Fleet Street opposite St. Paul's in the early morning hours. As he wrote to the artist William Hyde, who had done some drawings for a projected book on London in 1897: "My own mind turns especially towards the gloomier majesties and suggestiveness of London because I have seen it most peculiarly under those aspects." [16]

How much or how little Thompson managed to write during the almost nine months of his first period of vagrant street living it is, of course, impossible to say. He habitually carried bits and pieces of manuscript notes from place to place and it is likely that he did so then. It appears that he attempted to do some creative work in the Guildhall Library until the condition of his clothing compelled the librarian, Bernard Kettle, to ask him not to visit there any longer.

IV

Thompson's first important work in London was probably not undertaken until he had the good fortune to meet John Mc-Master. This devout Evangelical churchman was a warden of the Anglican church of St. Martin-in-the-Fields, which faces Trafalgar Square. In the crypt of that church homeless men were provided with a place to sleep on the wooden benches two nights each week, and some of its more zealous parish-ioners, like McMaster, devoted themselves to seeking out those down-and-outs who seemed capable of rehabilitation. Their approach was often crude, but their intentions were well meaning.

McMaster, who maintained a bootmaking shop at 14

Panton Street, Haymarket, encountered Thompson in August, 1886. Wandering along Wardour Street, carrying his load of guilt and feeling the effects of laudanum, Thompson heard McMaster's habitual query as if from a great distance: "Is your soul saved?" The tattered outcast who had once aspired to the priesthood, having been tormented by the same question in other forms through long nights of self-accusation, replied with unaccustomed force: "What right have you to ask me that question?"

It was a fair enough rejoinder, for Francis Thompson's religion led him to assume that God alone knew the answer. A less sincere man than McMaster might have taken offense. Instead, he quietly replied that if he could not save Thompson's soul, at least he was able to save his body. Before the simple goodness of this man, the poet's first sense of offended privacy quickly gave way, and he willingly accompanied McMaster to his shop.

The bootmaker was a prudent as well as a pious man. After communicating with the police of Ashton-under-Lyne, he accepted Thompson's account of himself and decided to rehabilitate him. The project was doomed to failure from the start. McMaster's experience with missionary work among derelicts led him to suppose that employment, food, lodging, and prayer meetings were adequate means of salvation. Since Thompson was a Roman Catholic and McMaster was a man who respected his right to follow the dictates of his own conscience, there was no question of prayer meetings. Within the limits of his knowledge and far beyond the limits of the charity of most men, McMaster did all that he could for his transient guest. For although Thompson was given a boy's work to do and a wage of five shillings a week, he was more a guest than an employee.

McMaster's family physician was of the opinion that all

Thompson needed was good food and pleasant surroundings. This simple diagnosis at first seemed accurate. Properly clothed for his work, well fed, and given a room, Thompson, according to McMaster's own account, "soon looked very different and he tried his best to please." Sent on errands, he was frequently accompanied by McMaster's niece, who was, as children always were, the poet's delight.

In her, to whom he gave the name of "Little Flower,"—which was something of an improvement over the family's "Rosebud"—Thompson must have seen the image of the sisters with whom his own childhood had been so largely spent. Wandering with her through St. James Park, he felt something of what he was to write of Monica Meynell some years later in Kensington Gardens:

> Eve no gentlier lays her cooling cheek
> On the burning brow of the sick earth,
>   Sick with death, and sick with birth,
> Æon to æon, in secular fever twirled
>   Than thy shadow soothes this weak
>   And distempered being of mine.
>   (*Sister Songs*, II, ll. 250-255)

In the "Little Flower" of the McMaster family, Thompson's romantic imagination saw the primal innocence which he, like Wordsworth and Traherne, always associated with childhood. And he wrestled with the mystery of his own downfall before the crucifix in his room, as each night he prayed aloud. Hearing him, McMaster supposed that the man who wore a medal of the Virgin about his neck must be saying "his Mass." In a sense, this was true, for in his night prayers Thompson's mind must often have returned to Ushaw and the vision he had once had of himself as one vested for the offering of the Church's liturgical sacrifice. It is impossible to say how regular Thompson was in the formal practice of his religion during this period, but the testimony of McMaster is evidence that he had not abandoned it.

Nor did he turn from his devotion to the "fierce Bacchante" of poetry. McMaster lent him such books as he had. What they may have been one can only imagine, but he later noted that Thompson had a fondness for "the classical poets and preferred Homer's *Odysseus* and *Iliad* to other books one lent him."

During this time it is quite possible that Thompson was at work on the first drafts of the poems and the essay "Paganism Old and New," which he was later to send to Wilfrid Meynell for eventual publication in *Merry England*. His notebooks display his habit of revision and according to his own testimony,[17] the manuscript of "Paganism New and Old" was in existence in some form before February, 1887.

In the bootmaker's shop and in the circle of the McMaster family, Thompson not only wrote but talked as he had not done for months. As when he had stood before the fireplace at school and talked until the boys had thought he would never stop, so Thompson gained the reputation among the McMasters of being a great talker. Yet, as the Meynells were to discover, the speech of this deeply introverted poet was seldom true communication. Instead, it took the form of endless and aimless discourse about trifles, for he seldom found it possible to find the spoken word he really wanted or a listener who would understand him when he did find it.

McMaster was far from satisfied with the results of his efforts to rehabilitate Thompson and was quite aware of his own inability to penetrate the poet's defensive reserve. Consequently, it was decided that Thompson might benefit from a visit with his own family during the Christmas holidays. The poet accepted this proposal with much the same docility which had marked his seminary years, and, neatly dressed for the occasion, he returned to Ashton-under-Lyne.

It was, of course, a futile procedure. At home he was a ghost returned to the scene of his former life; he was not any longer a part of it, nor had he been for a number of years. He told his family little or nothing of his experiences, which to them were inconceivable. But he probably learned that Mary was planning to become a nun, as she did in February, 1887, and he may have discovered that his father intended to marry Anne Richardson the following April. What effect this knowledge may have had on Thompson, whose attachment to his mother was so deep, can only be surmised. In some sense, it must have reawakened the feeling of desolate isolation he had experienced at the time of his mother's death almost seven years before.

In any event, his reaction was similar, for when he returned to McMaster in January, he had once again increased his use of laudanum, although his benefactor mistook the symptoms for those of alcoholism and treated them as such. Seeing, however, that his best efforts brought no improvement in Thompson's behavior, McMaster—disappointed in what he described as his "only failure"—decided that he could no longer keep Thompson in his home. Clothed in a clumsy brown overcoat, which he was to wear for years, the poet left to return to the life of the streets.

V

During the time when he lived at McMaster's it appears that Thompson had used most of the money he received to feed his addiction. Yet, judging by his general conduct and his creative efforts, it seems that he must have kept his consumption of the drug to a minimum. His condition obviously deteriorated after his return from the Christmas excursion, and when he re-entered the world of vagrant existence in the midst of the winter he reached the low point of degradation.

As with his early sufferings at school, when he had identified himself with Shelley, so in his addiction he had identified himself with De Quincey—although, unlike that author, he sought for no self-justification. There is, however, no reason to suppose that Thompson's account of the charity shown him by a nameless prostitute during the bitter winter of 1887 was imaginatively inspired by DeQuincey's similar experience with the girl he called Ann.

Sleeping in the arcades of Covent Garden, along the Embankment, or in the Catholic refuge in Providence Row, close to starvation and literally near death, Thompson found pity —if not McMaster's brand of salvation—in a forlorn young streetwalker, who lived in Brompton and nightly went by cab to the Strand. Such girls were certainly not rare in Victorian London. Beneath the dreary surface of its studied respectability, they formed a significant part of the background, as the so-called laws of classical economic theory continued to operate without restraint and England's wealth continued to polarize at one end of the social scale. Thompson's rescuer was the unhappy by-product of a society in which, as he wrote in "The Larger Hope":

> Brown, from the loins of Philistines,
> For six days laboured at his sins,
> And rested from his labours one day,
> And, to please Heaven, wore black o' Sunday;
> Sinned, but in proper time and place,
> And kept official hours of grace;
> Drabbed, swore, in decent due degree,
> Was drunk, but with sobriety;
> Made of his sins no vulgar rumpus

> But profligate by chart and compass,
> And, just as all good citizens are,
> Most regularly irregular;
> Lackeyed with vices, if you please,
> But in respectable liveries.[18]

The girl, whom he later described as little more than a child, gave him food and lodging, as well as her friendship and admiration. Theirs was in no sense an erotic relationship. Weakened though he was, Thompson's strong devotion to the concepts of love he had learned at Ushaw remained unimpaired.

It was during this period that he put "Paganism New and Old" into its final form. The fundamental theme of this essay is that Christianity transformed and elevated the concepts of nature, beauty, and love to such a degree that without it the whole body of our greatest poetry would have been impossible. Measuring what he described as the "distance between Catullus and the *Vita Nuova,* between Ovid and the *House of Life,*" he found Christianity to be the only adequate determining standard.

Thompson shared Swinburne's distaste for the almost universal Victorian ugliness and "the cold formalities of an outworn worship." But he had none of that poet's longing for the imaginary world of Arcadian Atalanta or for the ancient sacrifices whose "sanguine-shining steam" divided many an antique dawn.[19] Writing of those who sought in the revival of paganism a remedy for modern ills, Thompson— even in the lowest depths of his own personal disaster— surrendered nothing of his loyalty to Christianity:

> And those who, like the present writer, tread as on thorns amidst the sordidness and ugliness, the ugly sordidness and the sordid ugliness, the dull materiality and weariness of this unhonoured old age of the world,—can-

not but sympathize with these feelings; nay, even look back with a certain passionate regret to the beauty which invested at least the outward life of those (pagan) days. But in truth, with this outward life the vesture of beauty ceases: the rest is a day-dream. . . . Heathenism is lovely *because* it is dead. . . .

Christianity it was that stripped the weeds from that garden of Paganism, broke its statue of Priapus, and delivered it smiling and fair to the nations for their pleasure-ground. . . . She took Venus, and made of her the type of Beauty,—Beauty, which the average heathen hardly knew.[20]

With a few shillings that he had somehow acquired, Thompson paused in the bare struggle for existence to prepare the manuscript of his essay and on February 23, 1887, dropped it, together with a few poems, in the letter box of the Catholic magazine *Merry England*. The covering letter, written on a single piece of nondescript paper, explained that the soiled state of the manuscript was the result of "the strange places and circumstances" under which it had been written. This soiled packet, which the busy editor, Wilfrid Meynell, pigeon-holed for six months, was in many ways Thompson's last desperate hope. He had come to his last page of paper and his last halfpenny. As the weeks went by without any word from *Merry England,* it began to seem that he had also come to the frontiers of despair.

 VI

It seems probable that sometime during the spring of 1888, Thompson contemplated suicide. However, the only evidence for this is the testimony of Wilfrid Blunt, who quoted Wilfrid Meynell as his source. Meynell himself made no record of the story, possibly—as his daughter suggests—because "he may have been reluctant to make it common knowledge." [21]

According to Blunt's account, Thompson went to a rubbish disposal area behind Covent Garden where he planned to take one large dose of laudanum. Having taken half of it, he thought he felt a restraining arm on his wrist. Looking up, the half-conscious poet seemed to see the figure of Thomas Chatterton (1752-1770), the "marvellous boy," who had committed suicide before his eighteenth birthday and become the romantic symbol of genius suffering from poverty and neglect. Confronted with this image, Thompson recalled a legend that money had arrived for Chatterton the day after his suicide and resolved not to take his own life. The very next day he learned that his poem "The Passion of Mary" had appeared in *Merry England*.

As Reid says, this story is "a little too pat." Yet, the illusion of seeing Chatterton is not improbable, for Thompson was well acquainted with the romantic traditions surrounding him; and under the influence of laudanum, the inhibiting power of Thompson's Catholic conscience may very well have been symbolized by the figure of Chatterton. Since he had not abandoned his basic religious convictions, he would have regarded suicide as the ultimate sin of despair. In the very act of self-destruction, it may well have been that the enduring strength of his religious faith was, so to speak, shocked into an assertion of its command over him.

That the restraining figure should have been that of a dead poet rather than a canonized saint is in no way surprising. To Thompson, Chatterton was a martyr of art, one who, like the saints, suffered in a world which so frequently rejects the insights of the intuitive way of knowledge. There was, in fact, a close relationship between the way of the true poet and the way of sanctity in Thompson's whole theory of the creative process:

> The psychology of the poet, above all, (or of the musician, or, less strikingly, the artist), affords the closest natural parallel to the special psychology of the saint. . . . The weapon of poet or saint is intuition, and contemplation is the state, the attitude, which disposes the mind to receive intuitions.[22]

That he would not attain to sanctity in any generally recognized sense of the word seemed most painfully obvious to Thompson in the grip of his addiction. That he might, however, be worthy of the name of poet was a hope, which —together with the friendship of the girl of the streets— continued to sustain him until it appeared certain that he would never hear from the editor of *Merry England*.

Just when he discovered that "The Passion of Mary" had appeared, or was going to appear, in the April, 1888, issue of that magazine is not certain. It is, of course, possible that he actually received the good news in the dramatic fashion suggested by the story of his attempted suicide; but this possibility has been discounted on the ground that Canon John Carroll—who had been a family friend in Thompson's boyhood and attempted on several occasions to effect a reconciliation between Thompson and his father—told the poet of the planned publication of the poem before it actually appeared.[23]

In any event, Thompson wrote a letter to Wilfrid Meynell, dated April 14, 1888, in which he said that he had learned of the publication of his poem and asked the editor to communicate with him at the address of a chemist in Drury Lane, to whom, as it turned out, Thompson owed a small sum of money. Some months before, when he had first discovered Thompson's soiled manuscript in the pigeonhole of his cluttered desk, Meynell had written to the poet at the Charing

Cross Post Office address that had appeared on Thompson's first letter to him. No reply came, and the poem was published in the hope of stirring its author to make his whereabouts known.

Meynell, of course, went at once to the chemist shop where he began what was to be a familiar pattern through the coming years by paying the poet's bill. The chemist knew Thompson only as an occasional customer, but he promised to try to reach him.

A long interval followed before Thompson—who was almost an apparition of destitution, without shirt or socks and wearing a broken pair of shoes—hesitated outside the door of Meynell's office at 43 Essex Street. He opened the door halfway twice before he dared to enter, and when asked how he had been able to consult the books he quoted in "Paganism New and Old" replied, "Books I have none, but Blake and the Bible." Meynell concluded that all the quotations had been made from memory, but this may have been something of an exaggeration since, as we have seen, Thompson probably prepared the first draft of the essay while he was living at McMaster's.

Deeply moved by the poet's lamentable condition, Meynell appreciated fully the poignant significance of "The Passion of Mary." Technically, it is not one of Thompson's more memorable works, marked as it is by stock-responses that recall the Latin hymn "Stabat Mater," from the Sequence of the Mass for the Friday after Passion Sunday. It was inspired by a sermon Thompson heard preached by Father Richardson at Ashton-under-Lyne in September, 1885, and retains a certain homiletical quality which gives it a rhetorical cast that is happily absent from Thompson's better religious verse. Yet, as its author stood before him and he realized the circumstances under which the poem was developed in its final form, Meynell knew that sense of immediacy associated with writing that truly conveys human experience:

> Bitter the bread of our repast;
>   Yet doth a sweet the bitter leaven:
> Our sorrow is the shadow cast
>   Around it by the light of Heaven.
>
> O light in Light, shine down from Heaven!
>
> (ll. 35-39)

Despite the editor's understanding and his offer to publish more of Thompson's work, the destitute poet refused to accept a weekly stipend. Perhaps, the prospect was at once too overwhelming. The very idea that the tide of his failure had turned must have seemed incredible. The life of the streets, the torment of his addiction, which he must have been deeply reluctant to confess, had so great a hold that Thompson, who was actually near death, was unable to cope with the possibility of life that now confronted him.

Then, too, there was his attachment to the poor girl who had befriended him. He left Meynell after that first visit with nothing settled, and when on subsequent visits, Meynell proposed medical treatment for him, Thompson was evasive. Seeing, as he finally did, the life at the editor's home in Upper Phillimore Place, Thompson for a time insisted that he must continue to earn his living on the streets. All of his new experience was confided to the girl whose room was so often his shelter, and she urged him to leave her and enter the world that Meynell had opened up to him.

Finally in order to force him towards a new life, she left him, and although Thompson searched for her again and again, she became "a swift and trackless fugitive." Her memory remained with him, not only in the highly colored romantic imagery with which he later described her in an often quoted passage from *Sister Songs*,[24] but also in the tragic figure he portrayed in a poem called "Une Fille de Joie" which was found among his manuscripts and published in 1957:

> This is her doom! The ways are barriered which
>   Should lead to the All-Merciful's abode;
>   The house of penitence which Mary trod
> Long since is grown an appanage of the rich:
>   And though she strive, yea, strive and strive, *how*
>   strive!——
>   The gates of Hell have shut her in alive.[25]

In May and June, Thompson's "Dream Tryst," which dealt with the memory of a childhood secret love, and his "Paganism New and Old" appeared in *Merry England*. An essay on Bunyan followed in November, and the December issue carried the poem "Not Even in Dream," which recalls "Dream Tryst" but speaks of some other lost love that has not left the poet with so much as a "phantom memory of a vanished kiss."

Meanwhile, Meynell slowly won Thompson's confidence. The fact of his opium addiction was finally brought into the open, and Meynell persuaded Thompson to submit to medical examination and care. The physician who was first consulted expressed the opinion that Thompson was dying and too weak to withstand the rigors of being deprived of opium. His body, habituated to the toxic drug, would have to undergo the terrible battle involved in altering its chemical make-up to a normal state. He would have to go through weeks when no rest or comfort could be found. The dimmest light would have a blinding intensity. All the deepest feelings of guilt and conflict would rise to torment him, and he would be nauseated beyond endurance. And even if, by some miracle, Thompson were to survive all this, the victory would be a dubious triumph that might lead to even more defeats.

Yet, the alternative was extinction without a fight, and

Meynell was a fighter. He prevailed upon Thompson to enter a private sanitarium, from which the poet emerged near the end of the year barely clinging to life but pronounced cured.

The time of his dereliction was ended. His poetry was never to be marked by an abundance of evidences of the remembrance of that experience. Having lived as few other writers of his age in prolonged contact with the disinherited children of nineteenth-century industrialism, Thompson did not, however, forget what he had seen. His review of William Booth's *In Darkest England and the Way Out* (1890) gives a powerful picture of "the terrible welter of London misery." It is eloquent proof of Thompson's knowledge of what the unchecked avarice of commercial materialism was doing to the minds and bodies of the silent, brutalized, uprooted thousands who inhabited its lower depths.

The original draft of this essay, which is in the care of a Capuchin priest, Father Kevin Harrison, gives a detailed analysis of the Salvation Army program of rehabilitation. This clearly shows that Thompson had a very practical understanding of the problems involved, especially that of the marketing of the products of the Salvationists' workshops. Moreover, he suggested that any such program might gain in effectiveness if it were less centralized and more permeated with a religious outlook that was brighter and more attractive than that of the Salvation Army seemed to him to be.

To the end of his life, Thompson saw *laissez-faire* economic theory as the modern counterpart of Spenser's Blatant Beast,[26] a monster that is never satisfied. Against the uncontrolled spirit of individualism underlying it, he reaffirmed the social concept of human brotherhood:

> Rousseau said it. But so did Jesus Christ. It is the doctrine of the red cap. But it is likewise the doctrine of the red cassock. While on the antagonistic side is the con-

spicuous and significant figure of Professor Huxley. . . .
Individualism was simply Natural Selection applied to
the social order.[27]

In prose which recalls the fierce prophecies of Blake, whose
poems Thompson carried with him during his outcast years,
the review of *In Darkest England* poured forth its author's
memories of the ominous city:

> A region whose hedgerows have set to brick, whose soil
> is chilled to stone; where flowers are sold and women,
> where the men wither and the stars; whose streets to me
> on the most glittering days are black. For I unveil their
> secret meaning. I read their human hieroglyphs. I diag-
> nose from a hundred occult signs the disease which per-
> turbs their populous pulses. . . . I hear the shaking of in-
> visible lashes, I see men dabbled with their oozing life.[28]

Out of that world, Thompson finally came only to endure
the agonies of the cure that might easily have killed him. But
when it was over, Meynell found a place of refuge for him
with the monks of the Priory at Storrington in Sussex, where
he was to remain until February, 1890. There he returned
to life and creativity.

CHAPTER THREE

MERRY ENGLAND

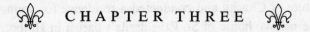

I

In the friendship which Thompson had found with the Meynells he had come at last to those who shared the two great loves of his own life—poetry and religion. Alice Meynell, a woman of striking beauty and a markedly creative intelligence, was the daughter of one Thomas James Thompson, but she was in no way related to the poet. Her father, who had a great passion for travel, as well as means to indulge it, was a friend of Charles Dickens and a man of some cultivation who devoted much of his time to his daughter's education during the many years they spent abroad, especially in Italy. A great admirer of the indomitable Dominican St. Catherine of Siena, Alice Thompson became a Catholic at the age of twenty in 1867. *Preludes,* her first volume of verse, was published in 1875 and admired by such critics as Ruskin and Browning. Consequently, she had already established some reputation as a promising young poet when she married Wilfrid Meynell, who was five years younger than she, in 1877.

Meynell, who came of Quaker stock, had become a Catholic in 1870. His strong social conscience, which was a family characteristic, attracted him to the work of Father William Lockhart, another convert, whose family was related to John Gibson Lockhart, the son-in-law and biographer of Sir Walter Scott. Father Lockhart was a member of the Order of the

60   FRANCIS THOMPSON: A CRITICAL BIOGRAPHY

Institute of Charity and conducted a residence for young men in the priests' house of St. Etheldreda's parish in Holborn.

Here Meynell made his first London home and his first contact with Catholic journalism by writing for *The Lamp,* a magazine which Father Lockhart edited. He also assisted in the social work of the parish and gained practical knowledge of London slum life, which later enabled him to have an intimate understanding of the world in which Thompson had been compelled to live during his outcast years.

Having been attracted to both religion and writing even during his adolescence at Ackworth School, Croydon, Wilfrid Meynell found the life of a Catholic journalist attractive. He was finally presented to Cardinal Manning by Father Lockhart and eventually became editor of the diocesan *Weekly Register* in 1881. Into the publication of this paper he and his wife poured their considerable energies and talents over a period of some eighteen years, even after the founding of *Merry England* in 1883.

The busy Meynell household soon filled with the activity of a large and growing family. It also became the center of what has come to be known as the Catholic Literary Revival, a movement in which the name of Francis Thompson has a place of the first importance.

The official ecclesiastical atmosphere which then prevailed was, however, quite different from that of more recent years, when the Church has welcomed and honored such artists as Eric Gill, Evelyn Waugh, Graham Greene, and Dame Edith Sitwell. After the re-establishment of the hierarchy in 1850, Victorian Catholicism was existing under what Wilfrid Ward —in an essay called "The Rigidity of Rome"—described as a "state of siege." [1] The Church had decided that she must accept a local situation in which no activity that could not be regarded as vital to the defense of her position could receive much serious official attention.

This attitude was, of course, reflected in the Catholic publications of the period. Under the editorship of Wilfrid Ward's father, William G. Ward, *The Dublin Review,* for example, was marked by a highly apologetic tone. Actually controlled by the future Cardinal Archbishop, Henry E. Manning—a militant convert—there was little room in it for any writing that did not directly serve the causes Manning espoused.[2] Similarly, when Father Herbert Vaughan, who, like Manning was to be Cardinal Archbishop of Westminster, controlled *The Tablet* in the years 1868-1884, literature and the fine arts were treated, if at all, as instruments in the service of immediate ecclesiastical concerns.

Writing a critical essay in May, 1890, Thompson could, it is true, point to some evidences that Victorian Catholicism was not "inimical to culture." He could also mention the fact that proof of this might be found in the work of such men as Newman, Aubrey de Vere, and others who had come into the Church when "the great flood of the Oxford Movement burst its Anglican banks."[3] Yet, it is significant that this same essay was rejected by *The Tablet*.

The official attitude was that of Cardinal Manning, who had been an Anglican archdeacon, but nonetheless could write: "I see much danger of an English Catholicism of which Newman is the highest type. It is the old Anglican, patristic, literary Oxford tone transplanted into the Church. . . . In one word, it is worldly Catholicism, and it will have the worldly on its side."[4]

Manning's was the temper that prevailed, and although he belonged to the Metaphysical Society (founded by Tennyson and James Knowles in 1869) and thus kept in touch with secular intellectual life, the Cardinal's outlook was essentially that of the ecclesiastical administrator and politician. The support which he gave to *Merry England* was given largely because Meynell's purpose in founding it included the presentation of a Catholic social philosophy rather than because the Cardinal had an interest in the editor's desire to promote the development of the work of Catholic literary artists.

No one was more aware of the existence of a widespread lack of interest in poetry among English Catholics than Meynell. In the spring of 1889, when Thompson was at Storrington, the poet was engaged in the preparation of a series of critical essays. They dealt with such varied topics as Crashaw, the realism of Zola, and the development of Irish poetry. It was during this time that he composed the first draft of his well-known study of Shelley, with its criticism of "Catholic Philistinism." Thompson, who felt that his essay would probably prove to be unacceptable to the "ponderous, ecclesiastical" *Dublin Review*, for which it was intended, asked Meynell whether or not the attack on the Catholic Philistines should be omitted. Meynell's reply was, "Leave it in." [5] The Shelley essay was, of course, rejected and did not appear in the *Dublin Review* until 1908, the year after Thompson's death.

Even the most intellectual Victorian Catholic publications, such as the *Rambler* and *The Month*, devoted themselves mainly to practical or speculative ecclesiastical interests. The *Rambler*, which numbered such luminaries as Newman and Acton among its editors and gained the respect of Matthew Arnold, was not especially interested in the creative arts. It was far more devoted to philosophical and theological discussion and debate. *The Month*, which began publication in 1864, at first published a good deal of poetry, including work by Aubrey de Vere and Newman's *The Dream of Gerontius*. But in spite of Newman's advice to the contrary, even *The Month* soon became far more concerned with strictly eccle-

siastical interests. This was markedly true under the editorship
of Father John Gerard, and belles-lettres received less and
less attention until he was succeeded in 1912 by Father Joseph
Keating, who was much interested in the work of Gerard
Manly Hopkins.

The literary activities with which Thompson and the
Meynells were associated were thus of scant interest to
official Catholicism, and the literary revival which flowered in
the period of Cardinal Vaughan (1892-1903) was in no sense
promoted by him.[6]

Furthermore, many Catholics accepted the current feeling
of other religious people that a devotion to the arts must
somehow be immoral. Many shared the opinions set forth in
Robert Buchanan's essay "The Fleshly School of Poetry," [7]
and concluded that writers like Swinburne and Rossetti had
proved modern poetry to be an erotic exercise. They associated
the newer writers with the supposed sensuality of George
Moore's *Confessions of a Young Man* (1888) or with the
morbid search for exotic sensations exhibited in Oscar Wilde's
Dorian Gray (1891) and the fictions of Frederick Rolfe.
Judging by what they heard of the avowedly decadent *fin-de-
siècle* leaders of aestheticism, it appeared to many pious minds
that modern literature and religious faith were destined to
move far apart.

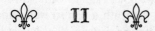

II

Thompson himself felt the tension between the widespread
aestheticism that was the vogue during the decade of his
greatest creativity and the demands of his own deeply religious
outlook. He never had any liking for the fad of studied artificiality, which, as Holbrook Jackson says, caused some of

its devoted followers to let their tea grow cold while they praised the Willow Pattern of the cup.[8] He would have been in complete accord with Hopkins' comment in one of his letters: "It seems that triolets and rondels and rondeaus and chants royal and what not and anything but serving God are all the fashion." [9] Believing, as he did, that any divorce of "shape from function" was the sign of a deplorable mental slovenliness,[10] Thompson was in no way identified with the fragile amusement of some of his contemporaries who could happily devote themselves to writing a villanelle in praise of the villanelle.

In the decadent writers, Thompson saw what he described as "etiolated poetry," created by men whose brains exhausted themselves in the "parturition of an epigram." [11] In an unpublished passage in his notes he wrote, "I hate the school of 'form,' who conceive that to play on poetry, as on a rustic whistle, you must first pith it. Their words have the marrow out of them." [12] This rejection of the decadent doctrine of form for form's sake he expressed most vividly in these lines from a poem called "Fool by Nature and by Art":

> Nay, this alone were prodigal Nature's plan;
> Behold the Artist supplement the Man!
> In the small line, with dainty exquisiteness
> Of feeble polish, polished feebleness,
> Wrought and perfected till each vein concealed
> Of native weakness shines with skill revealed.
> Scan thou the truth it can so well impart:—
> *A fool by nature, is twice fool by art.*[13]

Yet, Thompson was fully aware of the sensory delight espoused by those who spoke of "art for art's sake." In his own poetic development, as he himself confessed, "the stringing together of ingenious images" gave him the greatest pleasure. From the beginning, as his notebooks show, he never lost the love for sheer stimulation of the senses which he had found in the magic of poetry even as a child. To a sympathetic critic, like Alice Meynell, Thompson's imagery displayed the "splendid fault of excess." "How many poets," she asked, "might be furnished, not from the abundance but from the overabundance, of his imagery, and the prunings and chastenings of his fancy?" To less favorable critics, indeed, his poetry seemed—as *The Literary World* said, in a rather mixed figure of its own—to be "a dictionary of obsolete English suffering from a fierce fit of delirium tremens."

There can be no doubt that this overflowing passion for sensory images played an important part in the complex pattern of Thompson's tormenting sense of guilt. It is not too much to suppose that he may have associated it with the hours he had spent at Ushaw away from regularly assigned work as he searched the school library for more and more of the pleasure which he derived from poetic sound and the undisciplined play of the imagination. Thus he had moments when it appeared to him that the "fierce Bacchante" had come between him and the fulfillment of his religious vocation. In the aesthetic decadence of which he was so severe a critic, he also saw something of what he took to be a weakness within himself. Like Plato in his strictures against the poet, Thompson, by condemning aestheticism, was also protesting against an aspect of his own character.

As one who desired to overcome Philistine contempt for poetry and to arouse religious believers to a sense of its true worth, he nonetheless had times of serious inner conflict over the question of whether or not a life spent in the service of the sensory joys of the arts was likely to destroy one's chances of ultimate salvation. This truly Victorian problem, which was not unknown to Hopkins, is at the heart of that curious piece of self-questioning "To the Dead Cardinal of West-

minster," which Thompson wrote in 1892 shortly after
Manning's death. In this poem, the dead Cardinal is asked
to inquire of the angels as to what place there may be in
eternity for "One stricken from his birth/With curse/Of
destinate verse." Having loved Beauty with such intensity,
will it be the poet's ultimate fate

. . . .

> To find when all is known
>   That what
>   He solely sought
>
> 'Is lost, and thereto lost
> All that its seeking cost?
>   That he
>   Must finally,
>
> 'Through sacrificial tears,
> And anchoretic years,
>   Tryst
> With the sensualist?'

(ll. 158-167)

The mood which these lines represent may well have come
upon Thompson more than once during the times when deep
depression overtook him, as it did during the early days of his
stay at Storrington when he had first emerged from the world
of laudanum and the London streets. Yet, as he recovered
and frequently wandered up the steep path that leads to the
South Downs near the priory, he formulated an idea which
was fundamental to his essay on Shelley: The worship of
beauty is not evil but good. It becomes evil only when it is
separated from a sense of the "Primal Beauty."

Poetry, Thompson told himself, is a manifestation of that
primal, essential Beauty. Unlike Coleridge, who saw all the
arts as different species of poetry, and unlike Pater, who

thought of the various arts as striving to become what music
is, Thompson came to conceive of poetry, painting, and music
as the "trinity of beauty." He would have agreed with John
Symonds that there is a "prism of the arts," each one of which
expresses in its special way the same spiritual substance.[14]

In the essay on Shelley this spiritual substance, Beauty, is
pictured as a universal human need. Poetry, as one manifestation of it, is therefore a means of satisfying a truly
human hunger. As such it must be considered and evaluated
in itself—quite apart from all considerations of sectarian
controversy. Thus, unlike Newman, Thompson would not
raise the question of what English Protestantism had done to
influence the character of English conceptions of poetry. On
the contrary, he explicitly insisted that, "With few exceptions,
whatsoever in our best poets is great and good to the non-
Catholic, is great and good also to the Catholic." [15]

Just as Shelley had contended that poetry elevates man by
the way in which it causes him to know Beauty and to identify
himself with beautiful thoughts, actions, or persons, so Thompson felt that by keeping men mindful of Beauty, poetry elevated
them above the level of beasts. He was, in effect, in complete
sympathy with Ruskin's notion of "vital beauty" as the voice
of God, the concrete evidence of His presence. The Shelley
essay stands as his appeal from Storrington to the pastors and
"pious laics" of the Catholic Church to recognize that

> Poetry is the preacher to men of the earthly as you of
> the Heavenly Fairness; of that earthly fairness which God
> has fashioned to His own image and likeness. . . . Eye her
> not askance if she seldom sing directly of religion: the
> bird gives glory to God though it sings only of its inno-
> cent loves.[16]

III

The intense apology for poetry which Thompson developed at Storrington, like much of the writing he did there, was formed in the intervals between painful hours of enduring the continuing aftereffects of his withdrawal from laudanum. Far from being the considered reflection of an ordered time of objective analysis, it was a cry of affirmation in the midst of mortal combat. Tubercular and dyspeptic, he faced his struggle with every physical disadvantage against him. Introspective by nature, he confronted the added burden placed upon him by a mind which, when it was not distracted by work or reading, continually turned in upon itself.

The letters which he wrote to Meynell are the disordered record of his misery and the vital evidence of how great a part his attempts at creative and critical writing played in his effort to return to life. At the outset, he was incapable of finding much of the joy or peace which his surroundings at the Priory offered, but he felt that he would come to like Storrington as soon as he became capable of liking anything again. Yet even during what he called the "first sharp struggle," his love for poetry, and especially for Shakespeare, filled his letters with requests for the "absolute mercy" of books. If, as Everard Meynell says, "Thompson's muse rose from the penal waters fresh as Botticelli's Venus," those dark floods did not withdraw quickly. And they continued to engulf him from time to time with rising and falling periods of the deepest depression.

Painful attacks of indigestion swept over him during the half-sleep of the early part of the night or during the dawn. Medicine sent from London afforded but temporary relief and he would often sit up the greater part of the night simply to tire himself into a heavy sleep. At such times he wrote verse, some of which he sent to Meynell.

Such writings was for him "often nothing less than a confessional, a confessional far more intimate than ye sacerdotal one." [17] The sacrament of penance might touch one's sins while it left one's ignominious weaknesses in "merciful darkness." This deeply personal poetry, on the other hand, let the soul go forth in public, "like Anderson's Emperor, thinking herself clothed round with singing-robes," while in fact her "naked weakness" was utterly exposed "to ye visiting wind." Only those who, like the Meynells, loved and understood the poet's torment could be trusted with confidences so painfully given in the verses that rose up out of his secret self during so many sleepless nights.

He begged Meynell for work and directions in the formation of working habits. The first critical essays came slowly. At first he could not make any progress, although he tried "regularly enough" to settle himself to writing. Slowly his brain began to move, but, as he wrote in one of his Storrington letters, it did not seem to be very willing to serve him. When he felt that he had some power to write "in the teeth of nerves and mood and bilious melancholy," he wanted more to do so that he would not "lose a habit scarcely acquired."

There can be no doubt but that the physical and mental struggles of that time served to heighten his conviction that man is inevitably involved in a frequently painful paradox of being both body and soul. He was, as he wrote to Meynell, "often fairly sick of the being that inhabits this villainous mud-hut of a body."

The expression was typical, for he favored the language of Neo-Platonism. In the manuscript *Out of the House of Bondage,* for example, he wrote:

> Therefore, as a woman is committed to a eunuch, so
> is the spiritual soul to the unspiritual body. And from
> this clement servitude there is no flight on earth. . . . Nor
> by any profit of our study and diligence can we work out,
> as some have devised, a forestalled freedom from this
> gross control; nor in dreams, as others figure, slip its
> vigilance.

As a Christian Neo-Platonist, Thompson always was inclined to think of the body as "the clog which keeps us wing-
less"; [18] as a Catholic sacramentalist, he sometimes adopted
the Franciscan description of the body as a plodding ass, upon
which the soul must ride; but as one who had some knowledge
of medicine and a lifelong experience of illness, he knew that,
even as a beast of burden, "this sore-spent body is a Golden
Ass," whose energies must be protected. St. Paul's cry for
deliverance from "the body of this death" Thompson described
as the poignant outburst of one who rightly apprehended the
nature of the interaction of body and spirit. To that intimate
portrayal of the "internecine grapple between body and spirit"
the progress of psychological and physiological research
seemed to him to have added knowledge of the unsuspected
complexity of the relationships involved:

> We can no longer set body against spirit and let them
> come to grips after the light-hearted fashion of our ances-
> tors. We realize that their intertwinings are of infinite deli-
> cacy, endless multiplicity: no stroke upon the one but is
> innumerably reverberated by the other.[19]

The desires of the spirit, he observed in a notebook, are not
indefinitely credible and sufficing without the confirmation and
assurance of the body, and, in an unpublished portion of a
draft of the essay "Health and Holiness," he commented,
"Arius, one feels sure, was dyspeptic; a council of churchmen

pronounced on his doctrine, but a council of physicians should have pronounced on his liver." [20]

Yet, in spite of his own painful experience of the intertwinings and conflicts of body and spirit, which were especially acute in the first months of his stay at Storrington, Thompson may be said to have taken the corporeal aspects of life with a certain amount of equanimity. Even in his attack on the body in "Out of the House of Bondage," he admitted its importance in preserving that individuality without which there can be no creative activity. If the body inhibits self-expression, it nonetheless makes selfhood possible. Consequently, he wrote that if men were not "caged in matter" they would become like bubbles on water, losing their particularity in "brittle coalescence." The complete absorption of souls into one another, the perfect communication of self to self, would simply result in the solidifying of "the counter-revolving, yet harmonious, wheels of life" into a motionless mass. We can never "tell ourselves out . . . to the ultimate syllable." And if we could do so, we would finally create nothing but a sterile "communism of soul."

For Thompson, therefore, there was no desire to break out of the limitations of his frail mortality. He was resigned to the fact that just as men must fall back, uncomprehending, from the deepest mysteries of what he called "the ninefold universe and the threefold Eternal," so they would always encounter a providential frustration in attempting to break through the barriers of the flesh to achieve some imagined perfect communication with one another.

The dead weight of his bodily miseries hung on him at Storrington. But he knew that he must hold on to the physical frame of his life until, after much passive endurance, his body would serve his creative spirit. As the bitter days and nights passed, he began to have hope that "ye thing" was gradually loosening its hold upon him. By the middle of the summer of 1889 he was at work on the "Ode to the Setting Sun," and had evidently at least given thought to the theme of "The Hound of Heaven," which was finally to appear in *Merry England* in July, 1890. The fact that Thompson survived through all the anguish of the months that followed his treatment for the laudanum habit was evidence of his will to live; the creation of his splendid "Ode to the Setting Sun" was proof that all the infirmity of his nearly shattered body could not destroy the creative spirit that was in him.

IV

That creative spirit and the processes of the imagination which it animated were not only the sources of Thompson's poetry, but also the objects of his fascinated critical examination. The habit of introspection with respect to the life of poetic creation was strong in him from his boyhood. As his letters to Meynell suggest, that habit was deepened and intensified at Storrington. It became one of the major characteristics of his thought and permeated his writing.

Everard Meynell says, with some justice, that one can read Thompson's three volumes of poetry as if they were the prefaces to thirty-three, for so much of his poetry is about poetry itself. In "Carmen Genesis," for example, there is an extended comparison between the creativity of the poet and the creative acts of God. In "From the Night of Forebeing" there is a long passage on the winter of unproductiveness and the spring of poetic inspiration. In "The Cloud's Swan Song" there is an elaborate metaphor, comparing the formation of a cloud with poetry arising within the poet's mind; and such pieces as

"The Singer Saith of His Song" and "Contemplation" are concerned with the fruitful solitude of the poet in quiet, passive periods of retirement from activity. Poetic creation is an important theme in his "Mistress of Vision," and the relation between poetic insight and the experience of pain is essential to the argument of his ode "Laus Amara Doloris."

Poets, Thompson remarked in one of his manuscripts, are men of inner weather, with their phases, seasons, tides, storms, calms, aridities, and periods of fruitfulness.[21] Yet, as the changeful operations of their creative powers figuratively mirror the changes in the face of nature, so it is true that these very psychic changes are themselves actually rooted in the physical and the natural.

In this connection, Thompson described an experience which was, according to Wilfrid Meynell, the poet's own. There is the possibility that it may refer to an episode during his stay at Storrington. In any case, the passage is important and interesting not only because it serves to counterbalance some of Thompson's more "mystical" discussions of the creative process, but also because it reveals both a similarity to and a difference from Blake, who would not have offered so naturalistic an explanation of what took place:

> I recall a poet, passing through that process of seclusion and gestation already considered. In his case the psychological manifestations were undoubtedly associated with disorder of the body. In solitude he underwent profound sadness and suffered brief exultations of power: the wild miseries of a Berlioz gave place to accesses of half-pained delight. On a day when the skirts of a prolonged darkness were drawing off from him, he walked the garden. . . . Pausing in reverie before an arum, he suddenly was aware of a minute white-stoled child sitting on the lily. For a second he viewed her with surprised delight, but no wonder; then, returning to consciousness,

he recognized the hallucination almost in the instant of
her vanishing.[22]

This apparition of the child associated with the lily, Thompson says, came and went as the momentary product of a
nervous system worn out by bodily disorders and interior
struggles in a time of enforced withdrawal from actual writing.
But it was an experience which, when recalled, might well have
given birth to a lyric.

Clearly, Thompson was quite aware of the intimate connection between physical conditions and psychic phenomena.
Yet, one finds him saying in his *Analogies Between God,
Nature, Man, And the Poet* that some ideas which poets think
are their own actually have been inspired by angels. Such
inspirations, he believed, may come during sleep, but asleep
or awake, the mind receives such inspirations only when it is
allowed to lie fallow.

As an example, Thompson recalled his "virginal experience
of intuition in its fuller manifestations." [23] Reading an article
in a magazine with no apparent purpose in mind, the poet
encountered a description of how various recognizable forms
might be produced on sand when musical notes were sounded
over it:

> Some of these forms, it was stated, had a curious resemblance to trees and other natural objects. At that sentence, as at a signal, the peripheries of my mind were
> perturbed by a sensation new in its magnitude: as if,
> there, inter-isolated hosts of ideas were breaking up their
> camps and threatening convergence on my soul. From
> every horizon of consciousness, like far and wind-borne
> tramplings, the multitudinous rumour of their coming
> held me still. I laid down the Magazine, and said to myself: "Here is mystery." Not at once, but through several
> days, the convergence then begun developed itself: till a
> serried conception stood ranked in my mind. Then, for

the first time, I understood why the ancients thought our learning a remembering. The sensation was like nothing so much as the dire stirrings of forgotten memories, awakened by some sudden association. The air blew demons.

The "serried conception" arising from this experience was the idea that Nature, no less than man, is made in the image of God. This ancient concept, which Thompson here encountered as something fresh and new, became, as we shall see, a fundamental principle of his philosophy. It is, consequently, a forming influence in his poetry.

As a result of this and similar experiences—although the "demons" mentioned were metaphorical—Thompson felt obliged to take the word *inspiration* quite literally. However, if he had been asked why he could believe that a particular idea or passage in his poetry was supernaturally inspired, he said that he would have had to reply in the words of the disciples at Emmaus: "Did not our hearts glow within us while He was speaking."

This, most emphatically, did not mean that Thompson claimed any special sanctity or private revelation for himself. "Balaam's ass," he said, "is not yet on the calendar. His remarks after, as before, that episode were confined to 'heehaw': which may have much symbolic meaning, but seems a little wanting in variety. Did the Almighty speak through Balaam's ass, but never through Shakespeare?" Like Shelley, Thompson simply placed poets among those to whom there is sometimes given an intimate knowledge of the agencies of an invisible world.

He held to the general Romantic opinion that the poetic imagination has an intuitive power to see the secret identities of essence in outwardly separate things. Seeing the one in the many, the poet experiences powerful sensations of delight, which are recalled with passion during the actual composition of poetry, for the poet is not only a meditative man but also one who is passionate in his response to the image of remembered beauty.

Without passion there could be no poetry for Thompson, but he agreed with Shelley that poetic passion is not under the voluntary power of the poet, for verse does "no man's bidding." The writing of prose was, for him, like working with cold clay, but poetry, when the passion necessary to its making was aroused, was "molten metal." When he could work under the powerful, driving energy of this passion, Thompson experienced immense exhilaration in the feeling that the poetic medium was plastic to the lightest feather touch of emotional suggestion or to the most obscure stirrings of half-intentions or unconscious wishes. Sometimes, as he said in his notes, it was true that his metre might not "cool" to the intended effect because it had not been perfectly plastic to his feeling, but the rare times of his poetic creation in the white heat of the genuine passion for beauty were precious periods in which he knew the most "spontaneously easy of all media of expression." [24]

However, the fact that poetic composition involved much that was not "spontaneously easy" for Thompson may be seen in his notebooks. The drafts and revisions show the creative process to have been involved and laborious more often than not. Like an explorer, the poet searched out the possibilities of the language of imagination. For him, mere inventiveness was never enough, for as he remarked in a pencilled note, he believed that the poet is "an Elias," who must, when he comes, make all things new.[25]

Into his notebooks went Thompson's record of his explorations of imaginative utterance. At Storrington, as during his outcast days in London, they were the possessions he really valued above all others. To read them is to know Thompson, for as Everard Meynell said in an article for the *Dublin Review:*

> They were his other self; his companions through many solitary years; his life-work and his library; they were the only things he never discarded. The few volumes that came his way as a reviewer when they overflowed more than a small shelf would be sold, and if he changed his lodging, nothing of account had to be removed save the many dozens of shabby exercise books that filled a large tin box—dense piles of unstitched leaves covered with faded pencil marks.[26]

Typical of the jottings in those faded pencil marks is the following fragment, with alternative words in parentheses, relating to his memories of summers that are past:

> You taste the summer.
> Their fragrant garments (plumage) all a-blow (a-glow)
> Warm-wingéd summers in (through) me go
> I played with in the long-ago;
> Their plumage-tips (points) burn low, burn low.
> (Their fire-edged plumes)
> (Their plumage-edges burning low)
> (Their edgéd plumes burn low, burn low)
> So long it was, so long ago.
> So far they come from (the) long-ago.
> (For) the way is far (weary) from long-ago.
> (They are) weary out (from, of) the long ago.[27]

From many such fragments, as well as from extended first drafts, Thompson's fascination with the sound of words is as evident as is the delight in imagery for its own sake which sometimes marks, and occasionally mars, his poetry. Yet these working notes are significant for a much more important reason: They provide first-hand evidence of the process by which imagery often came to him from the subconscious to the conscious level, half-formed and highly plastic. His restless imagination was almost constantly forming and re-forming new combinations of images and sound, even when it appeared that he was in one of his fallow periods. For every fragmentary notation he made, Thompson must have been aware of a multitude of phrases and suggestions which never came into focus, or which were rejected.

For Thompson, a poem was the poet's "kaleidoscopic reproduction of himself and of external things." It was a middle ground between a thought and a thing. In the creative process he saw three stages: conception, mental expression, and objective reproduction.

The first of these, conception, he regarded as the most perfect, and it is evident that he agreed with Shelley's famous statement in his *Defence of Poetry:*

> The mind in creation is as a fading coal ... when composition begins, inspiration is already on the decline, and the most glorious poetry that has ever been communicated to the world is probably a feeble shadow of the original conception of the poet.

In Thompson's theory, the poet's initial conception is the product of his faculty of intuition, whose powers come into play only as the result of a period of contemplation, which is the time of gestation. As he remarked in a review,

> The insight of the poet springs from intuition, which is the highest reason, and is acquired through contemplation, which is the highest effort. For contemplation implies a concentration far greater than is needed for ordinary thought. We need not quote Wordsworth to show that such was the method used by him.[28]

Yet, Wordsworth is not the only influence at work upon Thompson's thought here. What Thompson calls "intuition" is very much like Coleridge's "primary imagination," described in *Biographia Literaria* as "the living power and prime agent of all perception . . . a repetition in the finite mind of the external act of creation in the infinite I Am." The secondary imagination, according to Coleridge, is an echo of this primary imagination, with which it co-exists and from which it differs only in degree and in the manner of its operation. It is this secondary imagination which Thompson seems to have in mind when he speaks of the stage of mental expression, which is less perfect than that of primary conception, yet synchronous with it and only theoretically separable from it. The poem itself, which, as we have seen, Thompson called the poet's reproduction of himself and of external things, is described by Coleridge as a totality in which the external has been made internal, the internal made external, nature made thought, and thought made nature.

To Thompson, Coleridge was "a critic the subtlest and most profound of his time," [29] and it is, therefore, not at all surprising that he should have found himself in such close agreement with that writer's views of the stages of poetic creation. Coleridge's idealism was, after all, a philosophical framework which was peculiarly congenial to Thompson's own Christian Neo-Platonism.

A true inheritor of the English Romantic tradition, Thompson never regarded the making of a poem as a process analogous to the work of an architect. His drafts show that his sense of the inner relations of the parts of a poem developed as he worked with each of them, and often, as Haecker says, his creative work went on in his mind even while he slept. At his best, as in "The Hound of Heaven," Thompson's poetry shifts from image to image along a line of development that states the theme through the implications contained in the imagery. Never obviously on the lookout for visual images, often quite indifferent to natural surroundings, Thompson nonetheless absorbed a vast amount of what he experienced. He stored it away at the subconscious level or recorded his imaginative interpretation of his experience in his notebooks, where it is evident that vivid impressions served him in composition as abstract ideas never could. For him, locality was never as important as imaginative effect.

The notebooks, which rapidly grew in number from the Storrington period onward, furnish few examples of poetic drill work. They rather record his endless effort to make the transition from initial conception to the medium of language with the greatest possible integrity. Their abundant disorder is the disorder of living matter growing and being formed. His drafts are the work of one who never really found communication easy, one who believed that "expression never fully expresses." At Storrington, however, he was well on the way to making what he felt intensely "in the brain" available to those who would listen and understand.

CHAPTER FOUR

TASTE OF SUMMER

I

Two of Thompson's poems written at Storrington clearly mark the progress in his work which finally caused the Meynells to advise him to return to London in February, 1890, so that he might be closer to the libraries and centers of literary life. The first of these, "Daisy," later appeared with "A Song of Youth and Age" and "To My Godchild" in an anthology, *The Child Set in the Midst,* which Meynell had published in 1892. The second was the "Ode to the Setting Sun," which appeared in its first published version in *Merry England* in September, 1889.

"Daisy" is the first of a number of poems about children, and the figure of a child as the symbol of primal, innocent trust is, of course, conventional. While it is true that St. Augustine in his *Confessions* discerned in the infant the traces of original sin, the devotional tradition in which Thompson grew up often uses childhood to represent the quality of ageless innocence, for as St. Clement of Alexandria expresses it, "Whatever partakes of eternity assumes the qualities of the incorruptible; therefore the name *childhood* is for us a lifetime of spring, because the truth abiding in us is ageless."

As we have seen, Thompson condemned the idea that childhood is necessarily the happiest time in life. Moreover, at school he had known something of juvenile cruelty. Yet, whatever he may have owed to Wordsworth or to Blake, it was natural enough that his religious training should have suggested to him a well established conception of the relation between childhood and innocence.

Consequently, when he happened to meet the child named Daisy in the course of a walk on the Storrington common, his reaction was like that which he had felt towards the "Little Flower" of the McMaster household in London. Daisy was one of a family of nine, four of whom had been given floral names. A simple village child, in the best Wordsworthian tradition, she gave the poet three wild flowers and, trustingly taking his hand, talked of toys and strawberries.

If it is true that sentimentality in poetry attempts to create an emotional response that is in excess of the occasion, "Daisy" cannot rightly be called a sentimental poem. The occasion was the poet's time of return to life, and the opening lines are permeated with the new taste of fresh air:

> Where the thistle lifts a purple crown
> Six foot out of the turf,
> And the harebell shakes on the windy hill———
> O the breath of the distant surf!———
>
> The hills look over on the South,
> And southward dreams the sea;
> And with the sea-breeze hand in hand
> Came innocence and she. (ll. 1-8)

"Daisy" exemplifies Robert Frost's declaration that a poem "begins in delight and ends in wisdom. . . . It finds its own name as it goes and discovers the best waiting for it in some final phrase at once wise and sad." [1] The dramatic situation is the happy circumstance of the meeting, which is so short-lived. The child goes on "her sunshine way," and the poet is left feeling "The pang of all the partings gone, / And partings yet to be." The lush coloring of the imagery of the opening stanzas, as is so often the case with Keats, gives way to the ancient Greek paradox of the "sadness in the sweet." This aspect of the experience is caught in the suggestive figure, "And the leaves fell from the day"; and it issues in the explicit final statement that

> Nothing begins, and nothing ends,
> That is not paid with moan;
> For we are born in other's pain,
> And perish in our own. (ll. 57-60)

As he says in "The Hound of Heaven," the theme of which seems to have developed at Storrington, Thompson could not find release from his sense of loss and guilt even in the eyes of children:

> I turned to them very wistfully;
> But just as their young eyes grew sudden fair
> With dawning answers there,
> Their angel plucked them from me by the hair.
> (ll. 57-60)

The consolation he wanted could not be supplied by the created universe. Having once aspired to offer the Host before an altar crucifix, he had failed. But standing in a field at sunset on the Priory grounds at Storrington, he found himself in the shadow of a large cross that had been erected there and knew that his very griefs and discontents with the world remained essentially what they had always been—the restless stirrings of a spirit which was of "the brood of immortality."

The "Ode to the Setting Sun," written long before Thompson had seen and been influenced by the odes of Patmore, was, according to his own description, "not unworthy of preservation, though it was my first published poem of any importance." The general movement is from a nameless emotion stirred by

the sun's setting behind the cross through a general reflection
on the paradoxical union of birth and death in nature, where

> It is the falling star that trails the light,
> It is the breaking wave that hath the might,
> The passing shower that rainbows maniple.
>
> (ll. 8-10)

The sun, which seems to die at each setting, is described as
the source of life to the earth from the first dawn of creation.
Much of the imagery is mythological and recalls Thompson's
excellence in classical studies at Ushaw. Finally, the theme
moves from the level of nature to the tradition of Christian
religious symbolism, in which the sun becomes "type memo-
rial" of Christ, and the poet draws the analogy:

> Like Him thou hang'st in dreadful pomp of blood
> Upon thy Western rood;
> And His stained brow did vail like thine to night,
> Yet lift once more Its light,
> And risen, again departed from our ball,
> But when It set on earth arose in Heaven.
>
> (ll. 219-224)

It is Christ Who gives meaning to the mystery of the paradox
with which the ode opens. There Thompson speaks of Death
and Birth as "Mystical twins of time inseparable." He calls
Death "the fairer thing," not because he is morbidly in love
with death, for his own will to live was strong. It is rather
because,

> The fall doth pass the rise in worth;
> For birth hath in itself the germ of death,
> But death hath in itself the germ of birth.
> It is the falling acorn buds the tree,
> The falling rain that bears the greenery,
> The fern plants moulder when the ferns arise.
>
> (ll. 227-232)

In the section called "After-Strain," Thompson developed an idea that is one of his basic themes: the poet's creative activity is inevitably bound up with pain. As with all things human; the shadow of the Cross lies over his path. Yet, he does not see life as a cheerless experience, for the "rigorous austerity" of the Cross is brightened by the devotion of faith so intimately associated in Thompson's Catholic outlook with the "tender Lady, Queen Mary." Grief and frustration are seen to be evidence that men, whose last end is God, cannot rest content with less than God.

The "Ode to the Setting Sun" is a prelude to "The Hound of Heaven," with which it is closely associated as the product of Thompson's own experience of near-death and the renewal of life. It contains numerous suggestive evidences of the course of that life which led to the Field of the Cross at Storrington. His intense response to sense stimuli, which marked him from boyhood, is in the lines:

> Thy visible music-blasts make deaf the sky,
>   Thy cymbals clang to fire the Occident,
> Thou dost thy dying so triumphally:
> I *see* the crimson blaring of thy shawns!
>
> (ll. 16-19)

His love of Aeschylus and the poets of Greek antiquity echoes in the central section of the ode, while his contact with nineteenth-century science in the Manchester years appears in such places as his reference to "the furnace of the mammoth's heart" and in the ambiguity of the question, "How came the entombèd tree a light-bearer, / Though sunk in lightless lair?" The years at Ushaw are, perhaps, reflected in the use of the word *maniple* in the figure which appears in "The passing shower that rainbows maniple," for the maniple is one of the vestments used during the Mass. Certainly Thompson's fearful burden of struggle against addiction is suggested in the "After-Strain":

Yet woe to him that from his burden flees,
    Crushed in the fall of what he cast away.

(ll. 15-16)

The weight of his effort lay heavy upon him, but he knew well
enough that to abandon it was certain destruction.

The "Ode to the Setting Sun," probably more than anything
else that Thompson sent from Storrington, convinced the Meynells of the emergence of the poet's talent. As their daughter
puts it, "To the Meynells it was a revelation, even calling for
action, and they took train to Sussex to congratulate Thompson." By the beginning of the year, it was thought, he would
be able to come to London, work as a journalist, and continue
his creative development in contact with the literary life of the
capital.

This idea proved to be only partially correct, although
Thompson welcomed it, and wrote of his return to London in
February, 1890, that he was "immensely relieved; for the re-
moval of the opium had quite destroyed my power of bearing
the almost unbroken solitude in which I found myself."

Meynell, whose patience with Thompson has been described
as "a marvel, a miracle," [2] at once began to promote the poet's
literary career. Alice Meynell having inherited some money
from her father, it had become possible for the family to build
a house in Palace Court, Bayswater, not far from Kensington
Gardens. A room was found for Thompson in a near-by lodging house and he began to be part of the small group of vol-
unteers that helped with the editorial work for the *Weekly
Register*.

This work, like all the rest of the almost constant writing that went on at Palace Court, was carried on in the library. Absent-minded and constantly worried about trifles, Thompson was not only an anomaly but something of a problem to the household. Shabby amid the Morris furniture, the tiles, and the Persian rugs, sometimes confused by the inevitable noise of a house filled with activity and children, Thompson often lost track of his own work and held up that of others.

In spite of his frequent confusion and habitual lateness, he actually produced a considerable number of reviews for the *Weekly Register,* while his contributions to *Merry England* became so numerous that he used the editor's own practice of writing under a pseudonym in order to avoid the impression of a monotonous repetition. The names "Francis Tancred" and "Francis Phillimore" were most often used, but at times he also employed "Philip Hemans."

The years 1890-1892, during which Thompson spent most of his time in London, were years of poetic productivity. He worked on *Sister Songs,* wrote the series of poems that came to be called "Love in Dian's Lap," and produced such work as "Corymbus for Autumn," "The Poppy" and "To the Dead Cardinal of Westminster." Above all, he completed "The Hound of Heaven," a poem that has been translated into most languages and much admired by readers in every part of the world, many of whom have not shared Thompson's faith or his cultural background.

Seekers after "influences" are always with us, and "The Hound of Heaven" has not escaped their careful attention. As Reid points out, both the title and the handling of the theme, which is the mystery of the pursuing grace of God, have been affected by St. Augustine's *Confessions,* St. John of the Cross, *The Spiritual Exercises* of St. Ignatius, Silvio Pellico's "Dio

Amore" and Shelley's *Prometheus Unbound* and *Epipsychidion*.[3]

Whatever its literary sources, "The Hound of Heaven" is supremely Thompson's own—the poem of a man who had felt a vocation to the priesthood to be his, only to learn that it was lost to him forever. Unable to serve God at the altar, he had fled like a rejected lover, who fears what he loves most and seeks consolation in lesser loves. The silence of his return to his family, the deepening of his introversion, the escape in opium—all these things are reflected in the lines:

> I FLED Him, down the nights and down the days;
> I fled Him, down the arches of the years;
> I fled Him, down the labyrinthine ways
>   Of my own mind; and in the mist of tears
> I hid from Him, and under running laughter.
>
> (ll. 1-5)

Having once offered his life to God and feeling what seemed to be the awesome darkness of the Divine refusal, he felt himself to be alien, not only to his family and society in general, but to the whole divinely ordered universe.

Like Wordsworth in "Tintern Abbey"—and even Byron in certain of his moods—he followed the Romantic retreat to nature; but unlike those earlier poets, Thompson looked much more to the imagined natural world of literary tradition than to the experience of nature itself. Yet, he was too deeply imbued with the theological distinction between the Creator and His creatures, too much filled with a sense of the distinguishing marks of man's peculiar dignity, to find satisfaction in the Romantic treatment of nature. As he remarked in the manuscript *Mystery, Mysticism, and Allegory,* the "nature-mysticism" of Wordsworth was for him utterly "tentative and incomplete." He sought, after his fashion, to find some basis of unity with nature's "delicate fellowship," but:

> In vain my tears were wet on Heaven's grey cheek.
> For ah! we know not what each other says,
> > These things and I; in sound *I* speak——
> *Their* sound is but their stir, they speak by silences.
> Nature, poor stepdame, cannot slake my drouth;
> > Let her, if she would owe me,
> Drop yon blue bosom-veil of sky, and show me
> > The breasts o' her tenderness:
> Never did any milk of hers once bless
> > My thirsting mouth.   (ll. 99-104)

He found no real solace in nature; nor was the world of drug-induced fantasy any place of satisfaction for the spirit that had known the love of Supreme Reality. Even the power of the creative literary imagination failed as a device to run from the thought of God. In words that recall the Psalmist's "For my days are consumed like smoke," he wrote:

> My days have crackled and gone up in smoke,
> Have puffed and burst as sun-starts on a stream.
> > Yea, faileth now even dream
> The dreamer, and the lute the lutanist;
> Even the linked fantasies, in whose blossomy twist
> I swung the earth a trinket at my wrist,
> Are yielding; cords of all too weak account
> For earth with heavy griefs so overplussed.
> > (ll. 122-129)

Somewhere, perhaps at Storrington or even earlier in London, Thompson had felt the force of the idea that although he had been rejected for the priesthood, he had not been abandoned by the grace of God, whose pursuing love would give him no refuge in the love of creatures or the creation of poetry. His refuge could not be in flight but in surrender to the mystery of a love whose purposes for him were but dimly and momentarily perceived. He had not found any complete solution to his personal dilemma, nor had he lost his sense of guilt and frustration, but he had asked the question, "Is my gloom, after all, / Shade of His hand, outstretched caressingly?" He had come to the point where he could say, "Naked I wait Thy love's uplifted stroke!"

Certainly "The Hound of Heaven" does not describe the rediscovery of a lost faith, for Thompson, in all his darkest London days, did not abandon his religious belief; he never doubted the reality of his Pursuer. It was, in fact, the sense of that reality which made his feeling of guilt so real. With the writing of his best known poem, he had not found ultimate peace of mind through some process of sublimation by which religion would do what opium could not. He had, for the time being, stopped running long enough to hear the words, "I am He Whom thou seekest! / Thou dravest love from thee, who dravest Me." He had achieved a moment of the deepest wisdom, but questions remained.

"The Hound of Heaven" is, therefore, anything but a piece of stock religious poetry, with easy, conventional responses to great issues. It is as complex in its integrity as its imagery is often startling in the way that John Donne can be startling. Its author's religious awareness was that of a tremendous mystery rather than of an easily understood source of assurance. Like Herbert in "The Collar" he ends in the mood of the child who must trust and follow what he does not hope to understand. As to the future, he says:

> And now my heart is as a broken fount,
> Wherein tear-drippings stagnate, spilt down ever
>   From the dank thoughts that shiver
> Upon the sighful branches of my mind.
>   Such is; what is to be?
> The pulp so bitter, how shall taste the rind?
> I dimly guess what Time in mists confounds;
> Yet ever and anon a trumpet sounds
> From the hid battlements of Eternity;

> Those shaken mists a space unsettle, then
> Round the half-glimpsed turrets slowly wash again.
>
> (ll. 137-147)

There is, of course, the moment of insight, for the clouds do
not obscure the poet's vision before he has seen "him who sum-
moneth" standing "With glooming robes purpureal, cypress-
crowned." And the Voice that is around him "like a bursting
sea" leaves him with an answer which—like that given to Job
—is itself the statement of a mystery:

> 'All which I took from thee I did but take,
>   Not for thy harms,
> But just that thou might'st seek it in My arms.
>   All which thy child's mistake
> Fancies as lost, I have stored for thee at home:
>   Rise, clasp My hand, and come!'
>
> (ll. 171-176)

⚜ III ⚜

It is probably true to say that more than any other of Thompson's poems "The Hound of Heaven" has been responsible for
his having so often been described as a mystic. Caroline Spurgeon, for example, remarks that "the spirit of mystic devotion
and aspiration" permeates his work.[4] Holbrook Jackson judges
Thompson in relation to such of his contemporaries as Ernest
Dowson and Lionel Johnson and argues that Thompson had
the larger perspective, for in him there was "a new avowal
of mysticism" that gave a special beauty and life to his religious
orthodoxy.[5]

That very orthodoxy must have contributed in no small
measure to Thompson's honest astonishment when he discovered that he had earned the reputation of being a mystic. In

the prose fragment called *Mysticism* he remarked on the looseness with which that word is employed. If one accepted current usage, a mystic might be any one, or all, of the following:

a) anyone who holds views of nature which scientists have not yet arrived at;

b) a person, engaged in the business of Gilbert and Sullivan's J. Wellington Wells, the sorcerer;

c) a Pre-Raphaelite;

d) an individual who says prayers and has faith in saints;

e) an individual who does not say his prayers, but who believes in medicine-men and devils;

f) a person who writes things which journalists do not fully understand.

Thompson's own conception of a mystic was, as Osbert Burdett says, "ecclesiastical." [6] He did not set up an opposition between the institutional and the personal elements in religion, and although he held the poetry of Blake in high regard, he did not share Blake's antinomianism. On his own terms, it is evident that Thompson could never have thought of himself as a mystic, for he understood what Aldous Huxley has so well demonstrated: The practice of ascetical mortification is an integral part of all authentic mysticism, both within the Christian tradition and outside of it. [7] Thompson expressed this perfectly clearly in a review:

> Mysticism is an interior ladder, at the summit of which is God. The mystic endeavours, by a rigid practical virtue, combined with prayer, meditation, and mortification of the senses, to arrive at a closer union with the Creator. [8]

His own lack of worldly goods, his evident indifference to food, his lack of regard for time and routine—these things in Thompson's life were scarcely caused by regular mortification for a supernatural motive. In his adult life they were frequently the result of his indulgence in opium, but at all times they were the product of habitual withdrawal into the world of his own imagination.

Knowing this of himself, Thompson could say that if one thought of a mystic as anything "between a 3-card-trick man and a Russian minister," then

> It seems possible . . . that, despite a virtuous life, I may be a "mystic"; but then it is clear I am (must be) a very little one. Parturient montes, nascitur ridiculus mysticus. (The mountains labored and gave birth to an absurd mystic.)

As a Catholic, Thompson accepted an intellectual environment in which one presupposes the ultimate necessity of knowledge given by the inspiration of God. By so doing, he willingly identified himself with a point of view that may properly be called mystical, but even here, certain qualifications should be observed. As Delattre was quick to see, there is something distinctive about the combination in Thompson of the Roman Catholic religion, with its ritualism and dogmatic objectivity, and an interior piety which is distinctly English in its reserve.[9]

If he recognized the limitations of British common-sense practicality, he was nonetheless sympathetic to the homely spirituality of Herbert, although his own work more often displays the flamboyance of Crashaw. For example, in a review of a book on Thomas à Kempis he wrote:

> But had à Kempis been merely a mystic, he would have had no more readers among us than other and greater mystics. His power is in his profound humanity. His appeal to the English mind is, in a way, somewhat like the appeal of Herbert's poetry. Both, in their diverse ways, bring mysticism down to earth, or leaven daily life with mysticism.[10]

Although he frequently failed to display it, Thompson unquestionably had a native respect for common sense. The possibility of a "whole tribe of young men" rushing to be "mystical poets" he contemplated as "a dismal forecast" that could mean only "bad poetry and bad mysticism." [11]

He did not think of the publication of "The Hound of Heaven" as initiating a mystical trend in English poetry, nor did it mark a turning of his own life in the direction followed by the truly great mystical poetry of St. John of the Cross. His mind was not thereafter wholly set upon God.

The very year in which "The Hound of Heaven" appeared was also the year when Thompson began the series of pieces called "Love in Dian's Lap," in which the central figure, Alice Meynell, is so idealized as to bear little or no relation to what she was in reality—the beautiful, mature, and gifted mother of a large family, who was kept as busy with journalism as she was with the care of her very active household and left with little time for the creative writing of which she was so capable.

Thompson, like a great many other people, fell in love with Alice Meynell. It was not a difficult thing to do. Richard Le Gallienne described her as having the charm of a beautiful abbess, and Meredith saw her as one who seemed to have walked in holy places. The first time that Thompson visited the Meynells, he had been given a copy of her *Poems,* which, according to one account, he sat up all night to read and put down with the exclamation, "Then I, too, am a poet!"

"Love in Dian's Lap" proclaims Mrs. Meynell to be far more than what Patmore called her—a queen among women. To Thompson she was one within whose "spirit's arms" he found a refuge from the "ravening of the gates of hell." [12] He dwelt on her portrait in youth and, in an image he was later to use to good effect in "The Kingdom of God," he declared that, "Her soul from earth to Heaven lies, / Like the ladder of the vision." [13] She floats through the poetic sequence like a figure in a Pre-Raphaelite painting and at times is almost indistin-

guishable from the Blessed Virgin in his imagination.[14] In
"Manus Animam Pinxit," she is the spirit that feeds his spirit:

> Like to a wind-swept sapling grow I from
> The clift, Sweet, of your skyward-jetting soul,——
> Shook by all the gusts that sweep it, overcome
> By all its cloud incumbent: O be true
> To your soul, dearest, as my life to you!
> For if that soil grow sterile, then the whole
> Of me must shrivel, from the topmost shoot
> Of climbing poesy, and my life, killed through,
> Dry down and perish to the foodless root.
>
> (ll. 10-18)

The extravagance of the language, the involved conceits that
recall all the imitators of Petrarch, the highly derivative and
sometimes eccentric diction of "Love in Dian's Lap" do not
convey a passion half so much as they surround an almost religious devotion that is, perhaps, embarrassed by the suggestion of its own idolatry. Like *Sister Songs* of the same period
—which Thompson wrote for two of the Meynell children,
Madeline and Monica—some of the poetry of "Love in Dian's
Lap" has a luxuriance which is ample evidence that in 1890 he
had still not outgrown the notion that to produce rich imagery
is to create poetry.

The riotous power of sense stimuli which Thompson, in "To
the Dead Cardinal of Westminster," says he both felt and
feared, is quite uncontrolled in *Sister Songs,* where the theme
of childhood innocence becomes smothered in flowery metaphors and such mythological conceits as

> Thou Perseus' Shield wherein I view secure
> The mirrored Woman's fateful-fair allure!
> Whom Heaven still leaves a twofold dignity,
> As girlhood gentle, and as boyhood free;
> With whom no most diaphanous webs enwind
> The barèd limbs of the rebukeless mind.
>
> (II, ll. 288-293)

As Alice Meynell said, Thompson had to learn "that these ceremonies of the imagination are chiefly ways of approach, and
that there are realities beyond and nearer to the centre of poetry
itself." [15] If he was not to practice the mortification of the
cloister, he had at least to practice that which would discipline
his imagination.

Taken individually, of course, some of the figures developed
in *Sister Songs* have a striking vividness. For instance, he writes
of a journeying Arab, who

> Sees the palm and tamarind
> Tangle the tresses of a phantom wind,——
> A sight like innocence when one has sinned!
> A green and maiden freshness smiling there
>   While with unblinking glare
> The tawny-hided desert crouches watching her.
>
> (II, ll. 228-233)

Yet, Thompson showed none of the disciplined command of
imagery which is evident in "The Hound of Heaven," where
it serves the thematic development so well. Similarly, in "A
Corymbus for Autumn," which appeared in *Merry England* in
April, 1891, the theme was lost amid what Thompson's friends
at Palace Court called the "foam and roar" of his phraseology.
The poem may display what one favorable critic has called a
quality of "demoniac energy," but it also displays a disordered
lushness which rivals Keats at his worst. Moreover the reader
is confronted by such obvious absurdities as "the glorious gules
of a glowing rust" and "Day's dying dragon lies drooping his
crest, / Panting red pants into the West." [16]

It is clear that the problem of the sins of the imagination
and the limits of volition, which seems to have affected the essay
"Health and Holiness" that appeared in August, 1891, was a
problem which, in Thompson's case, had not only moral but
aesthetic aspects.

IV

From the time of Thompson's return to London from Storrington, Meynell tried without success to gain a wider audience for his work in non-Catholic publications. The Catholic press generally continued to have little interest in Thompson or in poetry, and it was not until the publication of the review "Catholics in Darkest England" in January, 1891, that Cardinal Manning asked to see Meynell's protégé. The Cardinal may not have cared much about poetry but he was greatly concerned with the condition of the London poor and what he regarded as the proselytizing of the Salvation Army among them. According to the original version of "To the Dead Cardinal of Westminster," Manning invited Thompson to visit him often, but the poet, recognizing the world of difference that separated them, never visited the prelate again.

Two men could scarcely have been more unlike than Thompson and Manning, the practical ecclesiastical politician. Yet, Thompson saw that in one respect at last they were similar: Both lived lonely lives, the one in his eminence, the other in his introverted obscurity. "To the Dead Cardinal of Westminster," which was written at Meynell's request for an elegy at the time of Manning's death, develops this idea in its early stanzas:

> Anchorite, who didst dwell
> With all the world for cell,
> My soul
> Round me doth roll
>
> A sequestration bare.
> Too far alike we were.
> Too far
> Dissimilar. (ll. 17-24)

It is, however, the dissimilarity that is stressed. The Cardinal is pictured as close to God, while the poet's "weak gaze shuns" the eyes of his Creator, and he says,

> But I, ex-Paradised,
> The shoulder of your Christ
> Find high
> To lean thereby.   (ll. 41-44)

As with Dylan Thomas, upon whom Thompson had a marked influence, there is in this poem the strong and bitter foretaste of death:

> Beneath my appointed sod;
> The grave is in my blood;
> I shake
> To winds that take
>
> Its grasses by the top;
> The rains thereon that drop
> Perturb
> With drip acerb
>
> My subtly answering soul;
> The feet across its knoll
> Do jar
> Me from afar.   (ll. 69-80)

The curious versification and the difficult constructions of "To the Dead Cardinal of Westminster" carried not so much the expected tone of elegy as they bore the poet's own mood of depression. Such moods continued to afflict him. Meynell had sent some of his work to Browning in Italy in 1889, and Thompson had been greatly encouraged by the older poet's saying that, "Both the Verse and Prose are indeed remarkable." Yet, such recognition was scant and Thompson frequently complained of times of dryness when he felt no capacity for writing. His stomach disorders grew, and his frail, tubercular constitution made him frequently subject to colds and fever. A life of St. John Baptist de la Salle, which he undertook, gave him some opportunity to plead for the children whose miserable lives he had seen in the slums of Manchester and London, but it was largely a burdensome piece of journalistic hack work. Not very different was an article on St. Ignatius, which was written during September and October, 1891, and formed the basis for the biography he was to write near the end of his life.

It seems likely that late in 1891 or early in 1892 he began the intermittent use of laudanum again. It cannot, however, be said that he abandoned himself to the drug as he had sometimes done during his outcast years, and his continued productivity suggests that he was able to maintain some balance in his dosage.

Certainly the problem of consenting to sin plagued him frequently. From 1892 onward he displayed an increasing interest in theological thought and became acquainted with some of the philosophical notions of Patmore, although they did not meet until 1894. He felt a strong affinity with Patmore's esoteric idealism, but he was, at the same time, troubled by it.

Probably as a result of his interest in Blake, Thompson had read something of the work of Emanuel Swedenborg (1688-1772). Like Blake, Thompson was impressed by the Swedish theologian's statement of the ancient idea that the natural world is but a symbol or representation of an invisible universe; but just how extensive his knowledge of Swedenborg was prior to the eventual meeting with Patmore is uncertain, although the notebooks—especially *The Small Commonplace Book*—contain a number of references to Swedenborg's symbolism.

It is, however, evident that Thompson was never under the direct influence of Swedenborg to the degree that Patmore was. It is well known, for example, that the ideas of sex and mar-

riage in Swedenborg's *Conjugal Love* strongly affected Patmore's *Angel in the House*.[17] Indeed, Swedenborg's theology
colored the whole development of Patmore's thought. Striking
evidence of this can be seen in the writer's own copy of the
Index to the 1860 English edition of Swedenborg's *Arcana
Coelestia*. On the frontispiece of this book, which is now in the
Thompson-Patmore Collection at Boston College, Patmore
wrote, "a vast magazine of *known* truths stated from new points
of view—so as to have all the impressiveness of discoveries."
And he went further:

> The most important of these truths have died out of
> the knowledge of men. They are present, indeed, in the
> esoteric teaching of the Catholic Religion but popular and
> official Catholicism is opposed to them.

Both volumes of the Index are heavily annotated and bear
witness to the truth of Patmore's declaration that he never tired
of reading Swedenborg.[18]

Of course, Thompson had been drawing upon a tradition of
mysticism, allegory, and symbolism all his life. Furthermore,
the whole idea of nature as the multiplied representation of the
Divine Essence is a commonplace in certain traditions of
Catholic thought which show the influence of Neo-Platonism.
Yet, it is understandable that he may have found Patmore's
interest in the esoteric to be overly audacious. At any rate, he
decided to discuss the matter with the Franciscans of Crawley,
which lies midway between London and Brighton.

Thompson had visited there at Meynell's suggestion, in the
hope that the contact with the friars and the peaceful setting of
the religious house would help him in the continuing struggle
with his addiction. The Franciscan Provincial, Father Alphon-
sus, greatly admired Patmore's poetry, and one of the friars,
Father Cuthbert, assured Thompson that his suspicions of

some of Patmore's mystical ideas were simply the product of an incomplete knowledge of the whole body of his thought. Thompson was evidently relieved, for as he later told Patmore, "Yours is the conversation of a man who has trodden before me the way which for years I trod. . . ." [19] His own philosophical speculations were to go forward to the time when the minds of the two poets would truly meet.

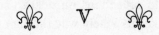

Preoccupied with his own concerns, Thompson had made no attempt to communicate with his family when he returned to London in 1890. He did not do so even after his work was a regular feature in the pages of *Merry England,* but from time to time he wrote to his boyhood friend, Canon Carroll, in the knowledge that the priest would probably convey word of him to his father. In many ways, it was true that he had found in Alice Meynell both his lost mother and a beloved woman, as in Wilfrid Meynell he had discovered a form of paternal understanding which he had never known and had not sought from his own father. If he had a home at all, it was with those who now protected him and assured him of the worth of the things he loved most.

Yet, even at Palace Court and in the company of other writers, like Lionel Johnson, he was essentially solitary. As Viola Meynell puts it:

> He was brought into things, however little he might seem to fit the part. The Meynell children were sent to skate on the Round Pond in his charge. He was made godfather to the youngest of them in 1891. All the Meynells' friends had to reckon with his presence. . . .

Thompson himself had to reckon with the ever-present sense of guilt and struggle, not only with opium but also with the always vexed question of religion and the artistic vocation. Bearing on this point is his "A Judgement in Heaven," written in the summer of 1892 and published in *Merry England* in October, 1893. This poem, like "A Fallen Yew," displays his continuing and deepening theological concern. The memory of the fall of the splendid old yew tree on the playing field at Ushaw led him into reflections on death and the survival of the soul, which makes its lonely way through the world to face its final relationship to God. In "A Judgement in Heaven," Mary Magdalen calls attention to the sufferings of the Poet, who has come "to win to the Father of Paradise" and who is, for all the apparent glory of his robe and wreath, a poor and sinful figure when stripped of all dishonesty. His poetic powers are not really his own; they are the gifts of God. But his sins are forgiven because he has suffered all the pains which the divine gift of poetry made him bear.

In the Epilogue, which shows a refreshing simplicity both in its diction and versification, Thompson deals with the mystery of grace, a mystery that escapes the "ethics of the text-book," and leaves even the "wisest moralists" competent to pronounce on little more than the "rough border-law of Heaven." After all human judgments have been passed, it remains true that

> There is no expeditious road
> To pack and label men for God,
> And save them by the barrel-load.
> Some may perchance, with strange surprise,
> Have blundered into Paradise.   (ll. 22-26)

The Poet, with the double burden of the "life of flesh" and the "life of song," could properly ask if there was not truly "expiating agony" in his creative work.

The theme of this Epilogue to "A Judgement in Heaven" is closely related to an article which Thompson did on Shelley for *Merry England* in September, 1892. It is much concerned with the question of the relation between a poet's character as a man and the worth of his verse. Shelley was for Thompson one whose idealistic sufferings as an artist might well be thought of as expiations for the sins of his life, a figure who might be the Poet of "A Judgement in Heaven," if that figure were not Thompson himself.

As his interest in the mysteries of art and salvation deepened, as his health declined and the pressures of his addiction increased, so Thompson felt, near the end of 1892, that his capacity for poetry was weakening. Meynell, too, was feeling the strain of having to care for him in London and finally decided to write to the Franciscans, who had a house at Pantasaph in Wales as well as at Crawley, to ask if Thompson might not become a guest in the Welsh retreat. He was thankful for an affirmative reply. The poet, in turn, accepted all the arrangements with docility and was put on the train for Pantasaph by an employee of *Merry England,* who made certain that he did not get lost on the way to Euston Station.

On his arrival at the monastery, Thompson was given living quarters in a small stone cottage known as "Bishop's House" to the left of the gateway, from which a road lined with trees on either side still leads to the monastic guesthouse, in which Patmore was later to stay during his visits there. From its windows one could easily see the impressive Capuchin monastery beyond, where for the next five years Thompson was to be a familiar figure. Indeed, one who was a young friar there still recalls how Thompson as a guest at the monastery table on some special feastday would become so absorbed in his talk as to forget to take his food until he was suddenly aware of the fact that his delay was holding up the serving of the community meal, since in a religious house dishes are not cleared away until all have finished eating the course before them.

At first Thompson did very little at Pantasaph. He was, as he wrote to Meynell, still "taking the turning which leads out of the debility consequent on ye breaking off" from opium. He was allowed no money and even his allowance of postage stamps was carefully checked. Mrs. Blackburn—a friend of the Meynells, whom he calls "Madam" in his notebooks—lived near by and visited him from time to time.

Another visitor was Father Anselm, one of the friars, who later became Archbishop of Simla. He came to Bishop's House as often as three times a day, and as Thompson recovered his strength, would often accompany him on long walks during which great silences sometimes gave way to extended discussions of theology. When the poet talked, even as he had done at Ushaw, he poured forth such a flood of words that Father Anselm years later said, "Thompson could easily have been a great orator." [20]

As the struggle against his need for opium became less painful, he set about the task of collecting and arranging the poems that had appeared in *Merry England* and adding others. Still greatly inspired by his devotion to Alice Meynell, he made revisions of "Love in Dian's Lap." Much of this activity was the result of the fact that Meynell had persuaded the publishing house of Elkin Mathews and John Lane, to put out a volume of Thompson's verse, which was to appear as *Poems* in 1893. The poet was not so intent upon this project as was his benefactor. Learning that the publishers had announced his work as forthcoming in their book list, he felt bound to go through with the editorial drudgery, but there were times when he was quite ready to let the book "go to the devil."

Had it not been for Meynell's patient labor, Thompson could not have reached the point in April, 1893, when his work was

ready for publication. Endless editorial discussion by correspondence had left him quite exhausted and the lack of opium
made his other physical ills all the more unendurable.

Yet, in May *Merry England* contained a new poem, *"Ex
Ore Infantium,"* which was the product of Thompson's medita-
tions before the crèche in the Lady Chapel at Pantasaph during the preceding Christmas season. Unlike his poems about
children, this piece uses an imagined child as the speaker and
is, in a sense, a child's poem. However, as with the *Songs of
Innocence* of Blake, the simplicity of the language is deceptive,
for the theme is the great Christmas mystery of God made man.
Underlying it, there is the knowledge that the analogical language of the theologians is a kind of baby-talk—an attempt to
state as best our minds can what is essentially inexpressible,
except in symbols:

> So, a little Child, come down
> And hear a child's tongue like Thy own;
> Take me by the hand and walk,
> And listen to my baby-talk.   (ll. 41-44)

Here—as in the essays "Form and Formalism," "The Image
of God," and "Sanctity and Song"—there is evidence of
Thompson's continuing concern with theological speculation.
Father Anselm, who was a professor of scholastic philosophy,
encouraged him in this and loaned him two volumes of St.
Thomas Aquinas, which Thompson soon returned with the
polite comment that if he became too interested in them, he
would write no more poetry.

The whole cast of Thompson's mind was little disposed to
accept the precision of St. Thomas' Aristotelianism. It is true
that in the essay "The Image of God," which appeared in
Franciscan Annals for July, 1893, there is an appreciative
reference to St. Thomas' teaching that there is in the human
body a real resemblance to God, *per modum vestigii.* This,

Thompson ingeniously suggested, means that the body has a trace of its Maker which is like the footprint a man leaves in the earth: what is prominent in the foot appears as a depression in the print, and it is possible to construct a concept of the foot from the footprint only when we understand the nature of the correspondence between them. Thus Thompson, characteristically, turned Aquinas' *per modum vestigii* into the Neo-Platonic doctrine of correspondence.

He was, as we have seen, a Neo-Platonist and at home in a tradition, which extends back in Christianity at least as far as St. Clement of Alexandria (c. 150-220). His intuitive perceptions and his eager pursuit of those multiple truths he found hidden in universal symbols sprang from a mind that was close to Augustine, John the Scot, and Anselm. Even the mighty *Apocalypse* of St. John was for him a "child's apologue" of that divine mind, "whose mature book is the Universe, and its compendium Man." Moreover he felt that in one idea of the divine intelligence "a whole wilderness of Platos" would be no more noticeable than "flies inside St. Paul's." [21] Consequently he was never attracted by the Thomistic methods of definition and division; the world as he saw it was a theophany that defied analysis.

If he studied scholasticism with Father Anselm, he did so "as people take the waters at Baden," because it was "the staple commodity of the place." [22] The only real fruit of such studies seems to have been a set of doggerel verses, of which the following is typical:

> And now in his Question Sixty-one
> The production of Angels is touched upon:
> But very much better had he, as I did,
> Left this knotty point undecided
> For the Schools could not tell, how it happened to be
> This production was just—just Somebody.

Thompson summed the whole matter up in a prose fragment called *Symbolism:*

> I am sensible that I have already tried the analytical Western mind to its utmost. But this is inherent in the subject. Were I not a poet—that is, an Eastern,—I could not have written this article. It has been well said that all men are born Platonists or Aristotelians. And Aristotelians—in Europe—are in the majority. For Plato was essentially an Eastern, Aristotle essentially a Western. Now, every true poet is an Eastern, most other men are Westerns. It is the difference of the synthetic and analytic minds.

Several months after his arrival at Pantasaph, Thompson had read Patmore's *Religio Poetae* with the greatest of care in preparation for a review in *Merry England.* Like Patmore, he greatly admired St. Bernard's treatise *On the Love of God,* a work which was basic to the religious thought he was following. He wrote Patmore of his sympathetic response to the ideas of *Religio Poetae,* and his mind turned more and more to the themes which were to be expressed in the poems known as "Sight and Insight." Working on drafts of such poems as "Assumpta Maria" and "Any Saint" near the end of 1893, Thompson at Pantasaph sometimes experienced the taste of a spiritual summer that had once seemed impossible to him.

CHAPTER FIVE

THE CAPTAIN OF SONG

 I

Poems was published in December, 1893. Richard Le Gallienne, who had read the manuscript for John Lane and strongly urged its publication, was enthusiastic about the book in a review in the *Chronicle*. Others were even more so, and often for the wrong reasons. John Davidson—who, with his predilection for Nietzsche, might well have been hostile—praised what Thompson did not have when he described *Poems* as a volume which displayed "domination over language." He went further in the direction of inaccuracy when he drew a parallel with Milton's "At a Solemn Music."

The frequently perceptive mind of Coventry Patmore, who had examined some of the work in *Poems* before its publication, rightly understood that in the England of 1893 many would want to read Thompson's work simply because of his personal history. Writing in the *Fortnightly Review* for July, 1894, Patmore remarked with typically aristocratic scorn that the defects of Thompson's writing would win him approval from the "crowd" and observed that "his abundant and often unnecessary obscurities" would help his popularity, much as obscurity had helped Browning "by ministering to the vanity of such as profess to see through millstones." The public, Patmore felt, would not appreciate Thompson's real qualities, which should place him on a level of permanent fame with Cowley and Crashaw.

Patmore was disturbed by what he thought of as Thompson's lack of contact with the world of concrete realities in his poetry. Reflecting his own somewhat more earthy attraction to Alice Meynell, he complained that, "The lady whom he delights to honour he would have to be too seraphic even for a seraph." Thompson, Patmore concluded, was "a Titan among recent poets." Yet, he admonished him to remember that Titans must refresh their strength "by occasional acquaintance with the earth." In a figure borrowed directly from Carlyle's "The Hero as Divinity," Patmore remarked:

> The tree Igdrasil, which has its head in heaven and its roots in hell (the "lower parts of the earth"), is the image of the true man, and eminently so of the poet, who is eminently man. In proportion to the bright and divine heights to which it ascends must be the obscure depths in which the tree is rooted, and from which it draws the mystic sap of its spiritual life.

The excess of "spirituality" in Thompson was, however, to be thought of as a noble defect and an eminent virtue "in a time when most other Igdrasils are hiding their heads in hell and affronting heaven with their indecorous roots."

As has continued to be the case with Thompson's work, the reaction to *Poems* was marked by extremes, from Arnold Bennett's declaration that Thompson was excelled in natural genius only by Shakespeare to Clement Shorter's description of him as the poet of nothing more than "a small Catholic clique." Thompson himself affirmed in a letter to Meynell that he thought his poetry "greater" than any new work which had appeared since Rossetti, with the possible exception of that of Alice Meynell. He would not "veil my crest" to Henley,

Bridges, or Watson, but he admitted that the "restraint and sanity" of his poems might have been improved if he had submitted to the influence of Patmore.[1]

The first edition of *Poems* was soon exhausted and Thompson was well on the way to being a controversial literary "discovery." It was, after all, the age of Oscar Wilde and J. K. Huysmans, a time when the appeal of exotic sensuality and religious ritualism thrilled and startled many weary Victorian appetites in search of something new and "shocking."

Perhaps Thompson realized that many of his readers were far more interested in his Bohemian background and his seclusion in a monastery than they were in his poetry, for the attraction was not unlike that of Thomas Merton's *Seven Storey Mountain* in our own day. In any case, he had been less than anxious to have the book published and his reaction to its success was less than joyful. Certainly he had moods when the warmest praise of his poetry could not compensate for his lost priestly vocation. There was the taste of dust and ashes in it.

Mrs. Blackburn, who busied herself working with the *Franciscan Annals,* must have been as much a trial to him as he evidently was to her. Writing to the Meynells in one of her regular reports, she said:

> As for Francis—I hardly know what to say. I gave him all your messages and I wish he would show some kind of human elation at his unprecedented success, but he seems to take it all in a dull mechanical sort of way which is distressing. . . . He isn't doing a stroke of work and stops in bed the best part of the day, and lately he falls asleep when he comes to see me in the way he used to do at Palace Court.

She suspected Thompson of returning to his addiction and concluded that if he was not taking opium, he must be taking something else. His failures to appear for tea were duly recorded. His walks made her report him as "flying over hill and dale and never to be seen." [2]

What he needed was not Mrs. Blackburn's concern but the company of Coventry Patmore, of whose article in the *Fortnightly* he had written to Alice Meynell, "I have got more help and self-knowledge from his article than from anything else which has appeared. Will you convey to him my warmest thanks for an article which cannot but remain a landmark in my life?"

However, before Patmore finally came to Pantasaph, Thompson had a visit from his old friend Canon Carroll, who had recently been consecrated Bishop of Shrewsbury. This visit took place early in 1894 and was intended by the bishop to result in a reconciliation between Thompson and his father. Dr. Thompson had been understandably pleased to learn that his son had successfully published a book of poems, although he did not pretend to understand what they were about.

Prior to the publication of *Poems,* the doctor had been on vacation at the seaside resort of Rhyl in September, 1893. Learning of this, Thompson had decided to go the short distance from Pantasaph to see him, but like so many other things in his life, the trip was put off until it was too late and his father had returned to Ashton. When Bishop Carroll urged him to make a real effort to bring about a reconciliation, Thompson offered no resistance to the idea, but in the end, he did nothing. There was little the two men might have been able to say, beyond saying that they had their mutual regrets.

Troubled by Mrs. Blackburn's gloomy reports, the Meynells came from London for a visit in April, 1894. The "Ultima" sequence, which finally was to form the concluding section of *New Poems,* owes much to this occasion. Thompson, referring to his love for Mrs. Meynell, wrote:

I yielded to the insistent demands of my conscience
and uprooted my heart—as I supposed. Later, the renewed presence of the beloved Lady renewed the love I
thought deracinated. For a while I swung vacillant. I
thought I owed it to her whom I loved more than my love
of her family to uproot that love . . . that I might be beyond treachery to my resolved duty. And at this second
effort I finished what the first had left incomplete. . . .
But it left the lady still the first, the one veritable, full-
orbed, and apocalyptic love of my life. Through her was
shown me the uttermost of what love could be—the possible divinities and celestial prophecies of it. . . . Surely
she will one day realize them, as by her sweet, humble,
and stainless life she has deserved to do.[3]

This devoted renunciation is expressed in the "Ultima" poems,
which properly form a sequel to "Love in Dian's Lap."

Seeing Alice Meynell again, he dwelt longingly on the touch
of her hand in "Love's Almsman Plaineth His Fare." But in "A
Holocaust" she is renounced:

> Henceforth this sad and most, most lonely soul
> Must, marching fatally through pain and mist,
> The God-bid levy of its powers enrol.   (ll. 6-8)

In "Ultimum" it is clear that his theological concerns have
strongly affected his outlook:

> And Lady, thus I dare to say,
> Not all with you is passed away!
> Beyond your star, still, still the stars are bright;
> Beyond your highness, still I follow height;
> Sole I go forth, yet still to my sad view,
> Beyond your trueness, Lady, Truth stands true.
>
> (ll. 30-35)

Thompson was willing to eliminate the "Ultima" sequence
from *New Poems,* but one feels that this may have been as

much because of some continuing personal conflict over what they said as it was a judgment upon their quality as poetry. In their completed form they actually display a greater economy of diction and a more disciplined imagery than the poems of "Love in Dian's Lap," although Thompson's characteristic faults are by no means absent, as in the final line from "Unto This Last" in which the poet is "Stung by those wild brown bees, her eyes!'

It may well have been, as Reid suggests, that the Meynells were disturbed by Thompson's emotional state during their April visit. Probably Alice Meynell best understood its cause, just as she had often seen more of the technical problems of Thompson's poetry than had her husband. She may also have understood that Meynell, who was really a journalist, could not give Thompson the advice he needed, while Patmore (in spite of his apodictic eccentricities) was a truly competent critic. More than that, however, Patmore had given every evidence of talking about philosophical matters in a manner that would continue to arouse Thompson's already stimulated interest and admiration. Patmore was, of course, devoted to Alice Meynell, while he never seems to have had any great interest in her husband, and it is more than likely that it was at her suggestion that he finally came to Pantasaph in 1894 for a visit of several days.

He was, at the time, seventy-one years old; Thompson was thirty-five. Patmore's self-confident individualism was overwhelming. He towered above Thompson's smallness and moved with an elegant grace of manner and dress which stood in marked contrast to the younger poet's hesitant shabbiness. Yet, they immediately recognized an affinity that sprang from much more than their common Catholicism and their mutual devotion to poetry.

II

Long before his conversion to the Catholic Church in 1864, Patmore had been deeply interested in symbolism and the mystical interpretation of reality. In the rather simple and frequently sentimental poetry of *The Angel in the House* (1854) as in the irregular odes of *The Unknown Eros* (1877), his apparent preoccupation with sex, and especially with married love, was inevitably related to a lofty interpretation of reality. In the tradition of the allegorical interpretation of the Biblical *Canticle of Canticles* established by Origen, St. Jerome, and St. Ambrose, Patmore celebrated the sex relationship as an analogy of the spiritual life.

In his essays Patmore described the creative artist as a man who is marked by the quiet habit of attention to unseen reality.[4] The poet, especially, is always aware of the analogies between external nature and the ideal world of ultimates. He is the meditative man, the man of insight, who shows us nature, but nature developed "by successive and intelligible degrees of growth and glory." For Patmore, the poet's language is essentially a vocabulary of symbols—a mixture of phonetic and objective imagery by means of which he seeks to convey the experience of the spirit in its response to the ideal order of reality. Consequently, every truly meditative mind is very close to the poetic outlook, and Patmore could say:

> Aquinas is to Dante as the Tableland of Thibet is to the Peak of Teneriffe; the first is not less essentially a poet, in the sense of a Seer, because his language is even more austere and without ornament, than that of the other.[5]

Thompson, of course, immediately responded to this view-point, and described Patmore as the only man with whom he could really talk. The contact of his own ideas with those of the older man was a dynamic experience; he listened and answered with what he described as "an after-train of illuminative corroboration." It was as easy for him to follow the agile steps of Patmore's mind the first time they met as if they had been old and practiced partners.

Discussing Patmore's philosophy in an article written six years after they came together at Pantasaph,[6] Thompson said that it was based on the system of the Neo-Platonists. Its first principle was that the whole natural order is analogous to man, as both man and the natural order are analogous to God. This first principle was arrived at by "intuition," which Patmore, "like all true poets and Platonists," held to be a higher power than analytical reason. Once the intuition had perceived the principle that man and the natural universe are mutually analogous because both are analogues of God, it would follow that all visible things point to an unseen, unifying reality.

For Patmore, at any rate, one of the most important of these visible signs which point to an ideal unity was nuptial love. He considered marriage not one of life's problems but "the image and key" of the relations between God and man, as well as the clue to many other problems. In marriage the full powers of humanity are harmonized and developed, for man—who represents the rational life—becomes united in love to woman—who represents the sensitive, emotional life.

Thompson, with his seminary training and his essentially clerical attitudes, did not share Patmore's lusty enthusiasm for matrimony. His reaction to it is well represented in a bit of light verse in the *Notebook of Early Poems*. These lines are concerned with the Biblical episode of the marriage in Cana, where Christ transformed water into wine at the wedding feast.

By so doing, Thompson says, Christ blessed matrimony and showed that nuptial love is "Jehovah's not Jove's child." But yet, he continues, in an almost Byronic tone:

> . . . the story has another side
> Too little by the multitude descried
> The Lord declared his thought by that his carriage,
> (Transmitted to us for a warning sign)
> That any man who ventured upon marriage
> Could not go through with it without much wine! [7]

Apart from this difference of attitude towards marriage, however, the harmony of outlook between the two men is perfectly evident. Thompson felt implicitly and knew intuitively that there is "a world within the world seen of eye and touched with hand." As the notebook he called *Pot-Herbs* shows, he delighted in Sir Thomas Browne, who loved the esoteric, and in the mystical theology of men like St. Gregory Nazianzen.[8] In the words of Wilfred Whitten, describing an evening he spent with Thompson in the Vienna Café in London, "The arts, the rites, the mysteries, and the sciences of eld gave him their secrets and their secrets words." [9] But it was Patmore above all others who made his thought really explicit.

In the fourteen-page prose manuscript which he called *On the Analogies Between God, Man, and the Poet*, the debt to Patmore is a factor. At the same time it is certain that much of what Thompson says is the statement of a world-view which he had held for a number of years. Moreover, some of its implications had been developed in his conversations with Father Anselm, whom Patmore himself called "a profound contemplative."

In the *Analogies Between God, Man, and the Poet* Thompson produced what he described in a letter to Patmore dated June 15, 1893, as "a fragment of a projected article, which has remained a fragment." [10] Yet however fragmentary, it is nonetheless a most significant key to this thought and important for an understanding of the poetry which he wrote at Pantasaph.

He begins with the axiom that all creation is reproduction, for the creator must work from a mental image of the object he is creating. In the beginning only God existed and all that He created was a "Protean reproduction" of His knowledge of Himself. God's self-knowledge was thus the model of heaven, of nature, and of man, who is, in Thompson's phrase, the "break-water of creation," a being who combines the worlds of the material and the spiritual.

In his adaptation of Himself to His materials, God has made what Thompson called "a vastness of phantasy" in all creation's differentiated parts. The divine imagination has, so to speak, created in every drop of water and in "that drop of fire we call a star" the parts of "a gigantesque *appoggiatura* upon Himself."

Thus every existing thing reflects one divine idea which sustains it in being and links it not only with its Creator but also with all other parts of the universe. Consequently, Thompson concludes, when we see that Nature is "applied Godhead," we may first begin to "surmise that God may be worth seeing." Furthermore, it follows that when we recognize creation to be the reproduction of God's "cognitions of Himself," we may begin to understand the vital importance to creation of that Word of God referred to in the first chapter of St. John's gospel, for the Word is to be identified with God's perfect self-knowledge.

This idea is quite in accord with the traditional Catholic interpretation of "In the beginning was the Word, and the Word was with God, and the Word was God. The same was in the beginning with God. All things were made by him; and without him was not anything made that was made."

(St. John 1:1-3). Thompson was quite aware of the limitations of language in expressing ideas and understood that this use of the term *Word of God* was based upon a psychological analogy: Before we can say anything we must have some mental concept; this concept, or "mental word" necessarily precedes the spoken word. Using this as a comparison between the human and the divine, it is possible to speak of God's idea of Himself as His "mental" Word, in which God sees both his own substance and every possibility of expressing Himself in created beings. The Word, so understood, is at once the totality of divine wisdom and the epitome of creation; and in the Catholic tradition, this Word of God is identified as Christ, the Son of God, who is God's perfect self-knowledge personified.

Following this line of thought in his *Analogies Between God, Man and the Poet,* Thompson said that nothing could have been created without the Word as its model. Nature and man were successive manifestations of God, neither of which would have been possible without the Word. However, God's crowning self-manifestation was the Incarnation, for with the actual coming of Christ into the world the human and the divine were united and humanity was elevated to the highest level possible. The first Christmas was, in effect, "the eighth Day of Creation." It was then that God's creation was truly perfected.

In the light of his theological speculations and strongly under the influence of Patmore, Thompson developed in his *Analogy* a basis for an understanding of the role of that poetic imagery which had both fascinated and sometimes plagued him for so many years. If man and Nature were made after the divine model, then it must be true that "Nature is made also to the image of man, and man to the image of Nature." In all the universe there must be a fundamental sameness underlying the outward differences, and the marvel of the created order is "that all things do not turn into each other, and this great Manyness, like a cluster of soap-bubbles, resolve into a little Oneness." From this common ground in one divine idea come those correspondences between man and nature which some have "set down to the fancy of poets."

All poetic imagery, then, takes its true justification from the fact that,

> Man is a symbol, Nature a metaphor, heaven and earth
> are written in hieroglyphs. The universe is a metonymy
> for God. It is a labyrinth, with God for its center, and
> the *gnothi seauton* (Know thyself) as its clue.

Those who think of the poet as a maker of merely fanciful images fail to understand that the imagery of poetry expresses the hidden identities arising from the divine idea which underlies the "separate provinces of being." The poet, by an intuitive perception of this system of correspondences, deals in basic analogies, "analogies rooted in the nature of things, *essential* as opposed to superficial analogies."

From this it follows that the very basis of metaphor, its justification and explanation, lies in a universal system of correspondences. Because of that system the poet is able to discover, between two different things, that similiarity which makes it possible for him to arrive at an implied comparison. His work rests upon the unity of Nature, the single idea in which all Nature participates. If Nature has no heart of her own—which, as Wordsworth once supposed, reaches out to the heart of man in silent sympathy—she is, nevertheless, not lifeless. The one underlying life in which Nature participates is, as Thompson wrote elsewhere, the being of God Himself. As man's life draws closer to God, he comes "into sympathy with Nature, and Nature with him." [11]

Reversing the familiar Romantic process, Thompson developed this idea in his "Outline of a Projected Poem," in which he imagines God speaking to humanity and saying that in the Incarnation He has converted bondage into a unity between God and man. Viewing the world from this standpoint, man can be reconciled with God and with Nature and come to the understanding that,

> All is on the one sufficing plan; and that plan is God. Yea, not only Man, but Nature also, is made to His image and likeness. Therefore Man, being in the image and likeness of God, is in the image and likeness, too, of Nature. And within himself is the key to Nature, which is less than he; as within himself is the adumbration of God, Who is greater than he. And from his relations with God, the action of God on him, he may learn the relation of Nature to him, his action on Nature. . . . To seek God through Nature is a way more tedious, devious, doubtful, and fallible. The one was the way of Wordsworth—yea, in a dim, instinctive, unwitting fashion, of Shelley. The other was the way of Francis of Assisi.[12]

That their age needed to be "reconciled" with God and Nature was, of course, a fundamental conviction with both Thompson and Patmore. As Patmore put it, the general notion that the Victorians were living in a time of great progress amounted to little more than the rejoicings "of a prosperous shopman over the increase of his business." [13]

In a discussion of the mystical outlook of Patmore's odes, Thompson caricatured the practical Victorian middle class, in a Carlylean variation on Shakespeare's characters in *Hamlet,* as Puddencrantz and Beefinstern. The always literal-minded Rosencrantz and Guildenstern of Shakespeare's play were the perfect prototypes for the unimaginative—and wholly unconscious—materialism of Puddencrantz and Beefinstern.[14]

These eaters of beef and suet pudding Thompson pictured as having strayed far from Nature because they had strayed far from God. Unlike their peasant ancestors, they had lost all sense of awe and wonder. Stolid Saxons, they distrusted "man's noblest faculty, imagination." For them nothing was august or high, and they would say what Thompson, in one of his notebooks, put into the mouth of any contemporary materialist speaking to a poet:

> . . . Go out from us, and leave our earth
> Utterly of the comfortable clay;
> Demand naught from us; let us hood our eyes
> With a strong veil of flesh, for this is wise,
> And but to peer forth is to pall in mirth;
> Disconsolate and hateful is your day.
> Your sights but trouble us: here in the mire
> Hognuts we have, if hognuts we desire. . . [15]

Poets like Patmore, Thompson said, had remained close to the mystery of Nature "and far from Puddencrantz." Their manner of speaking, which Puddencrantz would call lying, wiser men had once called soothsaying. Puddencrantz and Beefinstern must always regard the poet as a fool, because they failed to distinguish between a fool and a true "maniac." After all, the ancients had well understood that poetry is a divine madness.

In Patmore's *The Unknown Eros* Thompson saw the work of a man who had kept this "primal mania" of poetry for the mystery of the divine, a man who did not expect, or want, Puddencrantz and Beefinstern to understand him. Like the great Dante before him, Patmore spoke to those who knew that, "The practice of uttering things deep or high with a double—aye, even a triple tongue—has its roots deep down in Nature." But such a poet, like the prophet, must always be without honor among those whose range of vision is limited to the familiar world of material objects and sensory experience.

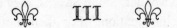

III

The Unknown Eros had appealed to Thompson not only because of its philosophical outlook, which was so congenial to him, but also because of its evident mastery of the technique of the ode, a form which Thompson had found most attractive even before his acquaintance with Patmore's work. Believing that poetic form is not an unchanging pattern into which emotion can be poured, Thompson saw in the irregular ode, in which the lines expand or contract with the movement of idea and emotion, an ideal form of poetic expression. Furthermore, the possibilities for effective use of metrical variation which it offered greatly appealed to him.

In Patmore he encountered a craftsman and a critic whose knowledge of English metrics was unexcelled by any writer of the nineteenth century. Just as it was true that Patmore's influence was fundamental to the development of Thompson's theological and philosophical speculation, so it was also true that Thompson's conception of the nature and role of metre awaited Patmore's guidance to become explicit. Anyone who is familiar with the essay called "English Metrical Critics," which Patmore first published in *The North British Review* in August, 1857, cannot fail to see how greatly Thompson was indebted to the older poet's teaching. There are echoes of it in many of his notebooks and all through his criticism, nor can there be any doubt as to its effect upon the odes of *New Poems.*

Recognizing as he did that much of the peculiar delight which poetry affords lies in its power to satisfy our natural

liking for measured rhythms marked by significant fluctuations, Patmore stressed the idea that the metrical time-beater
in a poem has its mental counterpart in the reader, for the
mind craves and responds to measure. Similarly, Thompson
notes in his *Large Commonplace Book* that although the
underlying metrical pattern in a poem may not be obvious, the
law of the metre remains something which is always felt in
the mind of the reader as a kind of invisible but potent "centre
of obedience." [16] This mental beat is what makes the reader
aware of the significance of the variations in metre which
arise from the poet's response to the ebb and flow of his emotions or from his desire for a particular emphasis. As in nature
there are fluctuations in any given species around a constant
norm, so in poetry the mind, responding to a basic metre, is
aware of significant inflections.

Like Patmore, too, Thompson said that the law of English
metre is that accent and quantity "should be lovers but not
wedded," in a relationship in which accent must always play
the dominant, or masculine, role.[17] Going back to its "native
bed-rock," as he recognized that Patmore had done, Thompson said that the "lost law" of English prosody was to be found
in the accentual measures of the Anglo-Saxons.[18] This opinion,
which he later found confirmed by Thomas S. Omond's *English Verse-structure* (1897), supported his belief that no
attempt to conform English prosody to analogies of classical
metres, such as that made by Bridges, could ever succeed, for
it was quantity that had given the law to classical verse.

First Patmore, and later the reading of Omond, thoroughly
convinced Thompson that "our metre is simply speech sys-
tematised." In language which is a paraphrase of Patmore's
own expression, Thompson upheld the view that English poets
must maintain "lovely interplay between accent and quan-

tity, approaching and receding from each other in a harmonious dance measure."

Thompson, of course, had recognized that the regular stress pattern of this "harmonious dance measure" is subject to variation in any given poem. "The Hound of Heaven" is proof enough that he had grasped the principle of such variety. His governing consideration in metrics was not some established precedent but the desired effect. It was, he noted in a review, mere pedantry to say that metrical variation must be used only where and how it had been used by some great poet of the past.

However, it appears likely that although Thompson experimented with metrical variation in his early book, it was Patmore who made him understand its theory. All that he says of metrics in his notes and later reviews shows that, as Everard Meynell says, Thompson followed Patmore as a son might bear a natural resemblance to his father.

Striking proof of this may be found in connection with a somewhat subtle point which Patmore made in his "English Metrical Critics." There Patmore pointed out that the real time of any syllable in combination is that period which elapses from the commencement of its enunciation to the beginning of the succeeding syllable. Consequently, the apparent equality of metrical intervals is merely general or approximate, and it often happens that pauses may displace regular syllables.

Thompson echoed this in one of his later notebooks in which he observed not only the importance of pauses but also the fact that the eye alone cannot perceive those subtle differences in metrical patterns which look alike but are not so. As he said in another note, all octosyllabics, for example, may be alike to the eye, but the ear, which must take account of the effect of pauses and various combinations upon the quantitative value of syllables, may reveal them as almost different metres.[19]

As Thompson gained from Patmore this deeper understanding of the principles of English metre, so, he also benefited from Patmore's penetrating understanding of Coleridge's organic theory of poetry. This doctrine, which has an important place in contemporary criticism, was developed in late eighteenth-century German aesthetic thought, but in the nineteenth century it was known to relatively few English critics. Thompson, however, speaks of "the supreme value of relation and organism" as an essential attribute of good poetry,[20] while Patmore wrote of Coleridge's "Christabel" that it is the living embodiment of a concept

> ... which expresses itself in every part, while the complete work remains its briefest possible expression, so that it is as absurd to ask What is its idea? as it would be to ask what is the idea of a man or of an oak.

Similarly, in commenting on a passage from Spenser, Thompson said, "It is all a matter of relation: the words take life from each other, and become an organism, as with Coleridge." [21]

From Patmore, Thompson learned that any poem which is a true organic whole has a special kind of integrity; it simply could not exist in any other form. Accordingly, he saw that there is about such a work the quality of the inevitable. After his friendship with Patmore had developed his critical powers, he could say of the poetry of Matthew Arnold:

> The austere and noble sonnet on Shakespeare, with other brief achievements of the kind, are worth more than poems full of fine thought, but only now and again inevitable in expression. For they are integral; and it is that quality which makes for permanence.[22]

After the years at Pantasaph were over, after his poetic productivity had all but ended, Thompson became an active and competent critic. In the process which gave him a grasp of the principles and techniques of criticism, Patmore clearly played no less a part than he played in the formation of Thompson's philosophy and the style of *New Poems*.

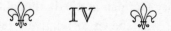

IV

The reception of Thompson's first volume led Meynell to think that *Sister Songs* could be published with similar success, a judgment which no one else—including Thompson—seems to have shared. With this project in mind, and the hope that in London Thompson might strengthen the reputation gained by the publication of *Poems,* Meynell invited the poet to come to the city for a visit. Consequently, during the last three months of 1894 he temporarily left his lodgings in Bishop's House—where he seems to have had a quarrel with the housekeeper—and went to be the guest of the Meynells.

During this interval, Thompson had some contact with his host's literary friends, such as Katherine Tynan—for whom he had written "The Sere of the Leaf" four years earlier—and Le Gallienne, who had been so favorably impressed by the manuscript of *Poems*. However, Le Gallienne does not seem to have been enthusiastic about *Sister Songs* and he did not influence Lane to risk the expense of the publication of that long, elaborate poem, which Thompson had already outgrown. Meynell tried without success to find another publisher and finally was compelled to plan a small private printing.

Early in 1895 Thompson returned to Pantasaph to work on the revision of *Sister Songs,* but he was apathetic about the forthcoming book and later wrote to Patmore that he regarded it "as a bad business." He had a room on the second floor of a building called Ivy Cottage. On the ground floor was a general store and the village post office. Frequently on his walks he would climb the nearest hill where he could look across to the horizon marked by the Snowden mountains and wander up the path that led to a white-washed stone house called Creccas Cottage. Set in a garden behind an arch of honeysuckle—isolated, as it seemed, above the world—this house attracted him far more than the lodgings over the post office, and he finally took a room there near the end of the summer.

His landlord was a man named Brien, the caretaker of the monastery grounds and the father of five daughters, one of whom looked after the house and Thompson's quarters. She was called Margaret Ann but was generally referred to as Maggie. About eleven years younger than the poet, she had known him before his move to Creccas Cottage, but he seems to have paid little attention to her. Yet, when he was a lodger in her father's house a curious attachment developed, which led Mrs. Blackburn to report to the Meynells the astonishing news that Thompson had fallen in love—a state of affairs which she regarded with less alarm than she usually displayed in describing his activities.

That Thompson actually did feel himself to be in love with Maggie Brien appears likely enongh. That she responded in some fashion is suggested by the fact that she kept the proof of a photograph of Thompson that had been taken at Chester in 1894 in her room, where it was found at the time of her death some years later. All that is known, however, concerning the course of this somewhat pathetic affair is found in a sequence called "A Narrow Vessel," which appeared in *New Poems*.

Written in a direct fashion that is quite different from such a sequence as "Love in Dian's Lap," the seven poems and the

Epilogue of "A Narrow Vessel" present a very human picture. The lover has been given a lock of his beloved's hair, and he imagines her saying:

> 'He always said my hair was soft——
>   What touches he will steal!
> Each touch and look (and he'll look oft)
>   I almost thought I'd feel.'
>   ("A Girl's Sin," I, ll. 85-88)

Like Alice Meynell, Maggie Brien is called a "tyranness," but she is called the "tender tyranness," of whom he can say:

> O hour of consternating bliss
> When I heavened me in thy kiss
> Thy softness (daring overmuch)
> Profanèd with my licensed touch;
> Worshipped, with tears, on happy knee,
> Her doubt, her trust, her shyness free,
> Her timorous audacity!
>   ("A Girl's Sin," II, ll. 39-43)

There is a moment, in the poem called "Love Declared," of passionate realization, expressed with some vividness in the following passage:

>   That falling kiss
> Touching long-laid expectance, all went up
> Suddenly into passion; yea, the night
> Caught, blazed, and wrapt us round in vibrant fire.
>   (ll. 7-10)

Yet the entire sequence is described in a subtitle as a little drama on the "aspect of primitive girl-nature towards a love beyond its capacities." Maggie Brien was evidently fascinated and moved to sympathy by the slight, bearded poet, whose great brown eyes spoke such strange sadness and whose soft voice expressed so much that seemed drawn from some higher realm of experience. But she gave herself "as children give, that weep/ And snatch back, with—'I meant you not to keep!' " [23] She was afraid of the consequences of the whole incongruous relationship, and while she seems to have always retained her attachment to Thompson, she withdrew from allowing the affair to develop:

> She did not love to love, but hated him
> For making her to love; and so her whim
>   From passion taught misprision to begin.
>
> ("The End of It," ll. 1-3)

In the Epilogue to the "Narrow Vessel" sequence Thompson characteristically turned the whole thing into what one friendly critic, who wished that Thompson had "always written as humanly," called "an unreal allegory." The hesitant flirtation, the meetings, the kisses, and Maggie's frightened retreat became an image of the soul's fear of the love of God. In "The Hound of Heaven" he had asked:

> Ah! is Thy love indeed
> A weed, albeit an amaranthine weed,
> Suffering no flowers except its own to mount?
>
> (ll. 130-132)

Commenting on the "Narrow Vessel" poems, he said that the soul fears complete surrender, which the love of God demands, just as a woman "recoils from a love which her all cannot equal." Like Patmore, Thompson was disposed to see human love as a symbol of divine love, but Patmore was in no way inclined to disregard physical realities, and it may have been that he was the nameless critic who found Thompson's attempt to allegorize the story of his relationship with Maggie to be unreal.[24]

The Epilogue is clearly an afterthought, for there is not the least suggestion of allegory in the sequence itself. Yet both the Epilogue and Thompson's later comments have their importance. The experience with Maggie Brien, for all its hesitant briefness, was a concrete point of reference for Thompson's development of the ideas which he shared with Patmore. Furthermore, there is in all that he says of the matter an opportunity to see how deeply his seminary training had affected his outlook. What he says of Maggie's fear of his love suggests the sort of clerical comment on the inadequacies of women sometimes found in the literature of the middle ages:

> Woman repels the great and pure love of man in proportion to its purity. This is due to an instinct which she lacks the habits and power to analyze, that the love of the pure and lofty lover is so deep, so vast in its withheld emotion, as her entire self would be unable to pay back. Though she cast her whole self down that eager gulf, it would disappear as a water-drop in the ocean. . . . The narrow vessel dreads to crack under the overflowing love which surges into it.[25]

His mind inevitably turned into the paths he had learned to follow at Ushaw, and it is typical of him that during the spring and summer of 1895, when he was working over the editing of *Sister Songs* and undertaking the more arduous and important writing that went into *New Poems,* Thompson should have tried to set up a careful schedule for his religious life. What he attempted sounds much like the program of a seminarian: early morning prayers; dressing; going to daily mass whenever possible; breakfast; later morning prayers; work and study; dinner; a walk for exercise, or work; the evening meal; correspondence and reading; evening prayers and examination of conscience. This program, carefully noted down, was not always so carefully followed, but it was in rough outline what he hoped his days might be and there is no reason to suppose that it does not represent the general pattern of his activity during this period.

In the correspondence, to which he intended to devote some of his evenings, Patmore was the central figure, and a number of letters passed between them. Thompson was fascinated by what Patmore had revealed to him of the idea of a large body of esoteric wisdom, stretching back into the pre-Christian ages and appearing in a variety of cultures that had mutually influenced one another. Such wisdom, both men believed, had been expressed symbolically, for as Thompson declared in one of his pencilled notes, the "style of double meaning" was a vital part of "the common inheritance of the ancient world." Among the Egyptians and Greeks, as well as among the Hebrews, symbolic forms both revealed and concealed men's deepest perceptions. As St. Clement of Alexandria had said, both Plato and Aristotle wrote on two levels, one for the general reader and one for the "fit and few." [26]

In Patmore, Thompson found a guide and an elder companion in the world of symbolism and speculative thought, and during the summer of 1895 he wrote a poem inspired by Sargent's masterful portrait of him. Called "A Captain of Song" this piece first appeared in the *Athenaeum* after Patmore's death in 1896, but as Thompson said, it cannot be properly understood without the knowledge that it was written to "a living man, and bears reference to spiritual experience and not to death." For him Patmore was pre-eminently one who "trod the ways afar":

> The fatal ways of parting and farewell
> Where all the paths of painèd greatness are
> Where round and always round
> The abhorrèd words resound,
> The words accursed of comfortable men,——

'For ever'; and infinite glooms intolerable
With spacious replication give again,
And hollow jar,
The words abhorred of comfortable men.

(ll. 11-19)

Patmore, who in the course of his highly individualistic life had known and abandoned the friendship of men of the stature of Emerson and Browning, might, had he lived long enough, easily have abandoned Thompson also. That, however, was one misfortune which the poet was spared; during the summer of 1895 and until Patmore's death in November of the following year, Thompson travelled with his admired friend on a journey along ways of thought where the simple humanity of Maggie Brien could not be expected to follow.

CHAPTER SIX

SIGHT AND INSIGHT

I

The fruits of Patmore's influence were not immediately evident in Thompson's published work. In fact, between the publication of "An Anthem of Earth" in *Merry England* in November, 1894 and *New Poems* in 1897 nothing that was really new or important to his development appeared in print. *Sister Songs* finally was published in 1895 only because Meynell insisted upon it against Thompson's better critical judgment, for the poet was well aware of the fact that even in its revised form *Sister Songs* displayed the worst faults of his earlier work. As he had anticipated, the book was poorly received.

Opinions about "An Anthem of Earth" tend, like the poem itself, to be rather extravagant. Rodolphe Mégroz has described it as "the greatest rhapsody in English poetry," and Alice Meynell, writing in the *Dublin Review* in 1911, said it was Thompson's "most magnificent ode." Some contemporary reviewers, however, drew unfavorable parallels with the work of Whitman, and *Pall Mall* called it "a terrible poem without form and void." More recently, Reid has suggested that "An Anthem of Earth" resembles the verse of the so-called "Spasmodics," Sydney Dobell and Alexander Smith, whose excited, verbose style had been satirized by W. E. Aytoun in 1854.

In Reid's judgment the work is engulfed in "clouds of rhetoric and cosmic attitudinizing."

Technically, it was exactly what Thompson called it—an "exercise in blank verse" in which he had transferred "whole passages" from prose articles he had written into irregular, unrhymed poetry.[1] Recognizing his lack of mastery over metrical variation, he sent the poem to Alice Meynell to ask how well she thought he had managed his experiment, for he confessed that he was among the "poor devils who write by ear."

There is an obvious similarity between "An Anthem of Earth" and the prose manuscript "A Threnody of Birth,"[2] in which Thompson described the men of his age as living in a time of decline when the blood had "grown flat in many veins." The child of the late Victorian world, he said, could not be "strong with all his fathers' strength, nor rejoice with all their joy." Yet science could offer him "poppies for his troublous thoughts,"

> For she has discovered life in putridity, and vigour in decay; dissolution even and disintegration, which in the mouth of man symbolise disorder, in the works of God has discerned to be undeviating order, and the manner of our corruption no less wonderful than the manner of our health. She has expounded the reflux and the influx of things; accounting the grave-ground the seminary of being, and extinction the Ceres of existence.

In "An Anthem of Earth" this prose passage was given verse form in the lines in which Thompson described science, the "old noser in its prideful straw," that

> Against its own dull will
> Ministers poppies to our troublous thought,
> A Balaam come to prophecy,——parables,
> Nor of its parable itself is ware,
> Grossly unwotting; all things has expounded
> Reflux and influx, counts the sepulchre

> The seminary of being, and extinction
> The Ceres of existence: it discovers
> Life in putridity, vigour in decay;
> Dissolution even, and disintegration,
> Which in our dull thoughts symbolize disorder,
> Finds in God's thoughts irrefragable order,
> And admires the manner of our corruption
> As of our health. . . .   (ll. 208-220)

Here the flavor of prose is scarcely concealed, and much of the rest of "An Anthem of Earth" is equally unsuccessful as poetry. Its mood was that of the period of depression Thompson experienced in the early months of 1894, and its attempt to make that mood come powerfully alive in an extended blank verse soliloquy largely failed.

Yet, the poem has its biographical interest and importance, for in it Thompson entered "The long arcane of those dim catacombs/Where the rat memory does its burrows make." The child, he says, comes to the world "in nescientness" and wears the "beggar's gown" of flesh with joy. Recalling the mood of "A Corymbus for Autumn," he speaks of a youthful time when it seemed that the earth set forth its seasons to "pamper me with pageant," and he looks back with a critical eye to his early obsession with imagery:

> Sleep I took not for my bedfellow,
> Who could waken
> To a revel, an inexhaustible
> Wassail of orgiac imageries.   (ll. 51-54)

Like many other late Victorians, he is weary and possessed of a sense of doom, not only for himself but for his world—a world in which

> Our souls go out at elbows. We are sad
> With more than our sires' heaviness, and with
> More than their weakness weak. . . .   (ll. 96-98)

Looking backward, like Kipling in his "Recessional," Thompson thinks of fallen Nineveh and other ancient cities; looking forward he speaks with a sense of prophecy of the great war that is about to come:

> Tarry awhile, lean Earth, for thou shalt drink,
> Even till thy dull throat sicken,
> The draught thou grow'st fat on; hear'st thou not
> The world's knives bickering in their sheaths? O patience!
> Much offal of a foul world comes thy way,
> And man's superfluous cloud shall soon be laid
> In a little blood.   (ll. 289-295)

Recalling certain passages in Tennyson's *In Memoriam,* Thompson pictures the earth as devouring whole species, such as the mammoth and the mastodon, for all living things are inevitably drawn together to "the thirsty grave." The individual man moves from the "little joy" of early youth through his allotments of sobering thought, brief strength, and limited knowledge to the "little peace" of death. Then, by an ironic reversal, he who has been nurtured by the earth gives sustenance to her.

The predominant gloom of this theme is broken from time to time by assertions of faith in a divine order behind the mystery of nature and the enigma of the individual; death is referred to as a bridge over the crevasse that leads to the "trifid God" and called the "broker of immortality." Such brief rays of light, however, do nothing to relieve the prevalent world-weariness, and the desire to "break the tomb of life" is the poem's true climax.

A very different mood, however, was to be dominant in *New Poems.* If in "To the Dead Cardinal of Westminster" he had found the shoulder of Christ too high to lean upon, "Any Saint" presented a changed picture:

> And bolder now and bolder
> I lean upon that shoulder
>   So dear
> He is and near: (ll. 13-16)

At Pantasaph, in spite of the dark times represented by "An Anthem of Earth," he dwelt more and more upon the wonderful paradox of man as a "swinging-wicket" between the world of sense and the world of spirit. Even before he had met and talked with Patmore, he had increasingly thought of human nature as a "secret metaphor" of God, a "Cosmic metonymy" [3]; and under Patmore's influence, he moved steadily in the direction of such poems as "Orient Ode," "The Mistress of Vision," and "Contemplation," each of which must be viewed in the light of their mutual relationship to the conviction that one unifying divine idea underlies all things.

This belief had led him to explore the whole subject of symbolism in poetry, for the literary symbol—which may be thought of as an analogy for something that is not directly stated [4]—reflects the kind of universe which both Thompson and Patmore habitually thought of as their dwelling place. If it was true that a unifying idea lies back of everything, then every part of the visible universe must point to an invisible reality—the ideal form or model of the entire cosmos. This ideal form must be known to us through our knowlege of the vast aggregation of visible things, each of which must have its esoteric affinities with the primordial idea. Consequently, all physical things can be said to have an analogical relationship to the unseen, ideal model from which the universe was made. Like Baudelaire, Thompson believed that nature is a forest of symbols which point to an ideal order of beauty. But unlike the French poet, Thompson conceived of that ideal order as being identical with the personal self-consciousness of the Christian God.

Thompson was actually never sympathetic to the French Symbolist movement and said that the very term *symbolism* had become a narrow label for a school of writers who, like Baudelaire and Mallarmé, were trying to make poetry a wilfully obscure mode of expression for an exotic group.[5] His own interest in symbols, which is markedly evident in his notebooks, was directed towards those which were both traditional and universal.

Unlike such moderns as Hart Crane or William Carlos Williams, Thompson was not seeking for a new focal symbol that would be as peculiarly his own, as Crane's Brooklyn Bridge or Williams' Paterson. In his poetry the most recurrent symbol is the sun, which is undoubtedly one of the most traditional and universal of all symbols.[6] Like Patmore, Thompson was concerned with the symbols that go beyond individual consciousness and claim to confront us with something which is universally valid. As he said in a fragmentary note to Father Anselm, a study of some of the most primitive symbols that have been widely used in a variety of times and places will show that "true symbolism" is never an arbitrary, conventional device but a means of expressing basic realities in a universe in which one divine analogy runs through all things.

When he had read the English translation of Count Goblet d'Alviella's *The Migration of Symbols,* which was published in 1894, Thompson set about the preparation of an article on symbolism that was never completed. In this article he expressed his belief that in any basic symbol, such as the sun, many parallel meanings may be found to resolve themselves into the same final meaning because the great symbols of mankind focus many significant ideas. They illustrate "that synthetic system of focus so difficult to the analytic Western mind

—unless one is a Plato, or a poet, which is much the same thing." [7]

In order to illustrate this point, Thompson undertook an analysis of a solar symbol which was employed by the Egyptians. It took the form of an egg-shaped disc on which were mounted wings and horns surrounded by two serpents. The flight of the sun through space was suggested by the wings, while the "ruling energy of the solar rays" was signified by the upright horns. Yet the very ovular shape of the disc carried with it the suggestion of the relation between the sun and fertility, while the serpents reinforced this association with the idea of sexual reproduction. Thus the sun symbol could be said to carry with it a manifold significance; fully understood, it appears not only as a conventionalized solar image but also as a symbol of the cosmic egg—the beginning in both men and nature.

If, as Patmore believed, nuptial love is the symbolic key to the mystery of creation, it would scarcely be surprising to find that such an ancient symbol of the sun was also used to signify the primal act of creativity by its association with suggestions of fertility. The Egyptian winged disc was therefore a most attractive bit of evidence for the "synthetic system of focus." Not only was it rich in suggestive possibilities but it also seemed to reinforce Patmore's theory with a piece of symbolic evidence derived from a very early historical period.

The correspondence between Thompson and Patmore gives ample proof of how eagerly Thompson responded to the pursuit of the interpretation of symbols in which the older man had engaged for so many years.[8] Thompson had long been convinced that a truly perceptive poet must inevitably turn to the use of basic symbols, not as artistic conventions but as effective insights into analogy. His contact with Patmore confirmed his belief that the poet must give serious attention to those universally recurrent symbols which continue to arouse manifold, significant echoes out of the long racial past.

Typical of Thompson's discussions of this topic, is one of his letters to Patmore on the symbolism of the points of the compass.[9] Patmore had told him that in the Bible and in "the mythologies" the North has always been given great importance, and Thompson replied that he already discerned this for himself but was grateful for Patmore's corroboration since Patmore's way of putting things always added "sight" to his "seeing." He then went on to say that he had learned from the study of comparative mythology that it is impossible to speak of the simple chronological development of the significance of any widely used symbol since symbols have recurrent multiple meanings which arise, disappear, and return again in a wide variety of times and places.

This apprehension of the multiple meanings attached to a given symbol has its evident importance for the understanding of such poems as "The Mistress of Vision" and "Orient Ode" where ambivalence abounds and depth of meaning is achieved through ambiguity. Thompson had, perhaps, first become aware of how a single symbol might carry a wealth of significance by the study of the allegorical treatment of the Bible which is so characteristic of many of the Church fathers, who, like St. Clement of Alexandria, greatly appealed to him. At any rate, in a manuscript called "Without a Parable Christ Spake Not" he noted that the Bible well illustrates the fact that in all "primaeval" symbol systems each term

> ... has many meanings, according to the department of thought in which it is used: but he who has learned a single signification of such a term, with the rationale of its use, can derive from that meaning—without further teaching—all other meanings.

As an example, he chose the symbolism of water. In the story of creation in the first chapter of Genesis, water is that from which all things in the material world originally came.[10] Water, then, may be taken to symbolize all of external nature, on the principle that nature as a whole may be symbolized by its aboriginal part, "just as we speak of a man's posterity as his 'seed.' " The rationale of the symbolic use of water is that it may be applied to anything which is primary to a particular order of thought. It might, for example, be used to denote truth in the theological order, while in other branches of learning it would have a different but equally basic significance.

With the growth of his own interest in the multiple meanings of the great symbols of nature, the Bible, and the tradition of literature, Thompson was more and more convinced that poets like Patmore and himself must create for their contemporaries a vivid and moving image of the universe as a vast symbol system pointing to God. Eyes that had for too long become strangers to the wonder of the invisible, intangible world of the divine reality must be turned in a new direction where they would not longer "miss the many-splendoured thing." [11]

※ II ※

The preparation of *New Poems* for publication was motivated in part by this desire to restore what may properly be called the sacramental view of the cosmos by which outward and visible things might be understood to be effective signs of God's presence in creative power. It was also motivated by the feeling that his brief period of poetic productivity was coming to an end. He wanted to bring together all the poetry that was the result of the time he had spent at Pantasaph in as com-

prehensive a book as possible, and he was not prepared to cut
out so much as half a line "to please a publisher's whim for
little books and big margins." Writing to Meynell he said:

> Treated in the sumptuous style, it would make a book
> about the size of Rossetti's first volume; but there is no
> reason why it should be got up more than just well and
> simply. I believe it will be my last volume of poetry—in
> any case my last for some years—and I am determined
> to make it complete, that I may feel all my work worth
> anything is on record for posterity, if I die. . . . [12]

That he had benefited from the critical admonitions of Patmore and Alice Meynell, as well as from what less friendly
commentators had written, is evident from one of the many
prefatory notes that he wrote and cancelled:

> Of words I have coined or revived I have judged fit
> to retain but few; and not more than two or three will
> be found in this book. I shall also be found, I hope, to
> have modified much the excessive loading both of dic-
> tion and imagery which disfigured my former work.[13]

Yet, what he felt that he had gained "in art and chastity of
style" could not make up for his feeling that he had also "lost
in fire and glow." After all the revisions and cancelled prefaces,
after the final arrangement of the fifty-four poems was completed, his conclusion was: "This book carries me quite as far
as my dwindling strength will allow; and if I wrote further in
poetry, I should write down my own fame."

From late in April of 1895 to the end of May, 1896, the
determined editorial work on *New Poems* went forward. But
just before it was completed, Thompson heard from Mother
Austin that their father was dying. The sequence of events
which followed was pathetically typical of the confusion and
misunderstanding that had marked the course of his relationship with his family for so many years.

Thompson decided that he must get to Ashton-under-Lyne as quickly as possible. Evidently he hoped that somehow at his father's deathbed there might be achieved a final moment of truth and understanding, a time when he could express his genuine regret for having been—as he told Wilfrid Blunt not long before his own death—such an "unsatisfactory son." Of course, Thompson did not have the train fare since he was not allowed to have any money. He had had to borrow from his father when he first went from Manchester to London; now he turned to the friars and was loaned twenty shillings so that he might reach his father before it was too late.

As it inevitably happened, however, Francis Thompson did not arrive in time. The faceless house where he had first hidden himself in his imagination offered him no hospitality. His stepmother—whom he had known only as Anne Richardson, the sister of the pastor of St. Mary's Church—refused to see him, and he finally was compelled to stay at the rectory of St. Peter's, Stalybridge. All through his father's funeral and for sometime after it was ended, Thompson stood apart in a mood of the deepest remorse. He could not express his feelings in a letter to Meynell beyond saying that it had been made very bitter for him, but in his prayer book he retained for the rest of his life a mortuary card asking prayers for the soul of Charles Thompson and bearing the motto: "The silent and wise man shall be honoured."

This mournful visit to the environment of his childhood was brief, but in the course of it he managed to lose the return half of his railroad ticket and had to buy another with what was left of his borrowed funds. Seeing his sister in her religious habit, he found her to be "the merest girl still, and sweeter than ever." This impression of youthfulness seems to have been characteristic, for even those who met Mother Austin late in her life usually remarked it. She, however, found her brother

to be much older and more worn-looking than when she had
seen him ten years earlier. She told him that he looked much
older than his recent photograph—an opinion that seems to
have been general, for as Thompson wrote to Meynell, "Every-
one made ye same flattering remark."

Looking at her brother, Mother Austin must have recalled
the pride and expectation of great things which Dr. Thompson
had felt when, on an occasion during the poet's boyhood, she
had heard him say to their mother, "I can't imagine where
that boy has learned all that he knows." She knew, too, that
what had been expected of "Frank" was never what he really
had to give—the poetry which without the tortuous course of
his life would have been impossible. Mother Austin was the
last member of the family Thompson ever saw, just as she had
been the one to whom he had written his furtive note when
he had left home in November, 1885. Margaret, who had
married Canon Richardson's brother, was living in Canada
and there was to be no time when their separate lives would be
even temporarily brought together.

Thompson returned to Pantasaph owing the friars their
twenty shillings and with a bill for a pair of new shoes he had
bought for his trip—"ye ones I had being quite impossible."
There was, of course, no one to care for these obligations but
Wilfrid Meynell.

Greatly depressed as he was, the last stages of the work on
New Poems became more difficult. There was much discussion
of the possibility of a change of publishers, and Thompson
was disturbed by the suggestion that two translations and a
redaction of poems by Victor Hugo, which he had done sometime before the publication of *Poems,* ought not to be included
in the new book. It was a sound suggestion, for the pieces in
question had no particular value or apparent importance. Yet
Thompson was adamant:

> I regret that I cannot consent to the omission of the translations. If anything is to be left out it must be the section *Ultima,* not the translations. . . . They were held over from my first book, and I will not hold them over again.[14]

The Hugo poems were taken from the series *Les feuilles d' Automne,* and Thompson may have found them attractive because of the sun imagery in the one he called "A Sunset" (*Soleils Couchants*) or because of the metrical challenge of what he described as the "splendid fourteen-syllable metre" of "Heard on the Mountain" (*Ce qu'on entend sur la montagne*). He was evidently pleased to learn that Patmore thought very highly of the diction and metre of this second poem in the group, even though it abounds in examples of Thompson's too frequent failure with effective rhyme, as in the following:

> I hearkened, comprehended,——never, as from those
>   abysses,
> No, never issued from a mouth, nor moved an ear such
>   voice as this is!   (ll. 11-12)

The redaction of Hugo's "Que t'importe, mon coeur?" may have seemed important to Thompson because of the first two stanzas in which he had expressed in his own words the belief that the material world is "a veil the real has." Yet it is difficult to escape the feeling that he displayed so much determination about the inclusion of the Hugo poems simply because he wished to assert his rights as an acknowledged poet. His petulant annoyance over the matter was rather like that of a child who grows weary of always being told what to do. Having literally nothing that was his own—other than his writing —and having to turn to others for the most elementary necessities, he would have been less than human if he had not wished to assert his independence on some occasions. It appears that the issue of the Hugo poems was such an occasion.

He insisted on having his own way, and in this instance managed to get it.

His opinion of the reliability of his own critical judgment was probably strengthened by the fact that in the very month in which his father had died, the *Edinburgh Review* had publish an excellent and balanced study which described Francis Thompson as an already great poet who could become even greater. This praise from such a respected journal helped to raise his depressed spirits after his return from the funeral and gave him the hope that all his work on *New Poems* might really be justified.

When that work was finally completed, Meynell invited Thompson to London where he went in June and stayed for the better part of a month. It was during this time that he finally met George Meredith, who had spoken favorably of his poetry. For Thompson, Meredith had been "the most unquestionable genius among living novelists," [15] but at Box Hill he discovered Meredith as a poet. He went there with Alice Meynell in answer to Meredith's repeated invitations and stayed in the little country cottage overnight.

Box Hill was a strikingly beautiful spot; his host was pleasant and his talk was entertaining, but Thompson remained uncomfortable. This direct encounter with the penetrating light of Meredith's clear, realistic mind was a strange and unaccustomed experience. He and Alice Meynell had been offered and given "Heaven's welcome to the elect," but when Meredith expressed a desire to see the proofs of *New Poems,* Thompson shyly refused. There could not have been much ease of communication between the poet of "The Mistress of Vision" and the great poet-novelist, of whom Thompson later wrote that he was one who believed in the hard doctrine that man must seek nothing beyond nature and conformity to her stern law.

Yet, Thompson was never to lose the great interest in Meredith's poetry which developed during and after his visit to Box Hill, and his critical judgment of it was perceptive and just:

> Mr. Meredith is a poet; a poet of a peculiar quality which has no parallel in English poetry save it be that of Browning. . . . In fact, chosen bits of Meredith or Browning would make a "missing-word competition" from which newspaper-readers would recoil aghast. . . .
>
> His metre has all the ruggedness of Browning's. . . . The deflection of law becomes the rule rather than the exception. . . .
>
> But with all these faults Mr. Meredith will not suffer you to forget his authentic powers; intermittently surprises you, in his most brambly poems, by passages of that sheer beauty which for its own sake he disdains. . . .
>
> And through sheer strength he secures that his poetry, despite its much formidableness, shall be read with strenuous delight.[16]

The contact with Meredith which developed so slightly during the Box Hill visit was never renewed, but when Thompson was buried, there were roses from Meredith's garden in his coffin and on the card which accompanied them was the inscription, "A true poet, one of the small band."

III

Thompson returned to Pantasaph in July and later in the same month visited Patmore at his home, The Lodge, in Lymington on the southeast coast opposite the Isle of Wight. Patmore, who was a member of the society of Catholic laity called the Third Order of St. Francis, had a great devotion to the great saint of Assisi, whose virtues he found it so difficult to imitate. One of the Patmore children was called Francis, and it was this member of the family who in later years recalled Thompson's visits to the Lodge, which apparently were fairly frequent after the two poets had met at Pantasaph. Francis Patmore found his father's guest to be simply "a weakly little man, with untidy red hair and unkempt beard," who had a great fear of Patmore's fierce retriever dog, which bore the heroic name of Nelson.[17]

Patmore had written Thompson in March that he felt himself to be "dying of having seen God, and of the vision having been withdrawn." He had been seriously ill for over two years and sometimes suffered acute pains, but as he looked at Thompson's haggard appearance he concluded that the younger poet might die first. He was, in fact, so worried after his friend had gone back to Pantasaph that he wrote to inquire whether Thompson was in need of his help:

Lymington, July 29, '96

My dear Thompson,

You were looking so unwell when we parted that, not having yet heard from you, I am somewhat alarmed. Pray let me have a postcard.

If at any time you find yourself seriously ill, and do not find the attendance, food, etc., sufficiently good, tell me and I will go to Pantasaph to take care of you for any time you might find me useful. It would be a great pleasure and honour to serve you in any way.

Yours ever,
Coventry Patmore

In his reply Thompson expressed gratitude for Patmore's great kindness and assured him that ". . . I never yet fell from any friend who did not first fall from me." As for the nursing care, Thompson was genuinely moved by Patmore's offer to come if he were needed, but he wrote, "Fortunately it has not come to that yet."

Four months later, Patmore was dead. No one has more perfectly described Thompson's feelings when he received this news than Everard Meynell: "He grieved for Patmore as a wife grieves for the husband who dies before the birth of her child." [18] *New Poems* had not yet appeared. Now the book, or the greatest part of it, would be "born dumb," as Thompson said, for the one man who could understand and interpret its language to the world was gone.

Writing to Mrs. Patmore at Lymington, Thompson spoke of the passing of "the greatest genius of the century," of a friend who could not be separated from him by years or distance. To Meynell, there was little he could say, for as the editor's daughter puts it, Thompson spoke a different language to her father than that which he spoke to Patmore. [19] It was not the language of high vision but of daily necessity.

Patmore had been the one person in Thompson's life of whom he could say in his notebooks that the contact between them was truly "dynamic":

> He reverberated my idea with such and so many echoes that it returned to me greater than I gave forth. He opened it as you open an oyster, or placed it under a microscope and showed one what it contained.

Even the lovely surroundings of Pantasaph that had become so closely associated with Patmore in his mind no longer appealed, and he wrote:

> O how I miss you any casual day!
> And as I walk
> Turn, in the customed way
> Towards you with the talk
> Which who but you should hear?
> And know the intercepting day

Betwixt me and your listening ear;
And no man ever more my tongue shall hear,
And dumb mid an alien folk I stray.[20]

Archbishop Kenealy, recalling a drive he took from Pantasaph to St. Beuno's Jesuit House of Studies in the company of the two poets, described the sheer delight with which Thompson entered into Patmore's mood, which on that occasion was one of hilarious laughter, during the trip. Yet the Archbishop, who, as Father Anselm, had known them both fairly well, concluded that although they were intellectually intimate, they were not friends "in the complete sense of the word." [21] There was, of course, a vast difference between the worlds in which each of them lived; their personalities were formed by utterly different experiences; and in the brief period in which they knew one another, Patmore's was clearly the dominant role. Moreover, in their very different ways, both men may be said to have been in love with Alice Meynell, a fact which could have produced a certain hidden resentment between them. Yet, when all this and more is taken into account, it remains that Thompson at any rate found in Patmore a man of whom he could write with evident sincerity that he was a "friend whose like I shall not see again."

Wilfrid Meynell, of course, remained to sustain him through the deepening depression that followed upon Patmore's death. It appeared that the years at Pantasaph had seen the end of the opium habit, and Meynell concluded that it would now be possible for Thompson to return to London without any danger of its return. Consequently, Thompson left his Welsh retreat, with its now painful associations with his lost friend, and came to Palace Court in December, 1896. The Meynell children, about whom he had written so much of his earlier poetry, remembered him years later as the sort of guest they never ran to meet with expectation, nor were they as attracted to him as he was to them.[22] Yet, they had always felt easily at home in his company; and they delighted in the tricks which his seeming gullibility allowed them to play on him.

His hosts at Palace Court introduced Thompson to their friend, Arthur Doubleday, who was a partner in the Constable publishing company. Through him it was arranged to replace Lane as the publisher of *New Poems,* and Thompson went for two short visits with the Doubledays, who lived in Westminster. Their home was a somewhat more formal place than Palace Court, where callers were likely to appear at almost any time and meals were always available, whatever their quality. The Doubledays dressed for dinner and Thompson sat at their table rather incongruously arrayed in dress clothes several sizes too large for him, which he had borrowed from Meynell. Although Thompson talked books and music with Arthur Doubleday and described his hostess as a "simply exquisite pianist," it seems evident that he was happiest during the day when he was left to his own devices, reading and smoking in the library.

Of course, Thompson was the sort of guest who would hang up his overcoat with a lighted pipe stuffed in the pocket (as he did on at least one occasion at Palace Court) and be startled to learn that he had caused a small fire. He preferred his own curious pattern of withdrawal, and the Meynell children, who might have found him amusing enough when they were quite small, hesitated about having their school friends see the strange guest who appeared to haunt their house.

Thus while he frequently came to Palace Court for meals in the evening, Thompson began inhabiting a series of rooming houses in the neighborhood of Harrow Road soon after his return to London. The first of these dimly respectable places seems to have been on Elgin Avenue, where his landlady was a Mrs. Maries, the wife of a printer employed by Meynell. She found him to be somewhat less than sociable, and may well have concluded—as did others after her—that her unusual guest was somewhat "mental."

The world of the London lodging houses was a world in which Thompson's poetic creativity finally all but expired, as it seems destined to have done had he lived elsewhere. There he began the last decade of his life, in which his writing was largely prose, written for various journals to help him to pay his landladies for putting up with the considerable inconvenience he often caused them.

The critical reception given to *New Poems,* when it was finally published in May, 1897, must have shown him how right he had been when he said that with Patmore's death there would be no one who could understand and interpret to others the meaning of most of the book.

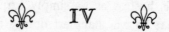

IV

Thompson had anticipated some difficulty with the critics, for he had remarked in a letter to the Meynells that the first section, "Sight and Insight," was so "terribly trying" that he had followed it with "a whole section of the lightest poems I ever wrote" in order "to soothe the critics' gums." Even so, it is not likely that he had expected his "stern, sober and difficult" work to receive quite the amount of abuse which fell upon it and seemed to obscure the favorable comments of critics of the stature of William Archer and Sir Arthur Quiller-Couch, who said that in reading "The Mistress of Vision" he had recalled "the wonder and delight" he had felt on his first reading of Coleridge's "Kubla Khan."

The critical charges against *New Poems* centered largely around the difficulties of his diction and the obscurity of his thought. These complaints were not new, for they had been made with some justice against his earlier work. E. K. Chambers, for example, had said of *Sister Songs* that its author showered out obsolete words and coined new ones at will. To an age that knew nothing of James Joyce and, with certain honorable exceptions, regarded Walt Whitman as nothing more than a vulgar eccentric, an abundance of coined words was especially offensive.

Yet, the number of true neologisms in Thompson's work was not as great as his critics supposed. According to G. A. Beacock's listing, there are 134 words in Thompson's poetry which cannot be found elsewhere.[23] However, when Beacock's list is checked against the authority of the *Oxford English Dictionary* no more than seven words are found to be specifically noted as Thompson's neologisms. The rest are compounds, obsolete, rare, or archaic forms put to new uses.

Thompson was well aware of the fact that Lionel Johnson had accused him of having done more damage to the English language than the American press and that even the sympathetic Archer had been offended by his supposed habit of word coinage, but as he remarked in his essay on Coleridge, the charge of strange or affected diction might well have been dismissed as having been levelled against any number of great poets:

> Wordworth wrote simple diction, and his simplicity was termed affected; Shelley, gorgeous diction, and his gorgeousness was affected; Keats, rich diction, and his richness was affected; Tennyson cunning diction, and his cunning was affected; Browning rugged diction, and his ruggedness was affected. . . . If this old shoe were not thrown at the wedding of every poet with the Muse, what would become of our ancient English customs? [24]

Yet, as we have seen, he had admitted to "excessive loading both of diction and imagery" in his early work, and he felt that in *New Poems* he had attained a greater "chastity" of style. Certainly, he had benefited from Patmore's guidance sufficiently to justify this opinion, but many of his critics did not agree. Their difficulty was, in fact, not so much one of language as of fundamental understanding, for they literally did not know what he was talking about. Terms, symbols, and whole concepts drawn from the Catholic liturgical and mystical tradition left them with a sense of complete obscurity in the face of the poems in the "Sight and Insight" group.

The *Saturday Review,* for example, found the splendid "The Mistress of Vision" to be one of several "nonsense-verses." The *Pall Mall,* as we have seen, attacked "Anthem of Earth" as "a terrible poem" and categorized it as being formless, "rhymeless and the work of a medieval and pedantic Walt Whitman." Under such a barrage, sales dropped rapidly, and praise of Thompson's earlier work in the *Bookman* during the year did little to help.

The importance and lasting value of *New Poems* lay in the "Sight and Insight" section on which the critics expended their most severe censures. In the writing of "The Mistress of Vision" and "Orient Ode" Thompson had not only given of the fulness of his deepest experience and conviction but had also labored to the utmost of his powers to serve the high demands of his art.

Of this labor, "Orient Ode" may be taken as typical. The evidence of his work on this poem appears in a notebook as a disordered collection of stanzas, phrases, half-developed figures, and whole lines, scattered over some twenty pages and inside both covers.[25] According to Thompson's own testimony in a letter to Patmore, the poem was suggested by certain passages in the liturgy for Holy Saturday and was composed during the Easter season.

On Holy Saturday a Catholic church is dark and silent as

the ceremonies begin; the tabernacle is empty; the altar is stripped of all ornament. Speaking in the awesome language of Jeremias, the Church laments the death of Christ in the Nocturns and Lessons of the Divine Office. As the ceremonies proceed, the darkness and the note of despair slowly give way to light until, in the *Gloria* of the First Mass of Easter, all is restored in the fullest possible liturgical splendor. All of the action, of course, symbolizes Christ's apparent defeat by evil and darkness and the ultimate victory by which He destroys these adversaries and brings light and life to men.

This liturgical pattern is the framework of Thompson's completed "Orient Ode," a pattern which is set in the first fifteen lines, in which the rising of the sun is compared with the elevation of the Host during the ceremony of devotion known to Catholics as Benediction and frequently performed in churches following the public recitation of the rosary. As the sun rises and gives light and warmth to the dark earth, so the Eucharistic Christ, lifted from the altar tabernacle during Benediction, sheds His blessings upon the faithful.

The risen sun is pictured by Thompson as calling forth the beauty and fertility of the earth, which responds to its warming touch; the heavens are then described as swept clear of all lesser bodies, while the sun, like a triumphant lion, progresses to its zenith. Standing gloriously in the heavens, the sun is the destroyer of darkness, the life-giver to men and all created things. The poet is his devoted worshipper and sees in the sun nothing less than a symbol of Christ. The poem ends with an exultant cry, as the poet apprehends—in the relation of the sun to the earth, which it illuminates—an analogue of the immanence of God, Who is present in all things, but not identified with them.

In the notebook draft of the poem, the first fifteen lines, with the imagery of Benediction, stand in the same introductory position as they do in the published version. There are, however, certain important variants:

Lines 1-2 of the published version are:

> Lo, in the sanctuaried East,
> Day, a dedicated priest

The notebook has it:

> Lo, in the sanctuaried East,
> Nature, a dedicated priest.

Day rather than *Nature* makes the metaphor more specific.

Lines 8-15 in the published version are:

> And when the grave procession's ceased,
> The earth with due illustrious rite
> Blessed,———ere the frail fingers featly
> Of twilight, violet-cassocked acolyte,
> His sacerdotal stoles unvest———
> Sets for high close of the mysterious feast
> The sun in august exposition meetly
> Within the flaming monstrance of the West.

The notebook has this variant:

> The earth with due illustrious rite
> Blessed,———before the fringes featly
> Of her twilight acolyte
>   weeds
> Her sacerdotal pomp unvest.
>   stoles

In the published version, the personification of twilight as the acolyte is clear; it is not so in the draft. Moreover, in another version of the same passage there is an even more ineffective variant:

And when the grave procession's ceased
And with due illustrious rite
    adoring
The   earth is blessed completely
    kneeling

The suggestion of *kneeling earth* seems strained, and the word *completely* is utterly prosaic and was wisely rejected.

Following the first fifteen lines in the notebook, there comes a section which deals with the metaphor of the sun moving as a roaring lion to dominate the heavens. This corresponds to the part of the poem which begins at line fifty-five in the published version, where it is preceded by forty lines that describe the sun as a warrior breaking through the ramparts of darkness and as a lover coming to his beloved. In the notebook, these two metaphors are developed elsewhere, but without any relationship to the lion-of-the-heavens section, to which they lead in the published version.

The metaphor of the sun as a triumphant lion, driving the satellites of the solar system before him, as if they were lesser creatures under his sway, raised a problem for Thompson: The sun consumes like a devouring lion, but it is also a life-giver. How were these two elements to be enclosed in the same metaphor? Like Shelley's west wind, this lion-sun must be a destroyer and preserver, not only because the sun is so in nature, but also because in "Orient Ode" the sun is a symbol of Christ, the Lion of Judah, who destroys darkness and preserves life. The answer to this problem lay in evoking the Biblical story of Samson, who killed a lion and returned later to find that bees were living in its carcass. Having eaten of their honey, Samson made up a riddle to trick the Philistines: "Out of the eater came forth meat, and out of the strong came forth sweetness" (Judges 14:14).

Recalling this Biblical episode, Thompson did not abandon the lion metaphor when he described the "deathfulness and lifefulness" of the sun's fire in his notebook draft:

> Ruddy lion, ruddy lion (lion, red-lion)
> Samson's riddling meaning merging
> In thy twofold potence meet:
> Out of the terror of thy (burning) might
> Comes the honey of all sweet,
> And out of thee, the eater, comes forth meat.

He was understandably unhappy about the word *ruddy* and began again:

> Samson's riddling meaning merging
> In thy twofold potence meet (join complete)
> Out of the terror of thy might,
> Burning lion, burning lion
> Comes the honey of all sweet,
> And out of thee, the eater, comes forth meat.

The word *burning,* which was taken from the fourth line of the first version, replaced the unfortunate *ruddy,* and modified the word *lion* in its new position in the third line of the second version. As a result of this process, *burning lion* now appears in the published version of the ode in line eighty-nine.

These examples of Thompson's studied efforts to make the transition from his initial inspiration to full expression with the greatest possible integrity could, of course, be multiplied, not only for "Orient Ode" but for the rest of the poems of "Sight and Insight." Sections of "The Mistress of Vision," for instance, may be found scattered through at least two notebooks, with many variants.[26]

In this poem he expressed most intensely what many of his critics failed to understand. It was, perhaps, the most perfect fruit of his contact with Patmore; it was the essence of the

world-view they held in common with few other men of their
time and place.

The first speaker and the narrator in "The Mistress of
Vision" is the poet himself. The vision which it describes is that
of an allegorical garden in the medieval tradition of "The
Pearl." In the garden of vision—at its very heart—is a Lady
of light, whose eyes hold mighty secrets which no man can ever
tell adequately. All through the vision the Lady sings, but what
the poet can re-create of her song is but a dim fragment. She
tells of "the land of Luthany" and "the tract of Elenore" where
the poet must learn his art. In the answer to his repeated question as to where this land may be found, the Lady tells him
that the key is in his own heart. To find his way to Luthany and
Elenore, he must obey her commands:

> Learn to dream when thou dost wake,
> Learn to wake when thou dost sleep;
> Learn to water joy with tears,
> Learn from fears to vanquish fears. . . .
>
> (ll. 128-131)

When at last he has gone beyond the limited vision of his
contemporaries, when his song reflects and conquers pain, then
he will know that he has attained the goal he seeks, the wonderful land of true poetic insight of which she has sung.

The words of the Lady, which are heard only by the ear
of the imagination and not through the physical sense of hearing, are understood by the poet in his inmost soul. He tells us
that when the magic of the vision is ended, he will weep, for
even in the songs of the greatest poets he cannot expect to hear
such music again.

Bearing in mind Thompson's conception of the multiplicity
of meanings that find their focus in a single symbol, one can
read this poem at various levels of significance. The garden of

the vision may be thought of as the realm of the highest poetic attainment, and the Lady may be seen as a personification of poetry. The poet must learn to dream when he is awake because the creative process requires not only imagination to see beyond the ordinary impressions of commonplace experience, but it also requires times of contemplative inactivity. He must learn to wake when he is sleeping because, as we have noted above, some of his greatest inspirations may come in sleep. He must abandon life as a "successful" man of the world in order to find it in the apparent failure of the life of a striving artist. In an age which is dominated by an exclusive scientific materialism, he must penetrate the web of matter to the true values which it distorts and conceals.

All these aspects of Thompson's thought concerning the poetic process of creation lie back of the vision described in the poem. Yet, there is so much more. The Lady tells ancient, hidden secrets, and the poet is reminded of Christ's crown of thorns, prefigured in a vine which Noah made into a garland or wreath after the deluge. The crown of thorns and the spear of Calvary, symbols of sacrificial pain, must be a part of the poet's life, for like the saint, the poet will have no true spiritual insight if he is unacquainted with suffering.

The Lady is a "Lady of fair weeping"; in her tears the vision is sustained and the "lily" keeps "its gleaming." She is, therefore, not only to be seen as a personification of poetry, but she is also suggestive of the Blessed Virgin Mary, of whom the lily is a traditional symbol.

"The Mistress of Vision" is not only concerned with the poet's life as an artist but also with the search for mystical insight, the longing after the Vision of God, which cannot be satisfied by the music of poetry. Underlying its complex theme is the basic Christian Neo-Platonic outlook, which he had shared with Patmore and developed to a great degree during the course of their exchange of ideas. The Lady of the vision says in verse what both men had said elsewhere both in verse and prose:

> 'When to the new eyes of thee
> All things by immortal power,
> Near or far,
> Hiddenly
> To each other linkèd are,
> That thou canst not stir a flower
> Without troubling of a star;
> When thy song is shield and mirror
> To the fair snake-curlèd Pain,
> Where thou dar'st affront her terror
> That on her thou may'st attain
> Perséan conquest; seek no more,
> O seek no more!
> Pass the gates of Luthany; tread the region Elenore.'
>
> (ll. 149-162)

The world is a theophany; everything is linked in one divine idea; and the path to an understanding of this truth lies through sacrificial pain.

In "From the Night of Forebeing," and "Any Saint" he spoke with some confidence of the true relation between "God's two worlds immense, / Of spirit and of sense," and of the poet's gaining true insight while still limited by the bounds of language. Yet, as he felt that he had made some little progress in spiritual illumination, so he continued to reveal—as in "The Dread of Height"—a guilty sense of his own incapacity for its higher and truly mystical reaches:

> Too well, too well
> My flesh doth know the heart-perturbing thing;
> That dread theology alone
> Is mine,
> Most native and my own;

And ever with victorious toil
When I have made
Of the deific peaks dim escalade
My soul with anguish and recoil
Doth like a city in an earthquake rock,
As at my feet the abyss is cloven then
With deeper menace than for other men,
Of my potential cousinship with mire.

(ll. 72-84)

It was not the sort of difficulty which the average reviewer for
the contemporary journals might have been expected to understand—as, perhaps, his confessor had understood at Ushaw so
many years before.

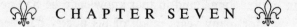

CHAPTER SEVEN

CRITIC'S WAY

I

Looking back on most of his early work, some of which had been so favorably received in *Poems,* Thompson had the feeling that much of his writing had been wasted on lesser themes. At Pantasaph he had confronted what he regarded as ultimate reality with an intensity and an awareness that were heightened by his contact with Father Anselm and with Patmore. The Lady of his vision, who had given him the key to a deeper knowledge of himself, was symbolic of the fact that he had not only grown as an artist but attained a greater spiritual maturity. In poems like "Grace of the Way" and "The After Woman," he longed to be able to write poetry that would be worthy of this newer vision, and in "Retrospect" he spoke of the poetry he would yet write:

> Yet shall a wiser day
> Fulfil more heavenly way
> And with approvèd music clear this slip,
> I trust in God most sweet.
> Meantime the silent lip,
> Meantime the climbing feet.   (ll. 40-45)

But with *New Poems,* he had virtually terminated his work as a poet. Apart from a very few of his later pieces, he was to do nothing of any importance in verse. As he said in "The Cloud's Swan-Song," he had learned "To make song wait on life, not life on song," and in that knowledge he had come to realize that for many years much of his poetry had been not an imitation of reality but a flight from it. The poems of "Sight and Insight" were, like "The Hound of Heaven," echoes of the confrontation of his mind by the most compelling of realities. The critical reaction which they produced, coupled with the loss of Patmore's understanding presence, convinced him that he was evidently speaking in "an alien tongue, of alien things." More than that, however, he felt his inability to go beyond what he had called a mysticism of "limited and varying degree." [1]

It is more or less futile to attempt to explain precisely how and why Thompson became "exanimate of quick Poesy," for no explanation can be altogether satisfactory. His own words are, perhaps, as suggestive of the truth as any could be:

> For who can work, unwitting his work's worth?
> Better, meseems, to know the work for naught,
> Turn my sick course back to the kindly earth,
> And leave to ampler plumes the jetting tops of thought.[2]

Thompson may not have found the systematic mind of Aquinas to be congenial, but he may be said to have shared the Angelic Doctor's experience of feeling that all he had written was worth no more than a heap of straw when compared with the vision he had been permitted to glimpse.

Of course, Thompson—unlike the saint—could never, as he said, "face firm the Is, and with To-be / Trust Heaven," and he had made what proved at length to be the fatal mistake of returning to life in London.

At first, however, things appeared to be going well enough there. Meynell had persuaded Charles Lewis Hind, who had become editor of the *Academy,* to employ Thompson as a reviewer and a contributor of critical articles. The extent of the work which he was to do in this capacity, not only for the *Academy* but for many other publications as well, can be appreciated only when one realizes that as a result of the most painstaking research Father Terence Connolly has found 455 such articles and reviews to be definitely the products of the last decade of Thompson's life. He wrote to survive; his income was measured in terms of the number of columns of print which he could produce. Since much of this work appeared anonymously, it has had to be identified through the evidence of the notebooks and other devices of scholarship. Gathered together by Father Connolly, it now provides clear proof not only of the burdensome work but also of the genuine intellectual productivity of Thompson's final years in the face of increasing sickness and recurrent despair.

In spite of the critical reaction to *New Poems,* Thompson, of course, continued to have a considerable reputation as a poet. Viola Meynell recalls how noted photographers wanted pictures of him "in his study"; how a journalist wanted to do a feature story on him as an example of the home life of a literary celebrity; and how an unnamed American woman tourist, who wrote poetry, was most anxious to meet Thompson for "a quiet talk *a deux.*" The recipient of these and similar requests had no study in which to be photographed, no home in which to exhibit the domestic habits of what journalists described as "a man of letters," and certainly no suitable place to receive a call from a lady poet on tour.

He did, however, respond favorably when H. W. Massingham of the *Daily Chronicle* wrote to ask for a poem to celebrate Victoria's Diamond Jubilee. This letter, dated June 6, 1897, set a deadline of June 21. In three weeks the "Ode for the Diamond Jubilee of Queen Victoria" was duly delivered, but the suspicion that the whole piece was probably written in three hours seems to have some justification.

As verse it is an undistinguished example of occasional hack work, celebrating the literary, scientific, and military accomplishments of the Queen's sixty years as sovereign and looking forward with almost unblemished optimism to the future. Yet, the ode has its biographical interest. In the procession of the dead poets with which it begins, Tennyson leads the "long Victorian line." He is the poet of beauty, while Browning, who follows him, is the poet of strength. Arnold appears, "with a half-discontented calm," only to give place to the "fervid breathing" of Elizabeth Browning and the "gentle-taken breath" of Christina Rossetti, whose brother is rather unhappily described in the following fashion:

> Rossetti, whose heart stirred within his breast
> Like lightning in a cloud, a Spirit without rest,
> Came on disranked; Song's hand was in his hair,
> Lest Art should have withdrawn him from the band,
> Save for her strong command. . . .   (ll. 48-52)

Patmore, as might be expected stands apart. He has no brothers in this company, but must go "Where the sole-thoughted Dante waited him."

Scientists, explorers, and statesmen are given a brief honorable mention, but no names are singled out. The political history of the period is briefly noted when at the very end of the procession of the great come those statesmen who have been famous from Melbourne to "The arcane face of" Disraeli, "the much-wrinkled Jew." Thompson, however, had never lost his boyish love of martial music and tales of military adventure. Consequently, he devoted a number of glowing lines to "the sabre's children." Recalling the Crimean War, the Indian campaigns from Cawnpore to Gujerat, and noting that further violence threatened, he pictured England as keeping the feast of the Jubilee with her "hand upon the sword."

Just as he had not lost his romantic affection for the profession of arms, so he also retained to the end of his life what seemed to some to be his utterly incongruous love for the game of cricket. As one observer remarked, "If ever a figure seemed to say, 'Take me anywhere in the world so long as it is not to a cricket match,' that figure was Francis Thompson's." Yet, he never seems to have ceased to write notes and verses about cricket and the great heroes of the game. In 1900 he could easily recall the names of the famous Lancashire eleven of 1878 and the victories he had witnessed at the Old Trafford ground. As late as 1904 he went with an air of great solemnity to participate in a match with some of the tenants of a rooming house where he was staying and presented a more pathetic picture at bat than he had when he tried to play the game during his early years at Ushaw. Seldom able to get to the matches at Lord's or the Oval, Thompson in his last London years nonetheless was habitually given to making plans to see them.

These plans, like many others which he made, either never materialized or ended in some incredible confusion. Much of his correspondence consisted of apologies for not arriving for appointments or not meeting his publishers' deadlines. Among the tenants of the rooming houses, he had some acquaintances, and he evidently became quite friendly with Saratkumara Ghosh, an Indian, who, in 1909, published a novel, *The Prince of Destiny, the New Krishna,* in which Thompson's personal eccentricities are described with great accuracy and his genuine interest in Eastern mysticism is recorded.

However, apart from Meynell, he had no friendships with other men after Patmore's death. His contact with people like the enthusiastic J. L. Garvin of the *Newcastle Daily Chronicle* or his associations with Lewis Hind and E. V. Lucas, the biographer and editor of Charles Lamb, were generally on a superficial level. He was as much an outsider to the world of the professional journalists as he was to that of the Bank of England. His withdrawal into himself was, in fact, so great that he thought nothing of breaking into a Shakespeare reading at the Meynell's home with a sudden and irrelevant exclamation over a lost check from the *Academy*.

Typical of the misadventures which surrounded efforts to draw him into the movement of London literary life is the episode of his visit to William E. Henley, whose edition of Burns Thompson had effectively reviewed. Henley, who generally preferred a more realistic poetic style than Thompson's, was nonetheless interested by the review, which may have appeared to him to reveal a different side of its author than he had supposed existed. His own crippled condition having made it necessary for him to learn to discipline his time, Henley arranged with Hind and Lucas to have Thompson brought to him at precisely three o'clock one afternoon. They were to meet the poet at a designated point and go at once to Henley's study. Thompson arrived at the rendezvous quite late and announced that he must have lunch before going any further. As a result, Henley waited two hours before his guests appeared.

The fact that Thompson arrived at all was somewhat unusual, but the success of the meeting was even more so. Henley despised many of Thompson's favorite poets and was especially hostile to Shelley. Yet the entire conversation passed most amicably, as Henley sat enthroned in a great armchair and Thompson sat at his feet. There was a sympathy between these two utterly different men, both of whom had known the meaning of intense physical suffering. Finally, Henley concluded matters by suggesting that Thompson should write for the *New Review*, and in November, 1897, some of his critical work began to appear in that publication.

Most of Thompson's conversations with those whom he met in connection with his journalistic work were not as satisfactory as that which he had with Henley. Hind, who in addition to a weekly check to Thompson's landlady also provided a few shillings for pocket money, wrote that Thompson would accept the coins without comment or even a pause in the nervous, almost hysterical, flow of his talk about utterly trivial matters in which he seemed to be absorbed. This surface chatter, which was noted by many who had occasion to observe him, was a covering for the lack of that communication which he found so complete in his association with Patmore.

Always living in the neighborhood of Harrow Road, he moved in his awkward, shabby way in a circumscribed area between his changing lodgings and the offices of the journals he served. Many of his evenings were spent at Palace Court, where he was as likely to talk about cricket, indigestion, or tobacco as he was to speak of poetry or music. Often he simply walked the streets at night, composing as he went and paying little or no attention to things around him.

It is not, therefore, surprising that on the night of November 25, 1897, Wilfrid Meynell should have received a police telegram informing him that one "Francis Thomason" had been knocked down by a hansom cab and taken to the Homeopathic Hospital, Queens Square, with a severe laceration of the head. The son of Mrs. Frey, one of his landladies, who had often observed Thompson "cross the road amongst traffic as in a dream" [3] thought it a marvel that he managed to escape death in the busy streets—an opinion which Meynell, looking at him as they emerged from the hospital, must have shared.

His grimy pipe and the matches which he was constantly lighting were as much a danger to himself, as well as to others, as was his indifference to traffic. Not long after his accident with the cab, he set fire to the curtains of his room on Elgin Avenue as he lay smoking in bed. His own account of it is found in a letter written to Mother Austin some time after—a letter which he never mailed but left among the disordered papers and notebooks that always accompanied his movements among the rooming houses:

> . . . I have had a year of disasters. You will notice a new address at the head of this letter. I have been burned out of my former lodgings. The curtain caught fire just after I had got into bed, & I upset ye lamp in trying to extinguish it. My hands were badly blistered, & I sustained a dreadful shock, besides having to walk ye streets all night. The room was burned out.

His shock was so great that he fled without arousing Mrs. Maries or his fellow lodgers, who fortunately discovered the blaze in time to have it brought under control. But when Hind later asked him why he had given no warning, his only reply was the singular comment that a burning building was no place to remain. Apparently his landlady took a charitable view of the affair, for later on she did not hesitate to accept him as a lodger again.[4]

These "disasters" left him, early in 1898, in one of his deep periods of depression. He had increasingly the feeling that his life must end, as it had begun, in tragedy, and he prayed that the final act, which he expected to come on the London streets, might be brief in its agony. He talked of the illustrated book on London, the text of which was finally done not by him but by Alice Meynell, and he even thought of the possibility of publishing a fourth volume of verse. But in his times of recurrent depression, he contemplated a return to the anonymity of the old vagrant life, and on such occasions it was all that Meynell could do to keep him from the inevitable self-destruction which that would have involved.

❧ II ❧

Even before he left Pantasaph, Thompson had entered upon the beginning of an episode that was to add one more to the total sum of minor tragedies which formed the pattern of his life. This was his friendship and love for Katherine Douglas King, whose widowed mother, Mrs. Hamilton King, had gained some reputation for her poetry and a volume called *Letters and Recollections of Mazzini.*

Katherine King followed her mother's literary inclinations and wrote short stories which were marked by a note of romantic realism that reflected her activities as a volunteer worker at a little hospital for crippled children in London's East End. Upon reading some of these stories in *Merry England* in 1896, Thompson, who was still at Pantasaph, had expressed an unusual desire to meet their author. He wrote to Meynell:

> I admire them strongly—not, I think for that which she would desire to be admired in them. I think she would claim admiration for their realism. I admire them for their idealism. In all the chief characters there is something which never was in any such character. And that something is Miss King. . . . There is a very striking and attractive individuality disclosed through all these stories. If it is of any value to her, pray convey to her my sincere admiration of her true gift.

They met during Thompson's visit to Palace Court in the early summer of 1896, and Thompson was at once struck by the vivacious combination of courage, integrity, and sheer femininity which he felt in "Katie" King. He also met and was charmed by her mother, who was notable for her delicate resemblance to the ladies of the Pre-Raphaelite paintings.

In one of the very few letters in which he ever complained of Meynell, Thompson told Patmore of his distress at having had to leave London before this new friendship had developed further:

> That was a very absurd and annoying situation in which I was placed by W. M.'s curious methods of handling me. He never let me know that my visit was about to terminate until the actual morning I was to leave for Lymington. The result was that I found myself in the ridiculous position of having made a formal engagement by letter for the next week, only two days before my departure from London. Luckily both women knew my position and if anyone suffered in their opinion it was not I.

It need hardly be remarked that Thompson was not generally known for his scrupulosity about keeping his social engagements, which makes his irritation in this letter all the more significant.

When Thompson and her daughter began a correspondence which included fervent verses from Pantasaph, Mrs. King felt a proper Victorian alarm. Some, she knew, looked upon Thompson almost as a saint, but others read in "The Hound of Heaven" what they took to be the confessions of a great sinner, who, like Oscar Wilde, had—as one pious writer later put it—thrown himself "on the swelling wave of every passion." [5]

Consequently, on October 31, 1896, Mrs. King wrote to Thompson, quite against her daughter's wishes, asking him not to "recommence a correspondence which I believe has been dropped for some weeks." Katherine was staying at a convent, and her mother felt that, as Thompson himself seems to have suggested, she might eventually stay there. This prospect did not please Mrs. King any more than did the possibility that her daughter might marry a Bohemian, but she used it to suggest to Thompson that, "It is not in her nature to love you."

For his part, Thompson had explained in a previous letter that there would be nothing but an honorable friendship between Katie and himself. At no time does he seem to have proposed marriage, and Mrs. King was evidently torn between a concern for her daughter's emotions and the desire to believe that the friendship might be continued without harm to her reputation. In any case, she told Thompson that she saw no reason why he might not see Katie again, "now that this frank explanation has been made & no one can misunderstand." She ended her letter with the assurance that she considered his friendship for her daughter and herself to be an honor, from which she could not part "without still more pain."

After Thompson came to London to live, he received a letter from Katie, which was dated February 8, 1897. She regretted what she described as the "unwarrantable & unnecessary" check to their friendship and said that she felt that they understood one another perfectly. This letter concluded with an invitation:

> I am a great deal at the little children's Hospital. Mr.
> Meynell knows the way. I know you are very busy now,
> you are writing a great deal & your book is coming out,
> isn't it? but if you are able & care to come, you know
> how glad I shall be.
>
> > Ever yours sincerely,
> > Katherine Douglas King

The invitation was accepted and other letters followed, in which she spoke of her concern for his health and her delight in seeing him so much at home among the crippled children she served. It is difficult to say what Thompson expected would come of their relationship, which had begun so soon after his emotions had been stirred by Maggie Brien, but when Katie wrote on April 11, 1900, to tell him that she was to be married to the Rev. Godfrey Burr, the vicar of Rushall in Staffordshire, the news evidently helped to deepen his discouragement over the failure of his hopes for a new volume of verse. In a letter to Meynell, which was written in June, less than a month before Katie's wedding, he was highly melodramatic in his despair and once again announced his intention of returning to the life of the streets:

A week in arrears, and without means to pay, I must go, it is the only right thing. . . . Perhaps Mrs. Meynell would do me the undeserved kindness to keep my own copy of the first edition of my first book, with all its mementos of her and the dear ones. . . . Last, not least, there are some poems which K. King sent me (addressed to herself) when I was preparing a fresh volume, asking me to include them. The terrible blow of the New Year put an end to that project. I wish you would return them to her. I have not the heart. . . . I never had the courage to look at them, when my projected volume became hopeless, fearing they were poor, until now when I was obliged to do so. . . . O my genius, young and *ripening,* you would swear,—when I wrote them; and now! What has it all come to? All chance of fulfilling my destiny is over. . . . I want you to be grandfather to these orphaned poems, dear father-brother, now I am gone; and launch them on the world when their time comes. For them a box will be lodgment enough. . . . Katie cannot mind your seeing them now; since my silence must have ended when I gave the purposed volume to you. . . . I ask you to do me the last favour of reading them by 8 to-morrow evening, about which time I shall come to say my sad good-bye. If you don't think much of them, tell me the wholesome truth. If otherwise, you will give me a pleasure. O Wilfrid! it is strange; but this—yes, *terrible* step I am about to take . . . is lightened with an inundating joy by the new-found hope that here, in these poems, is treasure—

or at least some measure of beauty, which I did not
know of. . . .

Thompson, of course, was persuaded not to take the *"terrible
step"*; Meynell once again paid his debts and it was Katie,
rather than Thompson, whose life was soon ended, for she
died in childbirth in April, 1901, in the first year of her marriage.

The "orphaned poems" mentioned in the letter to Meynell
comprised a group of five sonnets, which were published in the
1913 edition of Thompson's works under the heading "Ad
Amicam," plus certain other completed pieces and rough drafts
gathered together in one of the familiar exercise books. The
publication of Father Connolly's *The Man Has Wings* has
made more of the group available in print so that a general
picture of what it contained can now be had without difficulty.
Some of the poems express a mood of joy in a newly discovered
love; others suggest its coming loss or describe the poet's feelings when he learns of a final separation.

The somewhat Petrarchan love story which these poems
suggest cannot obscure the fact that undoubtedly they have
more than a little of autobiographical sincerity. When they
were first written, there was evidently no thought of their being
published, and those which refer to the writer's love for Mrs.
Meynell particularly have the ring of truth. In "My Song's
Young Virgin Date," for example, Thompson wrote:

> Yea, she that had my song's young virgin date
>   Not now, alas, that noble singular she,
> I nobler hold, though marred from her once state,
>   Than others in their best integrity.
> My own stern hand has rent the ancient bond,
>   And thereof shall the ending not have end:
> But not for me, that loved her, to be fond
>   Lightly to please me with a newer friend.

> Then hold it more than bravest-feathered song,
>   That I affirm to thee, with heart of pride,
> I knew not what did to a friend belong
>   Till I stood up, true friend, by thy true side;
>   Whose absence dearer comfort is, by far,
>   Than presences of other women are!

Taking into account Thompson's capacity for self-dramatization and the possibility of a wish to identify his own life with the misfortunes of other poets who had known unhappy loves, there can be no doubt about his genuine emotion for Katie King. That she was affected by his protestations seems obvious, but since she was evidently a sensible young woman —as well as an outgoing and sympathetic type—it would seem that for her the word *friendship* had a far less intense emotional significance than that which Thompson gave it. From the outset, she must have realized that marriage with him was out of the question, and although she was displeased by the "unwarrantable" interference, it seems probable that she did agree with her mother's suggestion that the poet was "perhaps" a man "most fitted to live & die solitary, & in the love only of the Highest Lover."

The poems which were addressed to her, while they are far more restrained than those of "Love in Dian's Lap," show no great technical advance over those of the "Narrow Vessel" group and are, if anything, somewhat more labored. Their interest remains chiefly biographical, for they throw some light on the utter despair which overtook Thompson in the spring and early summer of 1900.

Whether or not Danchin is correct in suggesting that Thompson's resumption of the opium habit also dates from this period is, of course, a matter of conjecture.[7] Reid simply states, without offering any supporting evidence, that "after he returned to London, he resumed his draughts of laudanum, and continued this right up to his death." [8] There is every reason to recognize that in the very last years of his life, as we shall see, Thompson did take the drug in carefully rationed doses to ease the pains of his illness, but the exact date at which this began has never been determined. If, as Reid says, "nearly all his poetry was produced when he was not taking opium," there may be some reason to doubt that he was under its influence in the period from 1896 to 1900 when he was writing the poems to Katie King and making plans for another book of verse. In any event, the critical productivity of that time is abundant proof that if he was taking laudanum, it was never in command of him to the extent that it had been during his vagrant years.

Meynell's remedy for Thompson's despondent mood was typically practical. He simply found more work for him to do, and the articles and reviews continued without an evident break.

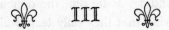

III

As a reviewer, Thompson generally displayed a judicious attitude. That he read some of the books assigned to him with a studied carefulness is evident from his notes, which are often so full that they provide an unquestionable basis for the identification of reviews that were printed without his signature. On the basis of this careful reading, Thompson frequently gave a clear, complete, and interesting description of a prose work or chose effective quotations to illustrate his discussions of poetry.

He was seldom an unmethodical critic, and his reviews generally followed a systematic pattern: a description of what the work contained, a treatment of the things that had especially interested him in it, and, wherever possible, a balancing of whatever artistic merits and faults he might have found.

It was, of course, in this drawing of the balance sheet of judgment that he most clearly displayed his desire to do full justice to an author. Reviewing Davidson's *The Testament of an Empire Builder,* for example, Thompson found that there was "too much metrical dialectic." Poetry, he said, must be "dogmatic": it must not stoop to argue like a "K.C. in cloth-of-gold." Yet Davidson impressed him as a poet capable of "sustained power, passion, or beauty," and he cited specific passages to illustrate not only these qualities but Davidson's command of imagery as well.[9] Similarly, he wrote that Laurence Housman had a "too deliberate manner" as well as a lack of "inevitable felicity in diction." But he admired Housman's "subtle intellectuality" and delighted in the inversion by which Divine Love becomes the most "fatal" allurement in "Love the Tempter." [10]

Of course, there were books about which nothing good could be said. Understanding, as he did, the difficulty of the art of poetry, and believing that the "only technical criticism worth having in poetry is that of poets," he felt obliged to insist upon his duty to be hard to please when it came to the review of a book of verse. He was—partly as the result of his own experience with *New Poems*—pained by the average reviewer, who passed sentence on poets "with a mere smattering of knowledge and study of the matter in hand." [11] But he was equally offended by the number of volumes of inferior verse that found their way into print. There was a time, he said, when "most clever and cultivated men" wrote verses and "only a fool or a poet published them," but he could see the day rapidly approaching when "only a poet will not publish." [12]

When he reviewed verse which he felt would have been better left unpublished, he especially displayed that power of

incisive expression which frequently marked his critical prose
but less frequently was evident in his poetry. One finds him
saying, "To love no poetry is merely a loss; to love poetry like
this, an evil." When he read the work of Robert Buchanan, he
remarked that diffuseness robs art of all distinction and observed that,

> Not since the author of "Thalaba" and "Kehama" re-
> lieved the public from asking, "What is Bob Southey's
> last new epic?" has a poet wallowed in poems of such
> dismaying proportions.[13]

Confronted by R. F. Horton's *St. John,* which was an unfortunate attempt to versify the gospel, Thompson was faced
with that bane of so much "religious" poetry, the stock response. He quickly pointed out that the religious feeling in such
verse never succeeds in prompting any artistic emotion, any
imagination. Religious sincerity, he continued, may often be
found where there is "poetic insincerity," for honest piety by
itself is quite powerless to create artistic integrity; the one kind
of sincerity does not generate the other.[14]

The incisiveness which one finds in Thompson's reviews
sometimes appears in his literary essays as well; the "Shelley"
is not at all typical. As Rooker, for one, has noted, he had a
certain gift for compressing all of his critical reaction to an
author's work in a concise phrase or striking comparison. For
example, when he was describing Coleridge's power to "bring
down magic to the earth," he said:

> He takes words which have had the life used out of
> them by the common cry of poets, puts them into rela-
> lation, and they rise up like his own dead mariners.[15]

Again, when he was expressing his admiration for Pope's satirical powers, he remarked, "He is like Ortheris fondly patting

his rifle after that long shot which knocked over the deserter, in Mr. Kipling's story." [16]

When he spoke of major figures, such as Pope, Milton, or Coleridge, Thompson often sounded like Hazlitt, for *impressionism, gusto,* and *appreciation* are terms which can be justly applied to his treatment of the great and near-great of English literary history. While it is true that he felt that Saintsbury's way of asking, "Is the delight there?" could lead to an excess of subjectivism,[17] he nonetheless believed that in the criticism of poetry the last word must be uttered by an "indescribable, intuitive faculty." Critical taste, he argued, can be educed or cultivated, but it can not be simply learned, for it is a native gift.[18] In exercising this gift, the critic should not be required to support his judgments by reasoned demonstration alone, for his is not an exact science. Consequently, he approached the major poets of the past with what he called a "warm, sympathetic intuition," and accorded them "discriminating praise, rooted in direct poetical insight."

It is not, therefore, surprising that he greatly admired the critical method of De Quincey, whom he once called, "the first to practice that mode of criticism we call 'appreciation'—be it a merit or not." Certainly, he had little regard for the "lofty reasonableness" of Paul Elmer More, of whom he said:

> If the whitened statue of Cobden, which looks seriously upon the Hampstead trams, were to speak, even thus would he comment upon books and life, after so many days of elevated and solitary immobility.[19]

More, he felt, lacked that inspiration which was almost as necessary to the critic as he believed it to be to the poet.

The "inspired" critic was one who was "passionately open" to impressions and possessed of a personality that responded to the artists whose work he discussed. Pure intelligence, like that displayed by More in his *Shelburne Essays* in 1905, produced analyses, which were objective, but "barren, like the critical exercises of schoolboys and professors." Similarly, those whom he described as "forever shearing the wild tresses of poetry between rusty rules" were equally barren and uninspired. They were the sort of men who had failed to appreciate Keats.

The best criticism, therefore, would not be so much concerned with comparing a work with "various categories of composition based on the practice of previous writers" as it would be to look for the effect upon the imagination produced by any given work as a whole. But even this was not as important as the necessity for the critic to identify himself with the artist's mind, to think the artist's conception again, to grasp his individual plan, and to criticize his work according to the extent to which that plan had been developed in an aesthetically pleasing manner:

> According to their [the critics'] capacity of assimilating his [the artist's] design, their criticism will be good or bad, complete or incomplete. And the measure in which a man possesses this sympathetic intuition is the test of his critical gift. "Appreciation," the wise it call, which we prefer to . . . "interpretation" as a name for the modern process of criticism.[20]

One suspects that if Thompson had ventured to write a history of English literature, it would have been marked by many evidences of the catholicity of his tastes and of his ability to appreciate writers differing as widely from one another as they did from himself. He liked Saintsbury's emphasis upon literary history as such, and was distrustful of Courthope's sociological approach to it. It was, he said, far better to understand the metaphysical poets, for example, as men who were trying to seek out and display the pure "poetic element" than it was to examine them as the products of social disintegration.

Saintsbury's powers of appreciative understanding, growing out of his wide acquaintance with many literary traditions, impressed Thompson very favorably,[21] just as his avoidance of such general categories as Arnold's "Hellenism" and "Hebraism" appealed to Thompson's own habit of trying to understand any author of importance within that author's own context.

His criticism of Macaulay is a case in point. Macaulay's prose, Thompson realized, was not likely to appeal to critics whose tastes were representative of the "delicate verbal instinct" which could best find its delight in the work of Stevenson or Mrs. Meynell. Men who, like Pater, had a passion for "verbal choiceness" were not likely to respond favorably to Macaulay's rhetoric. In the aesthetic final decade of the nineteenth century, Macaulay's love of the obvious was regarded as a kind of gaucherie. Thompson, of course, realized this and sympathized with it. Therefore, he called Macaulay "the most brilliant of Philistines"; he was the "Sauric deity of English letters, the artist of the obvious." Loving the surface view of things "with impatient middle-class thoroughness" Macaulay in purple would have been a "crowned bourgeois." Yet, Thompson saw him as one of the true "monuments" of English literature and expressed his distaste for critics to whom such monuments seemed to provide little more than an opportunity for malicious vandalism.[22]

Macaulay, he reminded his aesthetic contemporaries, had virtues that were sadly lacking in their own times and work. Thompson was delighted by the man's sheer vitality, his impulsiveness, his enthusiasm for the causes he espoused so vehemently. Admitting that Macaulay's style lacked a certain refinement, Thompson nonetheless described it as being like that of an able lawyer "fed by affection pleading for a client." Moreover, Thompson found Macaulay's martial ballads, while

not up to the best of Kipling, to be honest and able within their
very limited range. In fact, Macaulay's lines "On the Battle of
Naseby" supplied the model for Thompson's own "The Veteran of Heaven." [23] Summarizing his judgment, Thompson
gave the following well-balanced, concise, and justly discriminating estimate:

> As a critic he is naught; as a biographer or historian
> he is naught so far as exactitude of treatment, novelty, or
> philosophy of view is concerned. But he can revivify a
> period, a person, or a society, with such brilliancy and
> conciseness as no other Englishman has done.[24]

It has been said that a tone of religious bias can be detected
in some of Thompson's criticism of men who, like Macaulay,
were far from his own creed.[25] Instances of this, if they exist
at all, are very rare. More often, as in his treatment of Byron's
Don Juan, he was likely to display quite the opposite attitude.
He regarded *Don Juan* as one of the great poems of the century, a work whose author had managed to sustain "the warmth
and tension of a giant through sixteen cantos of miscellaneous
remarks." [26] Why, he asked, is there such a living appeal in a
poem that is filled with so much irreverence for things above
and so much contempt for things below? And he concluded
that its appeal lies in the fact that,

> We all savour Byron's opinions in moments and crises
> of our lives, and are pleased to find them finely phrased,
> and linked to a splendid personality.

Don Juan, he insisted, leaves no impression of mournful world-
weariness:

> It is not a sigh but a shout. . . . The negations and
> nihilisms with which it abounds are uttered as roundly as
> other men's faiths.

Looking at the world of 1903, Thompson found that Byron's satirical epic had a contemporary importance for a time that was experiencing visions of a new social order and the ferment of formative discontent, for against those who had wished to destroy similar visions and ferment, Byron had flung his own "picturesque denials" and passionate protests." To the "hesitant, geyser-like aspirations" of the struggling nineteenth century Byron had, in the reactionary years after Waterloo, given a "human reference," for he seemed to embody those very aspirations in his own career.

The case of Thompson's treatment of Bunyan in *Merry England* [27] was cited by Mégroz,[28] who is echoed by Reid,[29] as an outstanding example of how Thompson's Catholic concerns interfered with his critical objectivity. The Bunyan article was, of course, intended for a distinctly Catholic journal and might be expected to call forth some theological comment. However, Thompson's main objection to Bunyan was that he sometimes fails to give his allegory that inward imaginative quality which one finds in Spenser. Disagreeing with the thumping approval given to Bunyan by Macaulay, Thompson said that Bunyan had "inexhaustible invention, but no imagination." To call this, as Mégroz does, evidence of Thompson's desire to take part in "the Roman Catholic crusade of his time," with the Protestant classic *Pilgrim's Progress* as his target, is scarcely justified.

Writing ten years later in the *Academy,* Thompson said that his purpose was to abate some of "the undistinguishing eulogy traditionally poured out" upon *Pilgrim's Progress.* Yet, Thompson recognized that the position of the book would always be assured, and he pronounced his own judgment of its style with considerable restraint and perception:

> That very inveterate homeliness of conception, which makes Bunyan's weakness when he attempts the higher ranges of conception, is the main strength of his work in

the greater part. The familiar ingenuity of the imagery, the symbolism, the allegorical details, make them admirably suited to impress the daily understanding. Nor does the cultivated mind fail to admire them.[30]

Far from allowing his religious opinions to affect his critical judgment, Thompson often gives the impression of making a studied effort to avoid any such influence. Sometimes, if he did not agree with the ideas in a work, he would say so, but he did not for that reason condemn the work or deny its artistic merit. Thus he described Omar Khayyám as a "transcendental agnostic and ornamental pessimist," and admittedly disagreed with the substance of the *Rubáiyát*. Yet, he praised FitzGerald's creative translation and his power to make the English language convey the inner spirit of a society and an age "as remote from ours as those of Homer." [31]

In speaking of the letters of Robert Louis Stevenson, Thompson said that although that writer's views in religious matters were "not orthodox," they were nonetheless "his own, purchased at his own cost," and he quoted a letter to illustrate what he very respectfully described as Stevenson's "simple faith, and the limitations of his hopes." [32]

The fact that Swinburne showed contempt for Catholicism did not obscure Thompson's appreciation of him, both as a poet and as a critic. Speaking of *Poems and Ballads* as having a truly revolutionary significance, Thompson also praised *Atalanta in Calydon* as a "brilliant" performance.[33] *Songs Before Sunrise* he correctly criticized as sometimes approaching the rhetorical style of Swinburne's *"bête noire,* Byron," but he observed that few poets preserved their work from rhetorical alloy when they chose to make poetry a political weapon. Swinburne's "Genesis" he praised as a "memorable" work, "whether you accept all its teaching, or (like ourselves) do not." [34]

In general, Thompson avoided the use of theological tags in his reviews, and was mildly amused at what he referred to as the "Sunday-school tradition" of praising writers for being "Christian" or condemning them for being "pagan." [35] Furthermore, in dealing with the metaphysical poets, he showed no preference for the Catholic Crashaw over the Protestant Herbert. Actually, he found that Herbert was a religious poet who kept his best level with much greater consistency than did either the "winged" Crashaw or the "illuminated" Vaughn.[36] There can be no doubt about the fact that these and many others among his critical judgments were formed within the perspective of his deeply religious mind, but his unfailing respect for aesthetic values and his own lively intelligence preserved him from confusing literary criticism with Catholic apologetics.

IV

As a critic, Thompson obviously does not emerge as a major figure in a century that produced both Coleridge and Arnold, and he may have been guilty of a too great reliance upon subjective impressions and appreciative generalities. But thoughtless factionalism and the pursuit of literary fads were not among his critical vices.

It is, however, true that he displayed a blind spot when it came to much of the poetry of the eighteenth century, and he found the French influence upon some of the poets of the Restoration uninspiring. He made what he must have regarded as a valiant attempt to appreciate the worth of John Dyer's *Grongar Hill* by seeing it within the context of its own time, but it was a rather forced effort.[37] Of James Thomson's *The Seasons* he could only say,

We tolerate him for his last-centuryness. We have a certain curiosity in observing in him an observation of nature which was rewarded no more intimately than by a knowledge of the time-sequence of snow-drop, crocus, primrose. . . . We like to hear him speak of young birds as "the feathered youth"; of his women readers as "the British fair." . . . Such phrases speak to us from another world . . . a world which had taste that was not touched with emotion; from a world, in short, which lacked the one thing needful for poetical life—inspiration.[38]

That was his limited and, in its day, quite conventional view of the age of Pope, in whose "Rape of the Lock" he saw the apotheosis of all the "elegant . . . polished artificiality" of its time. For him the "Essay on Man" gave proof that the "pure and simple" didactic poem cannot escape the doom of eventual obscurity.[39] Cowper he could describe as an unusual eighteenth-century poet, who not only went "straight to Nature" before Wordsworth had done so but was able to make his readers accept him for his audacity. Similarly, he noted that in the "deadest time of the eighteenth century" Christopher Smart's "A Song to David" appeared with startling power:

It soars, and drops, and flops, and pitches skyward again; there are plenty of sufficiently tolerable stanzas, which are not more than terse moralities, and come with a shocking anti-climax after some burst which takes you off your feet like a waterspout. . . . But the best is great, and there is so much of it.[40]

Thompson was at his best when he was engaged in that part of a critic's work which R. P. Blackmur has described as the naming and arranging of what the critic knows and loves. The modernity of Jonson's *Timber,* its compact economy of language and its direct strength struck him forcibly. He loved it and he named it: "It is clean, hardy, well-knit, excellently idiomatic; pithy and well-poised as an English cudgel." Dryden's prefaces he called "beatific pot-boilers," a rebuke to the "slovenly work which overflows the press."

In the judgment of poetry he adopted an outlook which demonstrates his great debt to Coleridge. Two things must be looked for—an agreement with the "integral truth of nature" and the relation of ordered and carefully selected parts to produce an organic whole which gives pleasure to the reader.[41] These two principles, Thompson believed, were more trustworthy guides to any critic than that provided by Arnold's touchstone method, which he felt to be open to a perverted, mechanical application. He remarked, for example, that Frederic Harrison's *Tennyson, Ruskin, Mill, and Other Literary Estimates* (1900) was marred by its author's having set too much store by the comparison of detached lines and passages, as Arnold had sometimes done. Convinced as he was that each good poet's work must have its own peculiar identity, he could see little value in judging anyone's poetry by a detailed comparison with key passages from acknowledged masters. This, he said, more often than not, leads to conventional judgments which tend to underestimate whatever is novel.

Strongly influenced as he was by the Romantic critics of his century, Thompson really shared few, if any, of Arnold's leading critical ideas, except for the belief that there were undoubtedly certain racial qualities that could be detected in poetry. One finds him talking of "Celtic" poets as displaying a racial melancholy, pathos, and spirituality, and he points to the "Welsh" elements in the work of Herbert and Vaughn in support of this thesis. In the work of Herbert he found a blending of the Celt and the Saxon—a joining together of "Celtic poetic fantasy and imagination" with "homely sense and terseness of expression," which he thought of as being distinctly Saxon. The French he described as "modern Greeks," a people reliant upon the "sculpturesque" elements of form and structure, and lacking in their poetry that "spiritual intimacy," which he regarded as something that was "un-Greek and un-Gallic." The English muse, he asserted, does not take "more graciously to crushing her wings in a French corset than to rumpling them in a Greek chiton." [42]

Like John Addington Symonds, Thompson looked back to the Elizabethans—and especially the lyric poets of that period —as the voice of the English race speaking spontaneously in a time of young, fresh growth.[43] He did not go so far as Symonds in proposing a theory about the evolution and decay of national types of poetry, but he pictured the English lyric, with its supposedly spontaneous "Gothic richness," as having lost its distinct racial quality in the years between Marvell and Blake, only to emerge again in its true character in the work of the Romantics.

On the whole, however, Thompson's historical perspective was good. If he spent much time in the appreciation of the greatness of the "spacious dead," he was still quite alert to the potentialities of his own time and frequently quite forward-looking. Of course, it is true that he mistakenly shared the justly short-lived enthusiasm for Stephen Phillips, and he was overly impressed by the religious verses and dramatic monologues of Frederick Myers. Yet, he had the perception to see the worth of A. E. Housman, and he rightly insisted that Quiller-Couch's *Oxford Anthology* (1900) would have done better to have devoted less space to the academic exercises of Bridges in order to give a greater representation to Housman.[44]

The fierce realism of Henley's hospital poetry—so alien to his own work—Thompson praised for its "rugged directness," and he supported the experiments in rhymeless, irregularly accentuated forms which marked it. A poet working in such forms, he said, was not to be thought of as evading the challenge of more traditional prosody. To the many who failed to understand what problems Henley was attempting to solve, he pointed out that any poet who observes a well-known and codified law is "safe," even if he is quite often "undistinguished," but,

> No poet can guide himself through the uncharted and compassless ways of irregular metre, without an intuitive sense of rhythmic orientation.

Moreover, he added, such a poet must first master the conventional forms, just as Henley had done.

As for the work of Yeats—who was probably the most important young poet developing during the years of Thompson's critical writing—the judgment was given that Yeats' gifts gave every promise of a highly significant poetic development and growth.[45] This opinion was later much amplified in an *Academy* article that was prompted by an essay written by William Sharp ("Fiona Macleod") in the *North American Review* for October, 1902, under the title "The Later Work of Mr. Yeats." In reply to Sharp's saying that the obscurity of Yeats must be condemned because "the things of beauty and mystery are best sung, so that the least may understand," Thompson said that this was not really possible. On the contrary, that which was both beautiful and mysterious at the same time must be treated as Yeats had treated it, with the "indefiniteness of remote suggestion." Pointing out, with considerable acumen, that Yeats' handling of symbolism would have to undergo a process of "sobering," Thompson recognized that there was nonetheless a suggestive power in Yeats' early work that was quite unique —a power that might well stimulate the beginning of a "new motive" in poetry.

This "new motive" might be seen in what Thompson called "the uncontrolled set" of Yeats' poetry towards mystical experiences that were at once dangerous and exciting. Here was a poet whose words actually stirred echoes which reverberated "to the dimmest verges of consciousness," and one whose "clear passion" was the yearning to penetrate by his art to the infinitely far unknown. In the light of Yeats' later development, this prophecy could not have been more accurate.

There were few people indeed whom Thompson ever regretted not meeting, but Yeats was one such. Writing to Wilfrid Meynell, after having failed to appear at a tea where Yeats was to be present, Thompson said, "I am very sorry to have missed this chance of meeting Yeats, as I have long desired to do. You know I heartily admire his work." [46] Deep as his critical attachments were to what he loved in the established poetry of the past, Thompson was, as he said of himself, "in tune with most audacity."

For him it was a basic principle that no aspect of human experience is completely outside the scope of poetry. There were no specifically "poetic" themes. Accepting Victor Cousin's conception of poetry as a "criticism of nature," he felt that this expression was far more inclusive and satisfactory than Arnold's "criticism of life." Considered as the criticism of nature, poetry was not to be limited with respect to its legitimate subjects, for it must be thought of as interpreting all existing things according to its own peculiar mode of operation. Therefore, Thompson never spoke of confining poetry to "artificial" or to "natural" worlds. He could admire the world of Wordsworth as much as the pastoral construction of Theocritus.

To Arnold's doctrine that noble subject matter is essential to the making of the best poetry, Thompson did not give assent. He was guided by the belief that poetry is never so narrow "as partisans would have her." As for his own work, he summed up his attitude in one of his notebooks:

> I reason not of depth or height——
>   Let this for critics be!
> I know that where is my delight
>   There is my liberty.[47]

When he became a critic himself, he continued to respect the liberty in delight which he found in other poets and opened his mind to listen to very diverse singers, In this respect, at least, he practiced in criticism what he had preached in verse.

CHAPTER EIGHT

A JUDGMENT IN HEAVEN

I

As he entered his forties, Thompson the critic and reviewer found his occupation, and life itself, to be increasingly burdensome. His subsistence requirements called for at least thirty shillings a week and that goal was not always met. When Charles Lewis Hind turned the editorial control of the *Academy* over to Teignmouth Shore, Thompson—in one of his frequently bad puns—found the new editor to be a "doubtfully hospitable Shore." Increasingly, his work was being finished at the last possible moment and was sometimes done under the street lamps on his way to deliver it to the offices of his publishers.

Early rising had never been easy for him, but now the effort became next to impossible to make. He wrote notes to himself urging the importance and necessity of getting out of bed. These he pinned to conspicuous places among the newspaper portraits of other poets and writers with which he adorned the walls of his room. He was, for all his praise of the sun, habitually abroad in the dark or writing in the sleeplessness of the hours after midnight. One of his admonishing placards read:

> At the Last Trump thou wilt rise Betimes!
> Up; for when thou wouldst not, thou wilt shortly sleep
>   long.

The worm is even now weaving thy body its night-shift.
Love slept not a-saving thee. Love calls thee,
Rise, and seek Him early. Ask and receive.

It was the kind of message that a young seminarian might keep
on a card in his prayer book to help him in becoming accustomed to the disciplined pattern of his life. For Thompson,
however, the time when such devices could have been of help
was long past and lay buried in the memories of Ushaw.

Tuberculosis had already claimed one of his lungs and he
was more and more subject to painful dyspepsia. He took
laudanum in carefully measured doses—certainly not for the
pleasure of exotic dreams but as a relief from physical distress
and the feeling that he had (as Patmore once said of himself)
outlived the ambition for living. Pawn tickets for clothing lay
beside the druggist's bill for laudanum and the notebook in
which he kept a record of the dosages he allowed himself.
How comparatively small they were is suggested by the fact
that his bill for laudanum for the entire period of December 24, 1904, to February 28, 1905, was no more than six
shillings and fourpence.[1]

Much of what is known of Thompson's life in this later
period has its source in his first biographer, Everard Meynell,
Wilfrid's second son, who understood him, perhaps, better
than any of the other younger members of the family. Quiet,
meditative, and devoted both to poetry and to cricket, he could
talk to Thompson of the things that interested him most. Having begun as an art student at the Slade School, Everard had
shown some talent for painting, as may be seen from the portrait of the poet which he made about 1906. However, his love
of books and his knowledge of rare editions led him to become
a book dealer, and he opened the Serendipity Shop at the end
of a narrow entrance in Westbourne Grove. This establishment
later moved to more prosperous quarters in Mayfair, but at

the time that Thompson knew it as one of his regular ports of call, it was in its original location.

There he passed many congenial hours, and there he would appear with the installments of his biography of St. Ignatius, the arrangements for which Wilfrid Meynell had made with the firm of Burns and Oates. The elder Meynell eventually became the managing director of the company, and had sufficient influence to persuade the publishers to agree to the somewhat unusual practice of paying Thompson a pound for every three pages he managed to produce. These pages were often delivered at the Serendipity Shop, where payment would be made and pleasant conversation could be had in a leisurely and congenial atmosphere.

All through the last years of his life Thompson was involved with his study of the famous founder of the Jesuits. The work was completed only a little time before his death and he did not live to see it finally published. For him it was far more than a piece of hack work, a means of earning money, or simply a tedious chore. It was intimately involved with his own reflections on the relationship between the psychology of the poet and that of the saint. This interest, which is evident in such essays as "Sanctity and Song" and "Health and Holiness," had been much deepened by his contact with Patmore, but it had been with him from his youth and the years when he first struggled with the conflict over the sensory appeal of poetry and the ascetical aspects of Christianity.

In 1905, during the time when he was much concerned with his Ignatian studies, Burns and Oates published a little book called *Health and Holiness,* in which Thompson expanded the ideas of the earlier essay of that title and developed his conclusion that:

> Hypnotism, faith-healing, radium—all these, of such seeming multiple divergence, are concentrating their rays

upon a common centre. When that centre is at length divined, we shall have scientific witness, demonstrated certification, to the commerce between body and spirit, the regality of will over matter. To the blind tyranny of flesh upon spirit will then visibly be opposed the serene and sapient awe of spirit upon flesh. Then will lie open the truth which now we can merely point to by plausi-bilities and fortify by instance: that Sanctity is medicinal, Holiness a healer, from Virtue goes out virtue, in the love of God is more than solely ethical sanity. For the feeble-ness of a world seeking some maternal hand to which it may cling a wise asceticism is remedial.[2]

In St. Ignatius Thompson saw a combination which formed a striking example of how in a life integrated by sanctity and self-discipline for a supernatural motivation, the qualities of the soldier and man of action—which he loved but did not possess—might be combined with those of the creative thinker —which he was—and the great mystic—which he longed to be but was not. Having reached for the "maternal hand" of a "wise asceticism" and having held it so weakly and so fitfully, he nonetheless knew whereof he spoke and had experiential knowledge of the spiritual mastery of Ignatius that was, in its failures, perhaps even greater than that of many for whom *The Spiritual Exercises* were a regular, if somewhat formal, guide. Thompson, even in the misery and moral confusion of his pitiful addiction, had a love of God which entitles him to participate fully in the significance of Christ's words to the sinful woman who anointed His feet: "Many sins are forgiven her, because she hath loved much" (Lk. 7:47).

He was irregular in his attendance at Mass, but he might have been less so if the Church in those days had provided for the evening Masses that are so common now. Often he would arrive at one of the ugly, garish little churches in his district only to find that he was too late for the service, and

he talked of going to confession far more often than he managed to carry out his intentions of getting there. There is no
evidence—and there should be none—that he was ever much
impressed or even interested by the pedestrian preaching of
the parochial clergy. If he listened at all, his sensitivity to language must have made the experience painful, while what he
knew of moral failure and rare moments of high vision must
have made him wonder at times whether the preacher was
talking about the same religion as that of the great Ignatius.
The testimony of those who knew him best is that he was
generally impervious to most of his surroundings. Thus one
may safely conclude that hopelessly bad ecclesiastical archi-
tecture and pietistic adornments, along with the pulpit discourses for which they provided so appropriate a setting,
happily caused him little pain at those times when he did manage to carry out his formal obligations as a Catholic.

At least once, however, he arrived early for a church service. He was invited to Monica Meynell's wedding. Anxious to
be on time for so important a day in the life of a woman about
whose childhood he had written so much in "The Poppy,"
Sister Songs, and "To Monica Thought Dying," he came to
the church so well in advance of the ceremony that he concluded he was late when he saw the building empty and
went away in the conviction that once again he had missed
a liturgical function. The whole confused affair caused him
more than the usual distress, however, for as he wrote to the
bride,

> I can only say I love you; and if there is any kind or
> tender thing I should have said, believe it is in my heart,
> though it be not here.[3]

Monica's marriage was part of the process by which the old
life of what had been a growing young family at Palace Court

gradually came to its end. Meynell's role as managing director of Burns and Oates required his presence at their offices on the corner of Orchard Street and Granville Place; the journey by horsecar was time-consuming, and in 1905 it was decided that the store rooms on the top three floors of the Burns and Oates property could conveniently be made into apartments. There the Meynells moved, and there Thompson came with regularity, although the journey was a considerable walk from his accustomed neighborhood. Palace Court or the new address of 2A Granville Place—the change did not alter his pattern of visits, except that he was frequently later than usual. One finds Mrs. Meynell writing much the same gentle, witty comments on his lack of promptness from one place as from the other:

> Francis Thompson has just arrived, at about eight-thirty to the seven o'clock dinner, or rather to the one-thirty luncheon, for that was the meal he chose, as he was going to confession tonight. I think it is the same confession that kept him many moons ago.

Like the Meynells, Vernon Randall, the editor of the *Athenaeum,* showed a remarkable patience with Thompson's often transparent excuses, which were sometimes offered with every evidence that their author was himself fully convinced of their truth. In even less lofty company, too, there were always those who gave him the warmth of simple humanity, and many evenings he sat by the fire in the Skiddaw, a pub at the corner of Elgin Avenue and Chippenham Road, where he could watch the dart players and hear talk of cricket from a seat to which no one disputed his right.

There were, of course, his habitual periods of depression, and they became more frequent and profound as his health deteriorated. Often he shared the mood of Hardy's "The Darkling Thrush":

> The ancient pulse of germ and birth
>   Was shrunken hard and dry,
> And every spirit upon earth
>   Seemed fervourless as I.

He was frequently filled with what he referred to as an "un-conquerable forboding" concerning the outcome of his own "gloomy affairs" and the possibility of some universal disaster about to fall on the whole world. He wrote to Meynell: "Disaster was, and is, drawing downwards over the whole horizon. And I feel my private fate involved in it."

Such premonitions of doom are most evident in certain of the occasional pieces he was sometimes asked to do. In "The Nineteenth Century," which appeared in the *Academy* on December 29, 1900, he spoke of what lay ahead:

> Young Century, born to hear
> The cannon talking at its infant ear——
> The Twentieth of Time's loins, since that
> Which in the quiet snows of Bethlehem he begat.
> Ah! with forthbringing such and so ill-starred,
> After the day of blood and night of fate,
> Shall it survive with brow no longer marred,
> Lip no more wry with hate . . . ?   (ll. 175-182)

Planning his ode "To the English Martyrs" for the *Dublin Review,* his mind turned back to the Catholics who had died for their religion in Elizabethan times, and he prophesied that their martyrdom would yet bring terrible divine vengeance upon England. Some of his most extreme language did not appear in print, as an examination of the manuscript of the poem shows:

> We watch the avenging wrath
> Draw downward on its unavoided path
> Of the malignant sun.
> Our world is venomed at the flaming heart,

> That from its burning systole
> Spurts a poisoned life-blood. See
> The gathering contagion thence
> Sick influence
> Shed on the seasons, and on men
> Madness of nations, plague and famine stern,
> Earthquake, and flood, and all disastrous birth,
> Change, war, and steaming pestilence.[4]

At other times, however, the mood of doom was tempered by his immense devotion to the Tory imperial ideal. In his "Peace," written for the conclusion of the Boer War, for example, he speaks of how the builders of the state must learn the hard lessons of imperial responsibility if the peace they have won with so much sacrifice is to be worth all that it cost in blood and treasure.

In "Cecil Rhodes" he pulled out all the imperial stops. This poem was requested by Hind and appeared on April 12, 1902, in the *Academy*. It was written within a week, under considerable pressure. On the day when it was to go to press at eight o'clock, Thompson—in answer to a series of frantic telegrams—arrived at half-past six in the editorial offices with fragments of the poem on a dozen pieces of crumpled paper. These were pieced together by Hind and sent off to the printers, while the poet was sent off to a restaurant with some money for his dinner. When he returned to read the proof, he was apparently dazed and seemed quite incoherent. Swaying back and forth as he examined the work, he made no comment, except to say, "It's all right."

As a poem it was far from being "all right," but it is a perfect reflection of Thompson's attachment to the romantic splendors of the dream of empire:

> And sure this dream is great.
> Lo, Colonies on Colonies,

> The furred Canadian and the digger's shirt,
> To the one Mother's skirt
> Cling, in the lore of Empire to be wise. . . .
>
> (ll. 99-103)

He had played the soldier in his imagination as a child; he had even attempted to wear the Queen's uniform as a way out of his dilemma in the days after the failure of his medical studies; and to the end, he sometimes had the hope that soldierly discipline might yet save England from the excess of luxury and the temptations of power. As he admired the ascetical strength of Ignatius, so he responded to the stern strength of Rhodes, the builder of empires. He was no athlete, but he made the athletes of cricket into heroes. Neither saint nor conqueror, he paid the tribute of his weakness to those who were.

II

During the last years of his life, Thompson planned to do a series of "ecclesiastical ballads." In the only two which were completed, "The Veteran of Heaven" and "Lilium Regis," his love of the sound of martial trumpets is evident through the thumping beat of the long lines. In "The Veteran of Heaven" there is an abundance of military imagery. Christ is seen as a warrior whose hand held no sword in overcoming His enemies. His Name itself is "a going forth with banners and a baring of much swords." In "Lilium Regis," where Thompson's sense of a coming world catastrophe is clearly seen, he speaks of an awesome time when the nations will "lie in blood" and the kings will be "a broken brood."

This same attraction to the world of armies is also evident

in the curious little dramatic sketch called "Napoleon Judges, A Tragedy in Two Scenes." Thompson seems to have had some awareness of the vital awakening of the English theatre which, under the impact of Ibsen and Shaw, was taking place around him. After all, William Archer, who had praised Thompson's poetry, had also been among the intelligent defenders of *A Doll's House,* when it was under so much outraged critical attack. In the notebooks and elsewhere Thompson refers to Ibsen, and he was, of course, conscious of the fact that both Tennyson and Browning had made unsuccessful attempts to revive the poetic drama. Yet, apart from the cardboard marionette theatre of his childhood, which, it will be remembered, he kept with him as an adult, Thompson had no contact whatever with the stage. In fact, it seems unlikely that he ever witnessed a professional performance of any contemporary play.

This, however, did not deter him from experimenting with the dramatic form for a brief period during his journalistic work in London. He attempted to handle the sort of witty exchange that was the specialty of Oscar Wilde in an abortive little comedy of manners called "Man Proposes but Woman Disposes," but it was the highly romantic melodrama of "Napoleon Judges" that he submitted to Archer, "asking him whether it afforded any encouragement to serious study of writing for the stage."

The scene is laid in the camp of General Augereau during the Italian campaign of Napoleon in 1796, and the plot is a fantastic shocker. At a banquet in his tent, Augereau has a deserter shot for the amusement of an opera dancer, Madame Lebrun, who is his mistress. The general is a bombastic drunkard in the old tradition of *Cambises,* and the dialogue is incredibly forced:

MADAME LEBRUN. *(laughing uneasily)*. You are terrible!
AUGEREAU. As battle! Ah, you see it is a lion you roll in
those soft arms; they are mortal jaws that lick
those little hands! Aha, aha, my love! [5]

At the end of the first scene, Napoleon suddenly appears, and
in the following scene he condemns Augereau for what he
has done. The Emperor then orders that Augereau must be
shot as was the unfortunate deserter—at a banquet in full view
of Madame Lebrun. In an utterly incredible climax, the unfortunate opera dancer is accidentally killed and the general's
life is spared, to the accompaniment of long discourses by
Napoleon, who sounds like something out of Addison's *Cato*.

Archer, of course, politely informed Thompson that the
drama did not seem to be a medium in which he could hope
to develop his talents, and the verdict was accepted. The figures
of "Napoleon Judges" were made of cardboard, and their stiff-
ness entitled them to a place in the marionette theatre, but
nowhere else.

The tragic, real drama of Thompson's own life was approaching its end. In 1906, when he often came to Granville
Place flushed and lethargic in the extreme, Meynell turned to
the device that had worked so well in the past: It was decided
that Thompson should go to live near the Franciscans at
Crawley. This time, however, he was reluctant. It was winter
and he dreaded the journey, with all its little arrangements
that always seemed like great obstacles to him. He had come
to a time when a change of scene appeared futile. When, in
his docile way, he went, his mood was expressed in a letter to
Everard:

In my youth I sighed against monotony, & wanted
romance; now I dread romance. Romance is romantic
only for the hearers & onlookers, not for the actors. It is
hard to enter its gates (happily) but to repass them is

impossible. Once step aside from the ways of "comfortable men," you cannot regain them. You will live & die
under the law of the intolerable thing they call romance.
. . . One person told me that my own life was a beautiful
romance. "Beautiful" is not my standpoint. The sole
beautiful romances are the Saints', which are essentially
inward. But I never meant to write all this.

At Crawley, he complained of the cold weather and talked
of the shelter of his warm room. He stayed with a Mrs. Gravely
in a rooming house on Victoria Road, where his habits of
staying in bed until late in the day caused his landlady so
much inconvenience that she told him he would have to move
if he did not keep more regular hours. However, she agreed to
enter his room each morning to make sure that he was getting
up, and under this plan, he reported to the Meynells, there
was no further difficulty.

From time to time, he was able to get to the monastery
where Father Anselm, who had done so much for him at
Pantasaph, was the prior. The priest had looked forward to
Thompson's coming and to a renewal of their old discussions
of "all things in heaven and on earth and *in infernis,*" but
much of the poet's ability to hold up his end of any conversation was fading and the old delight was gone. When Father
Anselm left in April to go to Oxford, Thompson found nothing to keep him at Crawley and returned to London. He felt
himself to be "a helpless waterlogged and dismasted vessel."

His tubercular condition was so advanced that when he
made his increasingly listless visits to the Meynell apartment
he seemed to resemble nothing so much as a tiny, animated
corpse. He trembled constantly and was painfully sensitive to
the least noise. Finally, in August, 1907, Meynell turned to
Wilfrid Blunt and asked that Thompson might be given the
hospitality of his splendid estate, Newbuildings, which was in

Sussex—a part of the country that Thompson had loved since the days at Storrington.

Blunt, who readily agreed, was an eccentric fountain of human vitality. Both he and his wife, Lady Anne Blunt, had travelled widely in the Arab world and were completely devoted to it. Their estate abounded in incongruous combinations of Arabia and rural England. Exotic eastern plants bloomed luxuriantly, and the master of Newbuildings, who openly shocked people by proclaiming himself a follower of Islam, wore colorful desert garb and rode among his English tenants on the finest Arabian horses. A poet by avocation, Blunt was especially concerned with exploding the myth of the "White Man's Burden" and constantly campaigned with his enormous energy against the claim of the superiority of Western civilization.

Thompson's clothing, as always, was in wretched condition and it was necessary to get him new shoes and some shirts so that he might at least make a decent appearance when he arrived in the atmosphere of his host's luxury. Yet, even when he was arrayed in his new clothing, he presented a figure that could not be anything but bizarre next to the vital elegance which marked Blunt's every gesture. But the bizarre was commonplace at Newbuildings, and Thompson was to be received there with the utmost cordiality.

In a final burst of energy, the dying poet made himself ready for the trip from London. As he had written seven years before, the city's very streets seemed to weigh upon him:

> These horrible streets, with their gangrenous multitudes, blackening ever into lower mortifications of humanity! The brute men; these lads who have almost lost the faculty of human speech . . . these girls whose practice is a putrid ulceration of love—for their very utterance is hideous blasphemy against the sacrosanctity of lovers'

language. Nothing but the vocabulary of the hospital, images of corruption and fleshly ruin, can express the objects offered to eye and ear in these loathsome streets.

Out of that world he was to be delivered, but at a time when, as Blunt later observed, he was no longer able to respond to the beauty of the Sussex countryside around him. There were to be no more long walks like those of the years at Pantasaph.

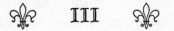

III

At eleven o'clock on the morning of August 24th, Wilfrid and Everard Meynell, together with an unnamed friend, called for Thompson in an automobile. They were prepared to find him in bed and expected to have to wait for him while he went through the process of dressing. Instead, they discovered that he had risen earlier than usual and had gone out on some errand, which his astonished landlady was at a complete loss to explain. When he finally turned up, it was discovered that he had walked a great distance to obtain a particular type of pork pie that he regarded as essential nourishment for so long a trip. He was generally quite indifferent to food and had on one occasion seen nothing strange in ordering a bowl of porridge and a glass of beer when he had found himself invited out to dinner in a fashionable restaurant. His pursuit of the pork pie is, therefore, worth noting, for it gives evidence of how seriously he had considered the simple details of going to Sussex.

Blunt had expected to receive a sick man, but he was not prepared for the spectral image which Thompson presented. As he later described it, the poet seemed to him to be "a poor frail spirit; in a body terrible in its emaciation, a mere shred of humanity, fading visibly into the eternal shadows." Thompson's face reminded him of that of a fifteenth-century Spanish saint, tortured by austerity, or, even more, that of "a prematurely aged and dying child."

The vigorous master of Newbuildings was not unacquainted with illness and sometimes required the services of a trained nurse, Miss Lawrence, who lived on the estate. She was prepared to care for Thompson, but Everard Meynell stayed on for a time to attend to his friend's needs until he could become accustomed to the new surroundings.

Pleasant as things were in the guest cottage which they occupied, this was not an easy process. Everard wrote to Grazia Carbone, whom he later married:

> I have just boiled the poet's eggs & toasted his cakes, which I hear him eating inside. He is very grateful for what I do for him, but he is so used to the very sorry comforts of his town existence that he has taken a little while to get into the way of being here. As it is, he never looks across the lovely landscapes, never goes out into the beautiful green spaces all round our cottage, & altogether presents a pitiable country figure. It is strange to see him twisting his moustaches & pulling down his cuffs when Mr. Blunt approaches, as if that could make him look less of a wreck. . . .[6]

Breakfast was prepared by one of Blunt's male servants, and Thompson managed to be up early to eat it, but he continued his nocturnal habits and would sit up in bed, candles burning beside him, clutching a prayer book in his thin hands, almost like one prepared for burial.

It finally became necessary for Everard to return to London to look after the affairs of his bookshop, and Thompson was moved into another cottage where he was cared for by two of Blunt's tenants. He was visited regularly by a physician, but showed no improvement. He was, of course, taking laudanum, and Blunt's judgment was that he had "quite given up" to it. Yet, Dr. E. Ulysses Williams, who attended him just eight days before his death, wrote to Wilfrid Meynell that when Thompson had told him it was his habit to take seven ounces of laudanum each day, the doctor had regarded this as a doubtful exaggeration because the small quantities given to Thompson in the hospital had a far greater effect upon him than they would have had if he had been habitually accustomed to a daily dosage of such strength.[7]

Whatever the truth of the matter may be, it is probable that the laudanum actually prolonged his life during its last stages and enabled him to endure his sufferings so that he was able to carry on his writing of essays and reviews almost up to his last hour. Blunt wrote to Meynell two months before the poet's death that, in spite of his evident lack of energy for the work, Thompson had "managed to finish an article for the *Athenaeum*."

The contact between Blunt and his ailing guest was sympathetic. In his diaries Blunt recorded that when he first met Thompson in 1898, he found him to be "a little weak-eyed, red-nosed young man of the degenerate London type." But he added, "On the whole however I liked him for he was quite simple and straightforward. Only it was difficult to think of him as capable of any kind of strength in rhyme or prose." At Newbuildings, where Thompson was frequently driven in a phaeton to the great house for lunch and tea, the two men established a common bond when Blunt dwelt on his favorite subject of "European civilization and the destruction wrought by it on all that was beautiful in the world." Thompson, in spite of his enthusiasm for the imperialism which Blunt hated, did, as we have seen, consider himself "Eastern" in his outlook as opposed to the analytical "Western" frame of mind. It was, therefore, much more than mere lethargy or even

simple politeness that enabled him to agree easily with much
of what Blunt had to say about the values of the Middle East
and India.

Blunt's religious outlook was, of course, a mass of incon-
sistency. He was a convert to Catholicism but proclaimed his
devotion to the Prophet of Allah; he is reported to have received the last sacraments of the Church before his death in
1922, but in his will he rejected the usual ceremonies of
Catholic burial. In talking with Thompson in August, 1907,
he expressed the opinion that the civilization of the West had
brought on "the despair of the intellectual part of mankind
with what life gave, and the craving for life after death."

Thompson was scarcely a conventional Catholic himself.
He wrote, for example, that:

> We are too much given to thinking that the Almighty,
> getting tired of His slow ways of teaching, came down
> suddenly from Heaven and finished off the whole of rev-
> elation in a neat and complete little compendium, with
> His Holiness the Pope as perpetual editor, to keep it up
> to date like an Encyclopaedia. . . . All the prophecies were
> wound up and fulfilled down to the last title; all was said
> and completed—needing just a trifling definition from a
> General Council or so; there was nothing left but for all
> mankind to get to Heaven as fast as they could, now that
> the way was entirely surveyed and mapped out for them.
> It looks a little odd, to be sure, if the Almighty had so
> completely changed His ways, that just when He had
> come down on purpose to wind up all the prophecies, He
> should give a new and more tremendous one than ever, in
> the shape of the Apocalypse. And accordingly we have
> never been easy with that Apocalypse; it would not fit into
> our succinct little theory: and accordingly we have now
> satisfied ourselves that it *must* have been fulfilled most of
> it about the time of Nero—with perhaps a trifle over for
> the reign of Domitian.[8]

Like Patmore, Thompson held the opinion that there might be "more light coming," especially with regard to the right understanding of the significance of natural love. He was not, therefore, likely to have been much put off by Blunt's theological eccentricities, but when his host inquired as to his views on the subject of life after death, Thompson replied, "Oh, about that I am entirely orthodox; indeed it is my only consolation." [9]

This led him to speak with affection of his early Catholic training and of his own failure to be honest and open with his father, whose conduct towards him he never found any reason to condemn. Instead, he expressed contrition for his youthful pride in his powers as a poet—a pride which is sometimes suggested in his verse:

> I hang 'mid men my needless head,
> And my fruit is dreams, as theirs is bread:
> The goodly men and the sun-hazed sleeper
> Time shall reap, but after the reaper
> The world shall glean of me, me the sleeper. [10]

Yet, as we have seen, his devotion to poetry caused him great pains of conscience. As Everard Meynell says, "His pride faces his distress; they stare each other out of countenance." Certainly in his mature years he was increasingly conscious of the limitations of his own range, as well as of those of poetry itself, so that he could say, "As a boy of seventeen, I was incredibly vain; it makes me blush now to remember what I thought of myself."

If, as is an undeniable fact, Thompson placed a high value on his poetry during the years before he felt that his inspiration had failed, he may be said to have valued what he wrote at least partly because of the pain which its making had cost him. In addition, however, there was also his inner distress over what he felt he could have done but never managed to do. The theme of the inevitable wedding of pain and the creative process is common in his poetry, and one detects in it something of that feminine strain that is so evident in him: To give birth to the offspring of the imagination was to share in the experience of maternity, which itself provided so much of his imagery. He was so well aware of this that he remarked in one of his notebooks, "I used to be afraid I was more woman than man. But I feel that less now." [11]

He treasured his verses, then, as a woman might treasure a child whose birth had been accomplished in danger and suffering, and he talked of his "heart's children" in his "Laus Amara Doloris" as having passed under the "sacrificial knife" of pain, his "pale Ashtaroth":

> Yea, thou pale Ashtaroth who rul'st my life,
> Of all my offspring thou hast had the whole.
> One after one they passed at thy desire
> To sacrificial sword, or sacrificial fire. . . .
>
> (ll. 22-25)

All creativity, since Adam's fall, must be associated with pain, for "both birth and death" have been given into its "lordship." For the poet, not to experience pain must be the sign of the end of his creative gift, just as a woman knows that without pain there can be no childbearing.

When he came to the time of speaking with "sieging Death, mine enemy, in the gate," [12] Thompson had gone beyond the days when the creative pressures within him were so unendurable as to demand all of the strength he could manage to summon. It was simply a question of the elemental pain of holding on to life. Towards the middle of September, Blunt noted in his diary, Thompson would come to lunch and sit without speaking on anything but the most trivial topics. In the afternoons he would half recline with an unread copy of *Martin Chuzzlewit* held upside down in his hands "three parts asleep, like a very aged man." At times, however, he would seem to rally somewhat, and a priest, Father Gerrard, who called on him said that even in his extremity he could show "keen perception and love of the Church," as well as his "power of language."

The summer was prolonged and particularly lovely, but it was evident that the sun, of which Thompson had often sung as a life-giver, was not to help him. In the middle of October, Blunt wrote that it would be best to get the poet safely back to London. Yet, in spite of his expressed fears that Thompson, under the influence of laudanum, was about to have "some sudden break down or break up," Everard Meynell, in arranging to come for him, expressed his father's typically optimistic hope: "I suppose I will bear back an extraordinarily stronger person than the lamentable poet we brought down to you." What his feelings must have been as he sat with Thompson in the train which took them back to London can only be conjectured, but when the journey—which was marked by the poet's disturbed reactions to the least annoyances—came to an end, Everard wrote, "I am just back from Newbuildings bearing with me the skeleton of F. T."

IV

Thompson died in the Hospital of St. John and St. Elizabeth as the sun was rising on the morning of November 13, 1907. His last portrait, which was made by Blunt's son-in-law, Neville Lytton, at Newbuildings, gives some indication of how utterly emaciated he had become. He weighed no more than seventy pounds, and as he lay in bed his forehead stood out in bold prominence.

His going to the hospital, like nearly every other practical need of his mature life, was suggested and arranged for by Wilfrid Meynell. In all the years of their association with one another, the word *laudanum* had almost never been spoken between them. Thompson had no desire to justify himself, as De Quincey had done, or to seek support for his private excuses. His closest friends knew, and he was aware that they knew, but the painful subject was studiously avoided. However, after Thompson had returned from Newbuildings and was once again at his London room, he finally broke his silence on the matter. His dosage having increased with his illness, he answered Wilfrid Meynell's concerned inquiry over his obvious decline with the simple declaration that he was dying of laudanum poisoning.

It is possible that Thompson actually believed this to be the case, although at an earlier time he had spoken of opium as "the saving of my life." [13] Of course, it was tuberculosis and not the drug that was killing him, but about that, too, he was always reluctant to speak. When, for example, a talkative fellow passenger on the train from Sussex had asked him, "Do you suffer with your chest, sir?" Thompson, who seldom spoke harshly to anyone, replied with a sharp, "No."

Perhaps as a result of his distasteful recollections of his medical studies in Manchester, Thompson had no liking for hospitals. Thus when Meynell realized how very serious his condition had become, it took some persuading to get him to consent to go to the hospital at all. Finally, however, having put himself entirely in his friend's hands, and upon learning that Madeline Meynell was a patient there, Thompson consented to the idea. Madeline had been the "Sylvia" of *Sister*

Songs, the child whose kiss had once brought back to him the remembrance of innocence,

> And spring, and all things that have gone from me,
> And that shall never be;
> All vanished hopes, and all most hopeless bliss. . . .
> (*Sister Songs,* I, ll, 303-306)

Once the decision was made, Thompson entered into the plans that were made for him without any further question. Apparently, the Meynells believed that the poet's self-diagnosis of "laudanum poisoning" was correct, for a few days after Thompson had gone to the hospital on November 1, Everard noted that he had "entered into the spirit of his cure admirably." Laudanum was actually keeping him alive, and for the twelve days before his death he showed pain only when his need for the prescribed light dosage made itself felt. When he was awake, he read from his worn prayer book or from William W. Jacobs' *Many Cargoes,* with its flavor of the world of the London docks. Sister Michael, the nun who nursed him, surrounded him with a gentle care, and Wilfrid Meynell often sat by the bed while Thompson held his hand in a long gesture of fraternal affection and the suggestion of farewell.

When he died in the dawn, there was no one with him, but he must not have had any sense of strangeness in that. He had chosen to live alone all his life. Moreover, it appears likely that the last person to whom he spoke was the priest who administered to him the final sacraments of the Church, which he had once hoped to administer to others. After that, there was nothing more to say. The failure of his priestly vocation was the key to his life, and he had written of himself:

> Ah God, a faithless sword, I broke
> In Thy right hand, for Thy great stroke
> Too weak; or rather, all a-rust

> In such a falchion was no trust,
> Which Thou, half-drawn, didst backward thrust
> Into the slothful sheath, where laid
> Roughed red with sin, the [recreant] blade
> Having Thy great intent betrayed. . . .

Yet, he had accepted what he believed to be the rightness of the divine will, and concluded with what might well have been his epitaph:

> Though Thou put by Thy recreant sword
> Yet Thou triumph'st, and Thou art Lord! [14]

Even as he lay dying, his reputation as a poet was strangely growing, although he had not published a volume of verse since the apparent failure of *New Poems*. When he was dead, a number of uninformed comments on his life and character appeared, and some critics, who were not willing to confine themselves to an evaluation of his poetry, appeared eager to indulge in the kind of judgment which belongs only to heaven. The stately *Times*, for example, remarked that conventional expressions of regret over his death would be a "mockery," because what the world ought to regret was "not the release of Mr. Thompson" but the fact that the cravings of his body had ruined "one of the most remarkable and original of the poetic geniuses of our time." Even Blunt, who had been asked by Wilfrid Meynell to write an obituary article for the *Academy*, gave the impression that Thompson had been intellectually dead during the last decade of his life. This opinion, based upon the brief period of time that Thompson had spent at Newbuildings just before his death, was given wide circulation. Others went even further and gave public credence to the rumors that Thompson had been morally decadent. Abroad, the *Mercure de France* proclaimed that his life had ended in the miseries of insanity.

Naturally, his friends rallied to his defense with the vehemence of righteous indignation. The *Athenaeum,* for example, published an article in which it was said that Thompson was a man whose life was marked by "the saint's intense, unfaltering preoccupation with eternal things." Wilfrid Meynell, writing in the *Nation,* defended Thompson's use of his creative gifts and stressed the fact that it was physical disease, not self-indulgence, which had killed him. The *Dublin Review,* in its turn, carried Mrs. Meynell's declaration that the dead poet had been an elect soul and "one of the most innocent of men."

That this controversy of moral judgment has unhappily been revived in recent times by J. C. Reid is regrettable, for it serves no really useful purpose. Father Terence Connolly, who undoubtedly has a greater knowledge of the primary sources for Thompson's life than any other scholar, is quite properly as disturbed by Reid's anachronistic suggestion that Thompson was a forerunner of the modern "beatniks," as he is by that author's attempt to link Thompson with the very decadent aestheticism which he so often condemned.[15] Yet, Reid rightly concludes that in spite of all evidence which he feels can be marshalled against Thompson as a man:

> This life was no disaster which was crowned with a good death, and with the achievement of the tranquil integration that saw Christ walking on the water of the Thames.[16]

One is inclined to wish that he had left it at that.

As to the place which Thompson holds in the history of English poetry, there can be no doubt that in the years before the First World War, it was somewhat exaggerated. When, in 1908, Meynell published a collection of Thompson's verse under the title of *Selected Poems,* the sales were astonishingly great. By 1910 they had gone to 18,000 volumes, and the editor wrote of his great surprise: "Having known the Poet during 20 years of obscurity, I cannot get accustomed to the new order of things."

Those who heaped praise upon Thompson's work after he was dead were, as Reginald J. Dingle points out in a recent issue of the *Dublin Review,* very frequently critics who did not share his religious faith.[17] Hardy, for example, wrote in 1913 that he found Thompson to be "packed as full of jewels as Keats." The three-volume edition called *The Works of Francis Thompson,* which included one volume of prose, appeared in that year, and Meynell was able to write to Blunt:

> A great thing as you say is the success of the books. Thompson can now be left to take care of himself. About 20,000 volumes of the Collected Works have been sold, & on Xmas day the Dean of Westminster proclaimed his name from the pulpit in Westminster Abbey—a mention which is nearly as good as a tablet on its walls, though that must somehow or other be brought about.[18]

If the Protestant Dean saw fit to quote Thompson with approval, the Catholic *Tablet,* in 1913, found him guilty of sensuality in his imagery and, with a clerical wagging of the finger, scolded the poet for having presumed to pose as a guide in spiritual matters.[19] Many Catholic critics, like Father Calvert Alexander or Agnes de la Gorce have been far too uncritical in their praise; but G. M. Turnell, writing in the *Catholic Herald* in 1936, after calling Shelley and Milton "certainly two of the most disasterous influences in the whole of English poetry," said that Thompson represented "the end of romanticism" and his "Hound of Heaven" belonged "not among English poetry but among devotional books." [20]

Danchin correctly points out that in recent years Thompson has been similarly described as one of the last examples of a school of poetry which is forever dead and buried. Reid, who speaks of Thompson's occasional power to write verse in which "precious experience is distilled in a bare simple style," concludes that the greater part of Thompson's poetry has "already faded." It belongs, he says, to a dead "trumpery tradition" of "multicoloured trains of images," "conglomerate vocabulary," and "cosmic vagueness."

He may, of course, be right, but the study of literary history would suggest that poetic techniques which one generation finds to be "trumpery" are not necessarily buried by the epithets of their critics. The cults begun by the Imagists may have already run their course, and we may come to another time when readers of poetry will find reason to agree with what Thompson said of the meaning of the word *simplicity* in his "Anima Simplicitas":

> Simplicity has been profoundly misunderstood, because it has been limitedly understood. . . . There is no true antithesis between simplicity and complexity. For simplicity is nothing else than the perfect coordination of parts, working effortlessly together towards a single unitive result. . . .
>
> These general remarks are no less apt to literary, and in particular poetical, simplicity. It is the single and unitive result of perfectly coordinated faculties, working effortlessly and without consciousness to their possessor. It is a seamless garment, woven of innumerable threads. When this simplicity works upon a plane of perception which is that of all men . . . all men recognize the result for simple, because all men can see round, can *comprehend* it. But when it works upon planes of perception which are given to few, the result is called complex, and universally denied to be simple; because the generality see the result in parts, but cannot see it whole. . . .
>
> A further procedure from the binding of simplicity to but one plane, is that most confound simplicity with the usage of what we are accustomed to call "direct lan-

guage." So that if a poet use words chiefly, images spar-
ingly, and those within the compass of easy understanding by the "intelligent reader," he is called simple; but if
imagery be a main note of his style, and his imagery what
we call "remote," he is thought to err against simplicity.
Now if he do so merely for beautiful adornment, the criticism is just; but if he do so for needs of expression,
unjust.[21]

This complex simplicity marks many poems of Thompson's
which are not on Reid's "approved list," a list which includes
"The Hound of Heaven," "The Mistress of Vision," "All Flesh,"
"Contemplation," "A Fallen Yew," and "In No Strange Land"
("The Kingdom of God"). It is found in the powerful unity of
"To the Dead Cardinal of Westminster," as well as in "Orient
Ode," "Laus Amara Doloris," "Any Saint," and some of the
shorter lyrics. It is, admittedly, not present in *Sister Songs*, or
"Love in Dian's Lap," and there can be no doubt that, with
the possible exception of "Daisy," the bulk of the poetry about
children is marred by an excess of both sentiment and deco-
ration.

Yet, as Dingle says, "The best poets have qualified for inclusion in an anthology of the worst verse, and Wordsworth's
place would be considerable." Thompson stands, like all the
Victorian poets, as one who continues, in his way, what had
been begun by Shelley, Coleridge, Keats, and Wordsworth.
Even more than Browning, for example, he owed a great deal
to Shelley, and like Rossetti, whose work he sometimes imi-
tated, he also went to school to Keats. Yet the poetry of the
Victorian age is as varied as the remarkable personalities that
formed it; and Thompson, in particular, was one who looked
back far beyond his immediate predecessors to Donne and
Crashaw, so that he became one of the first to revive the long-
dead accents of the metaphysical school. There is not one

among all the makers of the tradition upon which he drew who cannot be shown to have written some verse which at best can be said to have only historical interest.

Contrasted with the poetry of Oscar Wilde, Ernest Dowson, Lionel Johnson, Aubrey de Vere, Austin Dobson, and Edmund Gosse, all of whom had their admirers in his day, Thompson's work gains in stature. At least once he achieved poetic greatness, for "The Hound of Heaven" is a poem that is distinguished in its organic integrity and enduring in the universality of its appeal.

Sitting in John Todhunter's house in Bedford Square one night, Thompson found himself for most of the evening beside Dowson. It is reported that no one saw them speak to each other.[22] This is hardly surprising, for they lived in different dimensions, and Thompson had little or nothing in common with the precious young men of the "Rhymers Club." He was an authentic lyric poet, an explorer of the capacities of language to symbolize and re-create the qualities of personal experience. When he became pompous, it was because he departed from that role, but as Samuel Chew remarks, when he held to his true lyric line there was "nothing meritricious in his splendor." [23]

Thompson's informing vision, his theme, has its importance, but it is not by this alone that so much of his poetry still endures. Danchin, after a most exhaustive study of Thompson's technique and diction, sees him as one who helped to advance the modern effort to revivify poetry and give it newer harmonies. To achieve language that would throw a fresh and vivid light on the ancient and universal experiences of the human spirit, he did not hestiate to learn from the past—from Spenser, Milton, Crashaw, Keats, and Shelley. Yet he also learned the newer critical wisdom of Patmore, and he drew upon the language of the science of his day as freely as he

turned to what had become archaic. Often bold in his explorations, it is not strange that he could get lost in a wilderness
of words. He dwelt too much in the world of his own imagination and was too insensitive to the concrete objects around
him ever to have the precise powers of Hopkins. As Garvin
said of him, he would have been a poet even in the darkness
of a dungeon. Yet, however tentatively, he looked forward to
the best efforts of the twentieth century to wring from language a new and startling power and to strike the essence
which distinguishes poetry from all other discourse.

When the inflated estimates of writers like Mégroz have
been deflated by the perspective of that same balanced appraisal which Thompson himself displayed in his criticism, the
judgment of George Meredith stands. Whatever else Thompson may have been—competent critic, intuitive dreamer, and
great lover of God—he was, without question, "A true poet,
one of the small band."

CHAPTER NINE

VEIN OF LAUGHTER

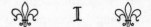

Perhaps the last verse that Thompson ever wrote took the form of a prayer, which, under the title of "Motto and Invocation," follows the Preface of Wilfrid Meynell's 1913 edition of Thompson's prose. This technically unimportant little piece was written during the time of the poet's last illness when he was still at Newbuildings. It is a private litany of his favorite saints and begins, as one might expect, with an appeal to St. John the Evangelist, in whom Thompson always saw the most authoritative source for his own Neo-Platonic Christianity. The "motto" of the poem—*Omnia Per Ipsum, Et Sine Ipso Nihil*—is an abbreviated version of St. John's "All things were made by him: and without him was made nothing that was made" (St. John 1:3). And Thompson begs the Apostle's pardon for the abbreviation.

The list of saints he invokes to aid him in his writing is very brief. There is his favorite Dominican, St. Catherine of Siena. She is followed by St. Augustine, who is called "Lofty Doctor" and "Glorious penitent." Then, in turn, come St. Francis of Assisi, St. Anthony of Padua, and St. Francis of Sales. The Blessed Virgin Mary is "last and first" in her "white Immaculacy."

Following upon this august company, another is added, as if his name had come as an important afterthought:

> *To which I add: Thomas More,*
> Teach (thereof my need is sore)
> What thou showedst well on earth—
> Good writ, good wit, make goodly mirth.

More, of course, was not canonized by the Catholic Church until long after Thompson's death, but the poet shared the hope of many English Catholics that he would be. It was not only the piety and the love of classical humanities in More that appealed to Thompson but, perhaps above all else, it was the extraordinary combination of sanctity and merriment, of intense devotion and urbane, sophisticated wit, that most drew him to the author of the *Utopia*. In "To the English Martyrs" he called More a "happy Fool of Christ," and gave him the title of "Jester in the Courts of God,"

> In whose spirit, enchanting yet,
> Wisdom and love, together met,
> Laughed on each other for content!
> That an inward merriment,
> An inviolate soul of pleasure,
> To your motions taught a measure
> All your days; which tyrant king,
> Nor bonds, nor any bitter thing
> Could embitter or perturb. . . .
>
> (ll. 104-112)

Thompson never possessed More's abundant capacity for friendship; when the poet was buried in St. Mary's Cemetery, Kensal Green, there were no more than a dozen people in the funeral party, most of whom knew him only slightly. But contrary to the impression gained by most readers of his poetry, Thompson had much of More's "inward merriment," and for many of the same reasons. The picture of him as living constantly in a state of melancholy self-pity is no less a myth than that of his having lived a life of immoral abandonment to a number of secret vices. It is astonishingly exaggerated to say—as did Wilfrid Whitten, the assistant editor of the *Academy* under Hind—that Thompson's presence was marked by a note of cheerfulness, which was evidence of "an overplus of sunny mentality and attention from a heart at leisure from itself." [1] Yet, Everard Meynell said that in writing Thompson's biography he had "a shamefaced feeling of dishonesty" about the "superficial look of disaster and pain" which that record conveyed.[2] As a corrective, he proposed his mother's statement in the *Dublin Review* of January, 1908. Alice Meynell's perceptions were both sensible and sharp, and her knowledge of Thompson was the product of her own intuitive experience of him in many moods and situations. Consequently, her judgment in this matter bears repetition:

> I affirm of Francis Thompson that he had natural good spirits, and was more mirthful than many a man of cheerful, of social or even of humorous reputation.[3]

She was obviously overly anxious to dispose of the idea that Thompson was to be numbered among the "unhappy poets," for the evidence is against her assertion that the "darkness and oppression of spirit the poet underwent was over and past some fifteen years before he died." Yet, a most important aspect of his personality is recorded in her remembrance of his laughter:

> It is pleasant to remember Francis Thompson's laugh, a laugh readier than a girl's, and it is impossible to remember him, with any real recall, and not to hear it again. Nothing irritable or peevish within him was discovered when children had their laughter at him.

Viola Meynell, who was one of the children who "had their laughter at him," says that he could not perceive absurdity, although he often provided it for her family by the curious incongruity of his own behavior. In his talk of his illness or his endless and incredible explanations of his lateness, he could be utterly humorless. In conversation he often displayed an absence of any quick wit, for so much of his talk was simply a nervous defense for his failure to communicate in speech. He would try to tell a joke, but his jokes were pedestrian, as his habit of making intolerable puns was almost pathetic.

Even in his attempts at light verse, he was frequently either childish or inept, as may be seen from some of the selections in *The Man Has Wings*.[4] Whole sections of his notebooks are devoted to doggerel verses, some of which run to thirty or more stanzas. One of the less poor examples, chosen by Father Connolly for publication, is called "The Voice of the Turtle Is Heard in Our Land." It concerns Charles Waterton's account of a ride on the back of a cayman in *Wanderings in South America* and Louis de Rougemont's story of riding on a sea turtle in *Adventures, as Told by Himself*:

> It was the gallant Waterton,
>   'Way down 'bout the Equator,
> That witched the world with horsemanship
>   Upon an alligator.

> 'Twas more the brave de Rougemont
>   (Unless our ears he dupe)
> That proved the turtle makes a steed,
>   As well as makes a soup.

The next to the last stanza concludes with a typically Thompsonian pun, put into the mouth of a turtle:

> "And though a turtle be no fish,
>   'Tis proved and cannot fail
> That here you have a turtle with
>   A very fishy tale."

It is in some of the prose manuscripts and certain of the reviews that one finds authentic examples of Thompson's share in that Comic Spirit which is so well described by Meredith in his *The Idea of Comedy and the Uses of the Comic Spirit*. This is the spirit of thoughtful laughter that pokes fun at the pretentious, the hypocritical, and the purely pedantic. It seeks out men's idolatries and their offenses against justice and common sense and subjects these things to laughter, along with false humility and the overvaluation of human attainments.

In the reviews Thompson's possession of this gift is a present quality, which most certainly serves to modify the legend of his loss of all joy in life. In his criticism of books and men, moreover, his ability to laugh intelligently was an important source of the balanced, proportioned appraisal which he normally gave to his subjects. In addition, it helped to preserve much of his criticism from pompous solemnity, for he did have the capacity to laugh at himself, in spite of Viola Meynell's suggestion that the contrary was the case. In the draft of a letter from Pantasaph, written shortly after his arrival there, he could, for example, say,

> Now, you'll think I'm in a state of light-hearted exhilarance, [sic] which is very improper in me, considering all I have to repent of. Therefore I beg to assure you that I am suffering like Old Nick. But when one is in this condition, one must laugh out or weep out! Too much of water hast thou, poor——; [5] therefore I'll grin through the very biggest horse-collar I can find. Don't think, though, that I repent having come here; if I were in London I should simply take a header into the Thames—only that it's such a damnably dirty place for a poet to drown in.[6]

As in certain other meditative, withdrawn personalities—like that of Emily Dickinson—Thompson's capacity for finding amusement in his own life and that of the world around him was the result of his unconventional scale of values. He smiled because he had turned the standards of commerce and mortal ambition upside down. He felt, as all who knew him testified, no bitterness toward the world. He had no sour *contemptus mundi*. He simply measured with what seemed to him to be a larger standard than that which the world generally employs.

This is clearly revealed in a passage in his *Large Commonplace Book,* which is among the most significant items in his private papers:

> I view all mundane happenings with the Fall for one *terminus* and the millennium for the other. If I want to grasp (gauge) the significance of a contemporary event of any mark, I dump it down, as near as I can, in its proximate place between those boundaries, where it takes up very little room, and (naturally) presents to me other relations and aspects than to one who views it from the thick of the present.[7]

Viewed beneath the face of eternity, the world seemed filled with ample matter for satire, and Thompson planned what he called his "ant satire," in which the leaders of a colony of ants were to be pictured as boasting of the huge fabric of their anthills. Like human beings in their pretensions to greatness, the ants would be awed by their pyramids, which would appear to them as towering and immense.[8]

Writing before Hardy's *Satires of Circumstance* (1911-1914), Thompson felt that no contemporary was maintaining the great tradition of English satire, and, in a review published on October 28, 1899, he lamented the severity of the British libel laws, which, he felt, had helped to kill personal satire.[9] These laws, he said, were administered by men who were indifferent to the question of literary justification, men who would "cast Byron in heavy damages and comment severely on the scurrility of Pope." Looking backward, he noted the "forest of flourishing trees" that would have been destroyed if the law had had its "awful libel thunderbolts" in earlier times.

In the same review there is ample proof of Thompson's critical appreciation of satirical wit. Samuel Butler, the author of *Hudibras,* he called the most "singular and unpatterned of satirists," and commented with great delight on Butler's capacity for the juxtaposition of unexpected ideas, which made his imagery always so "comically apposite." Congreve, too, he relished as a master of comic, fanciful analogies.

Dryden, whose serious influence may be detected in Thompson's "To My Godchild," [10] struck him as a satirical poet whose technique was so perfect that he could have made "a decent poem out of *Bradshaw's Guide.*" In Swift he found a writer who was less to his own taste, but he fully appreciated the grim power of that "terrible master of irony," and was much amused to find *Gulliver's Travels*—the work of a man who "had every gift of satire save mirth"—treated by so many as if it were a fairy tale for children.

For Thompson, Byron, whom he called "a magnificent satirist," appeared to be the last of the great line that had begun with Chaucer and the author of *Piers Plowman*. His own preference, however, was for "the delightful archness of Addison's finished raillery," and he saw in George Moore's "glittering arrow flights" of clever banter the kind of light satire which he hoped might eventually set a standard for his own age, in which the formal, rhetorical satire of Dryden's time, with its odes and extended pieces of didactic ridicule, was no longer possible. Calling for a "first-rate light satirist" to make his appearance, Thompson appears to have been all but oblivious to the work of Edward Lear, Lewis Carroll, or W. S. Gilbert, whom he once referred to simply as the creator of "topsy-turvydom." [11]

That Thompson himself tried his hand at the criticism of certain features of contemporary life and literature by the writing of light prose satire is evident in his notebooks and manuscripts. That he had more talent in this direction than in that of humorous verse is happily illustrated by a number of possible instances. There is, for example, his ironical treatment of the typically fashionable preacher addressing his upper-middle-class congregation on the imaginary text, "Be good and you will be respectable":

> It is not very difficult to keep from serious lies, if you are a healthy Anglo-Saxon. With a decent income, it requires only a firm self-command to abstain from pocket-picking, shop-lifting, or even coveting your neighbour's umbrella. A married person, with a little practice, can really keep from adultery in a way quite surprising to the frequenter of "problem-plays." . . . With assiduous cultivation you can, I affirm, arrive at praying to your Maker as much as twice a day without serious inconvenience; and an hour or two at church on Sunday, by means of a prudent selection of attire and preachers, can be made to pass not unpleasantly. Whence we must needs conclude that for a well-disposed person, and on about eight hundred or a thousand a year, the Kingdom of Heaven is an amazing bargain.[12]

Widening his range of satirical attack, in the manuscript he called "Modern Men: the Devil," he suggested that whatever is fashionable must be thought of as modern, so that it would be quite appropriate to speak of the subject of the sketch as "modern" since "the Devil keeps the vogue in a surprising manner." His progress in appearance from medieval portraits of him as "horned and tailed" to "the fine figure he cuts in Milton" could in fact be taken as a confirmation of the con-

temporary Darwinian theory of the evolution and perfectibility
of species.

In a biting comment on Victorian economic and political
life, Thompson remarked that the Devil's trade changes less
than his methods:

> He is still, like his ancient adversary St. Peter, a fisher
> of men. He deals in souls like a politician, and gets them
> nowadays for almost as little. Though no Royal Commis-
> sion has taken note on it, he is the primal employer of
> cheap labour; and has best advantage of these times,
> since he needs not to fear the Unions among his workers;
> for other *employés* unite to damn their master, but his to
> damn themselves. It is veritable that the output of sin has
> begun to exceed his demands; for the Devil's market is
> more glutted than any other, and there is grave fall in the
> rate of souls. So that . . . it were much o' these days if
> Faustus should sell his salvation for an Under-secretary-
> ship, or a mining swindle, or a laureateship in the *cortège*
> of Philistia, or a court-paintership to the Nonconformist
> Conscience.[13]

With a thrust at the natural realism of Zola, Thompson
noted that the Devil's technique had changed since the days
of Job. In Job's time he tempted men with the offer of taking
them off their dunghills, whereas in the world of the natural
realists the temptation was reversed. In fact, said Thompson
(in a passage that Swift would have approved), if the Devil
were to follow his ancient practice of leaving men to take up
his dwelling in swine, he would find that in the modern world
"it would be no change of lodging."

Admitting that there were some who might class the Devil
among those things—like the reality of Homer, the existence
of Shakespeare, and the virtue of the British nation—in which
so many no longer believed, Thompson insisted that if neither

the Devil nor the place of his habitation existed, it would have
been necessary to invent them:

> For we would ask any man if he does not feel doubly
> sure of Heaven when he has damned all his neighbours?
> And it is prettily demonstrable that if there be no hell for
> some men's persons, it would be necessary to have one
> for their works. . . .
>
> If the true diabolic note be the worship of ill for the
> sake of ill, then our aesthetics testify the Evil Principle.
> The old musicians perceived the *diabolus in musicâ,* and
> I cannot see how the present age should with any con-
> science deny him in art and letters. We have a devil of an
> Academy, a devil of a public, a devil of a stage, and are
> not unlike shortly to have a devil of a laureate. For the
> age, it should seem, is going about to restore the golden
> days when the laureate, like a geometrical point, had
> position without parts or magnitude.[14]

There might, he suggested, even be some reason to think
that "to the *diabolus in musicâ* and *in litteris*" there might
also "be added the *diabolus in ecclesia,* where, like many great
men, he has a freak of poking satire at himself." Not always
absent from the world of "fashionable congregations," the
Devil could be said to have come to the point where, through
"long familiarity," he was not any more frightened by crosses
than he was by horseshoes.

Thompson concluded, however, that while the Devil might
be the source of many ills in the churches, the social order,
and the arts, "he has some saving conscience—he is not responsible for the British Matron."

A British Matron, who is given the name of Mrs. Hiller,
plays an important role in the unsuccessful experiment which
Thompson attempted in his dramatic sketch *Man Proposes,
But Woman Disposes.* This piece, which he said was designedly
"as artificial as eighteenth century comedy," like another called

Venus' Fly Trap, attempts to deal satirically with those conventions of courtship which require women to appear to be the pursued, although they are actually the pursuers. Sometimes, as in the following passage from *Man Proposes,* the dialogue is amusing enough, but on the whole both of these abortive attempts show that Thompson had as little gift for dramatic comedy as the Napoleon play shows that he had for tragedy:

MRS. HILLER.   ... (*Aloud*) You owe me reparation, dear. Make it. Marry Willy Mortimer.

MISS. BLACK.   Again!

MRS. HILLER.   You refuse—let's see why. Firstly because he's hypothetically, a fool. That doesn't matter, my love. Fools make imperfect lovers, I admit; but excellent husbands.

MISS BLACK.   Stop this. I'm engaged.

MRS. HILLER.   That doesn't matter either, dear. An engagement is a chain and collar, which holds your lover, according to law, but only holds you until you let go the chain.

MISS BLACK.   Annette, I don't love him, and I love Jack.

MRS. HILLER.   That doesn't matter either, sweetest. I didn't ask you to love him, I asked you to marry him. To desire love with marriage, is like expecting butter on your wedding cake, my dear. Heaven works by compensations, and a woman shouldn't neglect the example of Heaven. To love one man and marry another—that's an equitable division of happiness, I take it.

MISS BLACK.   Your ideas of love, and mine, are a little different, Annette. Plato——

MRS. HILLER.   What is to be done with a girl that talks about Plato!

MISS BLACK.   Oh, any girl may talk about Plato, provided she hasn't read him. Nay, in these Girton days girls may, if they choose, read the Ancient Fathers, like Mrs. Browning.

MRS. UILLER.   My sweetest, women who love the Ancient Fathers are seldom loved by the youthful sons.[15]

Far more effective, and one of the best examples of Thompson's light satire, is the narrative essay called "The Trecentisti up to Date." This was directed against the psuedo-realism of the vogue of Jean Beraud (1849-1936), who, in the 1890's, did some representational paintings on New Testament subjects in which the Biblical characters, with the exception of Christ, wore modern dress in a contemporary setting. Thompson describes a visit to a London studio where an artist, who is probably imaginary, practices what he calls "The New Preraphaelitism." The artists of this school despise "outworn conventions" and "cheap sentiment." They seek to paint sacred history from the life of their own times as "naturalistically" as possible.

The results are evident. St. Peter is seen walking on the water. He is dressed in sea boots and sou'wester; his figure seems to give off the very odor of "grog and salt-water," and he gives the impression of moving with a nautical roll. His fishing boat bears the fine old English name, *Polly Ann,* plainly visible and clearly painted on its counter.

Standing before this canvas, Thompson meets a young man, who speaks in a voice "more lilied and languid than his appearance; a voice, indeed, which I can only describe as lotused." This youth, who is named Bertie, is utterly devoted to The New Pre-Raphaelitism and, together with his sister, moves devotedly from canvas to canvas.

Before one of the paintings, the Master of naturalism explains that it is called *Sermon on the Mount:*

> It showed the Disciples such as men tramping the country during an English summer would unquestionably appear. Their boots were realistically muddy and dilapidated, their trousers had realistic rents and stains, their faces were studied from Revival Meetings, and the holy women were Hallelujah Lasses *minus* the uniform. One Disciple, richer than the rest in zeal or money, held over the Saviour's head an umbrella. Here, for the first time, the Master's *confrère* broke silence. "I say," he said, "you've conceded too much there, you know, to the prejudices of the many. One of those girls is very passably pretty." [16]

The Master admits that this may be a weakness, for The New Pre-Raphaelites believe in the avoidance of beauty and the pursuit of the Realistic Mean. In the light of this "golden principle" he has painted *The Marriage-Feast of Cana,* in which the guests are seen to have "well drunk": Their formal evening clothes are in disarray; some have rumpled shirt fronts and a "winning disorder in their neck-ties." Beauty, which is nothing but an outworn convention of Greek art, is obviously absent.

Thompson's imaginary friend and guide during the course of this afternoon among the New Preraphaelites is described as being "burdened by the consciousness that he is an art-critic." This title, Thompson suggests, may best be understood in this fashion:

> An artist . . . is usually a man who understands nothing but art. A critic . . . is usually a man who understands nothing but criticism. And an art-critic . . . is a man who understands neither art nor criticism.[17]

Yet, the critic rightly concludes that "New Realism," as represented by the collection in the studio, "is uncommonly like Old Rowdyism"—a point which seems to be well established, as the afternoon ends when the Master informs the group that his chief recreation, when he is not painting, consists in visiting such "theatres" as the Gaiety and the Alhambra, where he can refresh "an artistic eye jaded by the realism" of his profession.

Such extended and developed pieces of satire as "The Trecentisti" were, of course, rare items among Thompson's collection of soiled manuscripts and accumulated notebooks. Generally his running satirical commentary is found in the most scattered bits and pieces. Here and there he talks of foreign relations, and suggests, for example, that the only "peace" which seems to interest imperial Russia is "a very large piece of China." [18] In one place, he gives the impression that he may, after all, have visited an actual theatre at some time in his adult life, for he describes melodramatic contemporary actors as having faces like "boiling porridge," where the "ready-prepared emotion" could be seen to heave its way to the surface, after which the "ponderous agglutination" would flop back into immobility." [19]

He had a liking for the imaginary monologue with a lightly ironical touch, which he used to portray the thinking of a hypothetical representative of the school of "pure poetry," in which all "ideas"—and especially those of religion—have been carefully avoided:

> Our poetry has been altogether disengaged from the narrow notions of virtue and piety, because it has been found, by experience of our professors, that the smallest quantity of religion, like a single drop of malt liquor in claret, will muddy and discompose the brightest poetical genius.[20]

Elsewhere, he imagined the reactions of an "illiterate literalist" who has been told that the figure of a dove is used to "represent" or "mean" the Holy Ghost:

> Means? You *said* it wur a dove. A dove mëans a dove, sure-ly. If it be a dove, it baänt noä 'Oly Ghoäst. And if it be a 'Oly Ghoäst, it baänt noä dove,——nor noä sparrer neither. You doänt fool me. I thowt there wur some noänsense. I'll be danged if I didn't! I thowt it wur a sparrer all along! [21]

Thompson never proved himself capable of sustaining a tone of light irony over an extended period in his published prose, nor did his satirical character sketches ever become much more than fragments. Yet it can be said that much of the incisive freshness of style that one sometimes encounters in his critical writing is the direct result of the vein of thoughtful laughter that was in him.

It was this quality which enabled him to comment that the very form of poor verse brings out the absence of real poetry in the same way that youthful costumes inappropriately worn by aging matrons serve to emphasize nothing so much as the absence of youth.[22] Called upon to review Clarence Ford's life of Madame Julie de Krudener, whose frank revelations of her inner life and varied loves rivaled those of the *Journal de Marie Bashkirtseff* (1887), Thompson illuminated his criticism with apt satirical wit. Ford had described the colorful lady as a "complex" personality; Thompson suggested that a better descriptive term would have been "disorganized." One does not, he remarked, describe a vessel as "complex" because it happens to be "cracked in all directions." Madame de Krudener's vanity, which Thompson found to be one of the few consistent things about her, was, he said, like that of the Welsh magnate who directed that a tablet should be erected in his memory in his local church "to inform the world how he hated pride." [23]

As he punctured the pretentiousness of Madame de Krudener, so he could dispose of the exuberant critic who had described one of the less impressive works of Sir Richard Burton, the Arabic scholar and explorer, as a worthy companion piece to the great story of Job:

> It is, perhaps, well for the reputation of the much-tried Patriarch that he was spared foreknowledge of this final trial. Had he heard the comparison, and heard the conventionally descriptive lines with which the poem opens, no one could blame him if he had flung his potsherd at the critic.[24]

Seldom departing from light, good-natured raillery, the wit in Thompson's criticism was neither harsh nor bitter. It conformed to the spirit of honest evaluation. He was not at all interested in making a play to the gallery by writing derisively or by becoming the critical champion of a wholly partisan viewpoint. Just as his habit of viewing the world from the totality of the Christian conception of the movement of history caused him to be mildly amused by much that others took quite seriously, so it also served to moderate his specific literary judgments. In the long reaches of history, over which he trusted that a divine will presided, he saw no reason for controversial critical frenzies.

By and large, he kept his balance, but he was capable of what he regarded as righteous indignation, as may be seen in the social criticism of "In Darkest England." He was also capable of overstatement, especially when he spoke of the work of those whom he loved—Alice Meynell and Coventry Patmore. Yet he was evidently aware of this problem as he gained critical experience, for he said in a review of Mrs. Meynell's *Later Poems:*

> The present writer finds a difficulty in approaching his task from a critical standpoint. These poems have moved and stirred him more deeply than any others read for the first time in recent years, with the possible exception of "A Shropshire Lad." That is, of course, a matter in part of subjective psychology, and not only of objective art. ... But, even allowing for the personal equation, it is hard to discover a critical test which Mrs. Meynell's work will not endure.[25]

It can be argued that Thompson's treatment of Baudelaire and Verlaine displays a humorless moral didacticism, and he was often absurdly chauvinistic in his talk of "bad French books." Furthermore, it must be admitted that the rhapsodic treatment of his favorite English authors, especially in the early essays which deal with the work of Shelley or Coleridge, might well have been modified by the saving salt of a wit which is conspicuously absent.

The fact seems to be that in prose, as in poetry, he learned much from Patmore, whose own essays are marked by examples of pungent expression. Certainly, Patmore encouraged him to develop his prose style and there can be no doubt of the fact that Thompson fully appreciated the effectiveness of the often brilliant, and sometimes biting, wit which spiced much of what Patmore had to say on a wide variety of topics.

When Thompson really matured as a critic in the years following Patmore's death, he obviously profited more by what his dead friend had taught him by example than by precept. With experience as a reviewer, he grew in his command of literary common sense and in his capacity to bring to bear upon his work the gifts of laughter. Fully developed, he was less pontifical than Patmore and much less given to allowing partisanship for his own views to color his judgments.

By 1899 he was well able to bring to bear both his powers of reason and humor on so sensitive a question as the religion of Shakespeare. In the *Academy* for June 17 of that year, he reviewed a book in which Father Henry S. Bowden, a priest of the Oratory, argued that Shakespeare was a Catholic.[26] This work, by its author's own admission, was based upon studies by Richard Simpson, but, as Thompson said, in it one could not easily distinguish "the voice of Jacob and the hands of Esau." Admitting that in a very general way one can find reasons enough for describing Shakespeare as the product of a culture that was still powerfully affected by a thousand years of Catholicism, Thompson described the book as "a monu-ment of undaunted special pleading." He sustained his argu-ment with careful logic and freshened it with wit:

> Shakespeare commentators with a pocket-theory—there should be a licence to carry pocket-theories or pocket revolvers, both weapons of uncertain and danger-ous use—are adepts in bringing surprising meanings out of a Shakespearean text, as you conjure remarkable odd-ities out of an empty hat. But this Bowden-Simpson union of forces easily surpasses them: leaves them and the reader gasping.

One of Father Bowden's—or Simpson's—strongest "argu-ments" was the absence of attack on Catholicism in Shake-speare's plays, even in *King John*. To this, Thompson replied by calling attention to the way in which Shakespeare "elimi-nated mere racial scurrility" in his treatment of Shylock, and he went on to conclude:

> Nowhere does Shakespeare cast wanton insult on the Jews. Extend Father Bowden's argument and a new solu-

tion comes in sight. Was Shakespeare a secret proselyte
of Judaism? We confidently await a book to prove it.
Surely some faddist is equal to the task!

The behavior of faddists never ceased to amuse Thompson,
and he lived in an age which provided abundant examples—
from Theosophy to the followers of Oscar Wilde. He would
have derived particular amusement from the knowledge that
for a time after his death he was himself to become the center
of a short-lived and somewhat sentimental fad. To live in a
world in which supposedly serious scholars could spend their
time arguing about whether Shakespeare was a Catholic, a
Puritan, a lawyer, or nothing but a pseudonym for Queen
Elizabeth was to add to the sense of incongruity in life, which
leads either to thoughtful laughter or to pity and terror.

If it is true that the world seems comic to the man who
thinks and tragic to the man who feels, Thompson may be
said to illustrate the point. In his poetry, where the expression
of feeling is the center of emphasis, a sense of tragic incongruity between what is and what ought to be is prevalent, and
the protagonist—who is Thompson himself—is intended to
be taken with the utmost seriousness and sympathy. Much
the same state of affairs is present in such a critical essay as
his "Shelley." There the author solemnly identifies himself with
his subject and feels intensely the tragic incongruity of Shelley's
role in a world where idealism seldom is seen to prevail:

> Less tragic in its merely temporal aspect than the life
> of Keats or Coleridge, the life of Shelley in its moral as-
> pect is, perhaps, more tragical than either; his dying
> seems a myth, a figure of his living; the material ship-
> wreck a figure of the immaterial.[27]

It is quite otherwise in many of the later essays and reviews.
There is no lyric feeling, as in the early "Shelley"; its place

has been taken by a critical objectivity that allows the comic view to come to the front from time to time and take its bow. Thompson did not feel for Chateaubriand what he had felt—and never ceased to feel—for Shelley. He could, therefore, treat Chateaubriand in the comic vein, in a passage which one feels might have applied equally well to Shelley:

> This brilliant young Frenchman was very unhappy and very discontented, for a great variety of reasons. He was tired of everything; his fellow-men were not geniuses like himself, and he was elaborately conscious of the fact. ... Especially he was deeply, tenderly sorry for himself. But instead of reflecting that there must be something profoundly wrong with his heart, and trying what might be done to remedy it, he hit upon a beautiful new idea. Since he was so hopelessly above his fellow-men, it must be his duty to become a missionary, and by the exhibition of himself lift other men to the same heights of superior misery.[28]

Similarly, in discussing the *Gioconda* of Gabriele D'Annunzio in 1901, Thompson quite consciously adopted the "quality of being plain" and found amusement in "affectations, poses, and exotics." Yet, he was far from having a fundamental sympathy with conformity and can hardly be said to have been governed by what he called the "precious instinct of common sense and social decency which always prevents the man of right reason from appearing too conspicuously different from his fellows." [29]

More often than not, reason and common sense played an inferior role in Thompson's estimate of his own experience. He found little difficulty in taking the tragic view of his life and could give the smallest episodes affecting him a dramatic importance. There were times when even an umbrella's falling against him in a train could make him say, in all seriousness,

"I am the target of all disasters." Nonetheless, beyond self-pity and the many moments when his sense of the eternal proportions of things became lost in the details of facing daily existence, Thompson's sense of the tragic quality of his life was more than justified. He was incongruously caught between a "veil of tutelar flesh to simple livers given" and the "brave-fledgling fervours of the Saint." [30] The tragedy of this situation he apprehended with a perception that was essentially neither melodramatic nor Romantic. He did not love himself, in the Romantic fashion, even to the point of contempt for God. He loved God, in the very core of his being, and knew the full meaning of contempt for himself.

The true comic spirit in Thompson was given its perspective and its foundation by his love of God, for it was in that love's light that his mind could take the measure of the world's—and his own—incongruous pretensions. It is, therefore, not only fitting but also most significant that beside the dynamic, and sometimes darkly tragic, religious passion of Augustine and Catherine of Siena he should have placed the wise laughter of the Christian humanism of Thomas More.

CHAPTER TEN

THE LAUREL TREE

In "To a Poet Breaking Silence," Thompson wrote:

> Ah! let the sweet birds of the Lord
> With earth's waters make accord;
> Teach how the crucifix may be
> Carven from the laurel tree. . . .
>
> (ll. 19-22)

As we have seen, a concern and a conflict over the relation between religion and poetry form an essential part of the course of his life and thought. Crucifix and laurel tree were symbols of the two forces, sometimes opposed but fundamentally reconciled, which most affected him as a man and as an artist.

That Thompson had a sense of religious mission cannot be anything but obvious, for he believed that it was a poet's duty to see and to restore the divine idea of things to a fallen world. Certain of his poems—most notably "The Hound of Heaven"—have been almost constantly employed by preachers, both Protestant and Catholic. He has been described as "the epic poet of modern Catholicity," and as one who was devoted to the single purpose of making known the union of all things in Christ by the application of liturgical imagery to the natural universe.[1] From the popular level of Hutton's

Guidance from Francis Thompson in Matters of Faith, through the rhapsodies of Mégroz, to the scholarly research of men like Father Connolly and Pierre Danchin, Thompson's religious message has been thoroughly explored.

This is, no doubt, as it should be. Thompson once said of himself, "My aims are as truly part of the age, as the child in the womb is portion of its mother." [2] It was an age that was intensely concerned with messages, a time when old beliefs were being subjected to searching analysis and many stood in need of assurance.

There is, however, a certain danger in becoming absorbed in Thompson's religious message. It leads to the false impression that he believed poetry's chief importance lay in the service it could give to the spread of Catholic doctrine. A study of his critical work proves that if he was aware of what poetry can do for religion, he was even more conscious of those qualities which make poetry important in itself.

Thompson was driven to write poetry, not because it seemed to be a means for preaching the gospel, but because of an inner personal necessity. The artistic process, as T. S. Eliot has said, has an intensity, a pressure, of its own—by which the fusion of the component parts of its end product must be achieved. [3] That pressure is not easily borne; yet without its demanding intensity there can be no significant re-creation of human experience in verse.

Thompson knew the pressure of the "implacable sweet daemon," and he acted under the need which it created in him. Nothing else could ever satisfy that need, for poetry has its own essential quality, its distinctive being and specific powers. Thompson was drawn to the metaphysical poets of the seventeenth century precisely because they had tried to "quintessentialise poetry." [4] He saw them as having initiated a basic, fruitful experiment that pointed out the direction which English poetry must eventually take. In Crashaw, for example, he felt that there was an exploration of the possibilities of imagery, which, early in his own career, he had regarded as the distinct quality of poetic statement. More than that, however, he recognized in the metaphysicals, particularly in Donne and Herbert, evidence for his own belief that:

> The existence of a delicately organized human being is diversified by divisions and revulsions of sensation, ill-defined desires, gleams of intuition, and the whole gamut of spiritual notes descending from exultation to despair, none of which has ever been adequately translated except in the hieratic language of poetry.[5]

Marked by its own essential quality and function, poetry, as Thompson came to think of it, had its sovereign rights and its own great dignity. Its "hieratic language" was not to be thought of as performing, in a less precise fashion, the work of philosophy or theology. On the contrary, it must be understood that philosophers and theologians employ a medium which is not only different in kind from that of poets but also different in its aims and objectives. Specializing their language, defining their terms, philosophers and theologians must always employ the single word to denote the single thing. They are men who, like the natural scientists, must speak analytically.

The poet, on the other hand, must, in Thompson's view, speak synthetically, using "one sign to focus many collateral things." Unlike Arnold, therefore, Thompson did not stress the role of poetry as a special means of stating ideas. The poet might illustrate the beauty, or even the truth, of philosophical thought, but it was not his business "to lecture on dry bones." [6]

Thompson understood that, like any other artist, the poet is not concerned with the act of formulating supposedly precise concepts. His concern is with the making of an object of art according to the inner necessity and particular good of that object. This concrete thing, the poem, must be seen as in itself no less an expression of reality than are the formulations of science. Thompson would, in fact, have agreed with Allen Tate that the poem displays the true content of the world's phenomena, for it re-creates "the totality of experience in its quality." [7]

Whatever its subject matter, poetry must concentrate upon the task of combining the separate elements of thought or sensation into wholes. It must be true to its synthetic character and avoid the attempts of analysis. Thus Thompson believed that Browning had chosen an almost impossible task for a poet when he chose to analyze conflicts of motivation in the characters he created. It was the analytic mode of the dramatic monologues and the extended narrative pieces of Browning which Thompson blamed for what he called "the intrusion of innumerable extra-poetic matters" in Browning's poetry, with the result that one found there many things which "weary and are like grit between the teeth." Yet, Thompson, unlike Hopkins, was willing to call Browning a true poet:

> No man ever took a stranger road to be a poet than Robert Browning, and only he could have compassed the feat. So analytic a mode would throw by the heels any imitator—as it has done; and thus we have not to fear the immeasurable calamity of a Browning school.[8]

He obviously respected Browning's individuality and generally displayed a sense of the inevitable and necessary interplay of tradition and individual talent in poetry. That was one of the reasons why he reacted against any indication that the Victorian successors of the Romantics might be attempting to establish, through usage, some canon of poetic diction. He complained of the growing dominance of a select company of words, "the Praetorian cohorts of poetry," that were currently thought of as essential "by every aspirant to the poetical purple." As Tolles rightly observes, Thompson's own verse abounds in examples of the very thing he here condemned,[9] but such inconsistencies are not uncommon in poets turned critic.

Words had fascinated him from his earliest boyhood, and he held that the poet must be distinguished by his true taste for language and by the desire to penetrate to "the sensitive roots of words." [10] But he also knew that concentration upon the diction of poetry, like concentration upon the study of some supposedly special body of "poetic subject matter," does not advance one far in the understanding of poetry's essence.

As we have already observed, he recognized that a very important source of the special delight of poetry lies in its measured rhythms and significant fluctuations, and he was deeply indebted to Patmore in this regard. However, he did not believe that metre provides "the proper distinction between poetry and prose." With a just allowance of the claims of free verse, he wrote:

> And it is rhythm which really is the *necessary* medium of poetry, not metre. But rhythm varies gradually and imperceptibly through numberless gradations, from the highest to the lowest, till it disappears in the pedestrian progress of average prose. . . . Poetry and prose can, and sometimes do, play into each other. Prose, therefore, becomes a vast *spectrum,* fading into poetry at one end, into journalism at the other. . . . To which of these extremities a given style shall approximate depends wholly on the author's aim.[11]

The poet must, of course, have an intense interest in the refinement of the "exterior mechanism" of poetry. He must absorb the law of his art until he becomes identified with it so completely that he needs no external guides of metrical rule. Having learned to fly, he has no need to call attention to the movement of his wings:

> To fly, the bird must set in action an intricate multitude of nerves, and through the nerves an intricate action of muscles. At first it takes practice to coordinate all; and when it succeeds, how proud it is of itself! . . . Then the folly passes, and it busies itself with flight. If it once began thereafter to think how the fine impulse must be transmitted along each nerve . . . it would cease to fly. . . . When I see a poet of any standing shivering his tail like a peacock, and crying "Art, art!" I think of Nebuchadnezzar, and conclude that he will presently be driven out to eat grass.[12]

The basis of the poet's claim to greatness and the attention of mankind must not be thought of as arising from his command of an evident and distinctly "poetic" technique. For Thompson, it lay rather in what he called "intellectual insight, or intuition, combined with emotional sensibility." The union of these two in the poet he described as being so subtle that "the poet may be said in a manner to see *through* his sensitive nature." The poet's feelings awaken sympathy in other men because what is in him in a highly developed state is at least latent in them also. He is attuned to a higher range of reality than most men and his discernment of this higher order of experience stirs in him an emotion which, in its turn, may lead on to even deeper perceptions. The poet and the real order of things become "so interfused that they reciprocally illuminate each other." [13]

For Thompson, then, to read a fine poem was to be confronted with an existing object which was marked by its own organic integrity and capable of giving to the reader not only delight but insight through its ordering of some aspect of experience into an effective wholeness. For the poet who made it, such a poem might very well be a means to what Thompson called "the poet's ideal, which is sensitive and candid self-realization," [14] but it would also be more than that: It would be a center of intellectual and emotional significance to the reader as well.

The poet, as Thompson conceived it, never deals either in purely aesthetic or purely personal values. He is engaged in communicating a particular experience of life that, of necessity, in some sense reaches beyond himself. The poet is inextricably related to a society, which, however obliquely, he must evaluate and which, in its turn, evaluates not only the poet but poetry itself. Some poets may think that it is possible for them to say to the world, "We will not argue about it. The true value is there for those who have the eyes to see it." But such was not the case with Thompson.

To its utilitarian critics, Thompson said that the very universality of poetry was evidence that men had always felt the need for the experience which it affords them:

> There is no utilitarian but will class a soapmaker as a worthy and useful member of the community; yet is there no necessity why a man should use soap. Nay, if necessity be any criterion of usefulness (and surely that is useful which is necessary,) the universal practice of mankind will prove poetry to be more useful than soap; since there is no recorded age in which men did not use poetry, but for some odd thousand years the world got on very tolerably well without soap.[15]

But as we have seen, to those who were, unlike the utilitarians, primarily concerned with the salvation of souls, Thompson pointed out that this universal need of men for poetry was not only an evidence of its utility but also a proof of its importance as a support of man's very humanity against the brutal drag of his animal nature.

Thompson, in fact, could not conceive of any art that was beyond considerations of moral good and evil, any more than he could accept an aestheticism which was little more than a longing for "a hot-house seclusion of beauty in a world which Nature has tempered by bracing gusts of ugliness." Even though he believed that the creative process by which a poem comes to be is governed by its own laws and has the good of an object of art as its proximate end, he nonetheless could not think of the poet as other than a morally responsible worker, whose acts are subject to a higher law than that of his art alone. Like Symonds, with whom his ideas so often accord, Thompson saw the soul of the artist as inevitably involving him in moral considerations.[16] Citing Homer, Virgil, Dante, and Shakespeare, Symonds said that the chiefs of poetry owed their superiority to the "completeness of their representation" and to their grasp of the "harmony of human faculties in large morality." Similarly, in commenting on Ruskin's saying that an artist must observe the law of "essential morality" in his art, Thompson wrote that the poet must conform his work, "to the laws which underlie the unchanging government of the universe, laws of which there is a constant tradition among the great poets—Homer, Virgil, Dante, Shakespeare, Milton." [17]

Although Thompson believed that there was such a necessary connection between poetry and morality, he agreed with Patmore's saying that just as metre shows inflections of an underlying pattern, so the poet may show inflections—and even actual infractions—of the moral law.[18] He is not bound only to the display of virtue, but in his handling of virtue and vice he must at least be expected to exhibit some knowledge of an existing difference between them.

We have already observed that Thompson was far from feeling that the personal behavior of a poet provided an adequate principle for judging his poetry, either as to its artistic integrity or its power to elevate the human spirit. Yet, at the same time, he fully agreed with Ruskin that if there was excellence of technical execution, the informing influence of a "lofty ethical spirit" would give a poem a quality of "fineness" or "nobility" which it would otherwise lack. Consequently, he regarded the *Epithalamion* of Spenser as superior to the "exquisite *Epithalamium* of Catullus because he felt that Spenser's work was suffused by a "beautiful austerity of ethical spirit." [19]

It was particularly to the poetry of those who, like Spenser or Dante, had combined technical excellence with a lofty ethical spirit that Thompson wished to call the attention of his co-religionists. Among these poets were, of course, most of the great names of poetry, and—as in the case of Shelley—many who most clearly did not present themselves as teachers of specifically Catholic doctrines or moral ideals. Yet, he believed that in all such writers there were demonstrated the distinct qualities of poetry, its special powers, and its capacity not only to meet certain distinctive needs of the spirit but also to present the evidence of man's peculiar dignity and significance with great vividness and force.

Furthermore, Thompson recognized that in poetry there is not merely a special medium for stating various aspects of experience, there is also a way of confronting the world. And it was his belief that most poets were more likely to confront the world with an outlook that was far closer to a religious interpretation of reality than they were to see it in the pattern of an exclusive, scientific materialism.

The reasons he advanced for this belief were, of course, to be found in his acceptance of Coleridge's theory of poetic intuition as a subtler and higher form of reason than that of scientific analysis, as well as in his conviction that poetic imagery displays the correspondence between the multiple parts of Nature, conceived as an analogy of one divine idea. As he put it in a review, "Plato's repository of ideals is the poet's true goal." [20] And for Thompson, this meant nothing less than God, "where one centre reconciles all things."

Yet it is important to recognize that although Thompson saw certain parallels between the psychology of poets in their approach to reality and that of the prophets and mystics of religion, he did not confuse poetry either with prophecy or with mysticism. He rightly understood that poets, prophets, and mystics not only have different ends in view but must employ very different means to attain them. Moreover, their work and its worth must be examined and finally evaluated in the light of the standards that belong to their specific knowledge and special experience.

If a poet kept these careful distinctions in mind he might properly regard himself as no mere representative, returned by his age to speak for its majority, but rather, like the prophet, he might well be a teacher of advanced or unpopular ideas which only a few would accept or understand. There was, in effect, nothing democratic in Thompson's conception of the poet's function, and he expected that the great poet was more than likely to share with the great prophet the role of a proper target for the disapproving stones of the majority. Furthermore, we have seen that Thompson was inclined to accept the idea that poets are sometimes quite literally "inspired." Consequently, he did not hesitate to suggest that they might be given insights to see well beyond the age in which they lived.

Yet, unlike the prophet, the poet could never have the single-minded concern of one who concentrates upon the delivery of a message, which he regards as his chief consideration. Prophet and poet might share in the use of the great symbols of insight, but for the poet the demands of his art—rather than the requirements of any doctrine or message—must always govern their employment.

Like a mystic in one of the great religions of the world, a poet might, even in his role as an artist, seek a personal union with a personal God, but, as long as he desired to create true poetry, he must never so lose himself in the quest as to fail to devote himself to the demanding requirements of the objective works of art by which he states his experience.

Thompson appreciated the fact that prophets—like Isaias —and contemplatives—like St. John of the Cross—had created great verse. He spoke often of the power of the rhythms of the Bible and was aware that a passionate seeking after God had often produced a truly spontaneous poetry. But he also knew that in creating poetry as a conscious and self-directed activity, prophets and contemplatives must give themselves, like lesser men, to the severe demands of that high and difficult art.

There can be no doubt about the fact that Thompson thought of poetry as a valuable ally of religion, but he never wanted it to be a domestic servant of the Church. Poetry, he insisted, must remain "untroubled by the necessity of formulating a creed." It must be forever free to penetrate 'into the complexity of human sensation"; it must have the liberty to "describe with delicate accuracy, and under a veil of artistic beauty, the amazing, the unfamiliar, and even the portentous phenomena which it encounters." [21]

Poetry, then, must be thought of as casting light upon areas of experience that no materialistic theory and no scientific analysis can fully explain or explore. Indirectly, it may strengthen the claims of religion, but its aim is not didactic. It is important for a right understanding of Thompson's developed critical theory to have this point clearly in mind, for there are passages in his writing which might suggest the contrary, especially to any reader who shares Thompson's belief in the truth of Catholic doctrines.

A notable example of such a passage is a manuscript of a proposed lecture on poetry.[22] Here one finds Thompson saying that the first thing a poet has to do is to express his "vision of truth," in language which cleaves as closely to it as possible. He then goes on to say:

> The object of all poetry is truth; but the source of all poetry is love. We love before we know. John the Beloved outstripped Peter in the race to the sepulchre. Peter indeed entered first, because John awaited him, for if love show the way to knowledge it is knowledge which must attain truth. Yet I do not say that you are wrong in esteeming the manner of a . . . poet's saying. I say only that you should mind *first* the truth of it. If so you attend, there will emerge upon you a beauty which you would else have missed; the inward beauty of a true thing said with utter justness, not the obvious and outward beauty which takes the ear for its own sake; a beauty which follows the sense, not the beauty which goes before the sense. Beauty may be a trumpet, preparing the ways of Truth, or a handmaid by her side: but the trumpet may draw your attention not *to* Truth, but from her, the handmaid never. And this handmaiden beauty, believe me, is the higher beauty; and the more you grow to regard and love her, the nobler will be your understanding of all things beautiful, which are the most beautiful when they are in vital relation to truth. Otherwise, you are but sophisticated worldlings, who prefer the cut and sterile flower on their dinner-tables to the flower which is anchored fruitfully in its living and related field.

Elsewhere, too, Thompson says that poetry is "essentially dogmatic or rather prophetic—a teaching instrument . . . when it assumes its highest function of dealing with truth." [23] The question is: What is this "truth" with which poetry deals and how does it deal with it? Here the word *dogmatic* is especially dangerous, for Thompson was not using it in its technical, theological sense but in a more general and much less precise fashion. What he means is that poetry does not argue; it does not seek to persuade by the use of dialectics. It states what it states, as the ancient prophets did not argue, but proclaimed, "Thus saith the Lord."

The poet's "vision of truth" is his underlying theme; it is not equivalent to the ontological truth of philosophers. As Aristotle long ago made clear, the poet can deal in "probable impossibility," which, for him is always preferable to the "possible improbability." What he writes may not correspond to what actually is, for he may deal with what ought to be, or even with what can never be, except in the little world which the poet creates for us. What is required of the poet is an inner consistency, an interior probability of order, in the work he creates. He must be faithful to that in the development of his theme. In the last analysis, his poem will have an order which life itself never shows. This order, which is beauty, must, as Thompson says, follow the sense. The legitimate poem is indeed "a true thing"—an integrated whole—presented "with utter justness."

Under the influence of Coleridge, Thompson came to his understanding of the "truth" of poetry. It is, as Jacques Maritain says, a real kind of knowledge which a good poem presents to us, but this knowledge is "existential knowledge" or "knowledge-experience." [24] It has its intellectual aspects, for the poem is a center or organized significance, but it has an emotional side, which is vital to it. To use Thompson's own words, "the source of all poetry is love." The union between the poet and some aspect of experience which the poem represents is always an affective union.

It is especially significant that in the manuscript for the proposed lecture on poetry, Thompson concluded with the image of the flower that is anchored fruitfully in its living and related field. It took him some years to see the necessity for an organic relation between theme, or sense, and poetic beauty, or ordered form. But when he gained that apprehension, he held to it firmly in his critical discussions. The living poem must have the "truth," the organic integrity, of the living flower, which draws its life from nature and fully develops in all its parts and aspects the potentialities of the seed from which it began.

In the beginning, poetry for Thompson was little more than a world of delightful fancy. It was his escape as a child, and it continued to be so well into his early manhood. He fell in love with it for its sounds and its images, and he found it a world of order whose splendors carried him away from confusion and anxiety. In the teaching of Coleridge he discovered the difference between mere fancy and the might of the imagination to perceive the one in the many and the hidden similarity between apparently very different things. Under Patmore's guidance, this apprehension deepened and extended; it found its expression in a truly sacramental view of the world.

But even the poems of "Sight and Insight" were not the statement of a theological system. He responded to Augustine, not Aquinas, and he said:

> Your true poet dreads a system as the gates of Hades. A system is only for the philosopher, for a system implies analysis. . . . We do not say that a system should not underlie poetry, if it be philosophical; but the system should be suggested, not elaborated. It should be caught at the nodal points, the points of intersection, and indicated by pregnant, inclusive suggestion of those points.[25]

If divine truths were to be treated, they must be treated indirectly through the "handling of life." Thompson did not set about the task of being a "Catholic" poet. His poetry is pervaded by Catholicism because, as Patmore said of him, he was "of all men I have known most naturally a Catholic. My Catholicism was acquired, his inherent." [26] Like Hopkins, his religion illuminates and sustains the shape of much of his best verse, but it is not the primary cause of it.

Just as Thompson rejected the didactic motivation for poets quite as strongly as he rejected the aesthetic theories of the decadents, so he also had his doubts about much that passes for "the teaching of poetry." He objected to the very expression itself and commented caustically on "the quite modern belief that poetry can be taught":

> No previous age has conceived such an idea. It is a democratic mania of this democratic age, when the democracy demands to be "taught" everything—from science to pastel-painting, from philosophy to poetry—in a neat little series of handbooks. . . . We believe, with . . . almost every poet, that poetry cannot be taught.[27]

He was as contemptuous of attempts to teach English literature by studying the lives of authors, with lists of their works and dates, as he was of "the setting of crabbed passages from a writer, as a kind of mouse-traps, to see whether the scholar will find his way out."

He believed that a primary and necessary love for poetry must always precede its study, and one suspects that he would have had little sympathy for the extreme forms of the so-called New Criticism, with its immense emphasis upon analysis, for he remarked that the endeavor to "teach" poetry "by analysis" is a reversal of the natural order, in which the love of beauty and truth in their concrete expression should come first.

Most of the "canons of criticism," he noted, have been "spiked by poet after poet," since in actual poetic practice "the end—or at least the result, which is the same thing—does justify the means." To lead the young to believe in the fixed existence of such "canons" seemed to Thompson to be doing them, and poetry itself, a great deal of harm.

His own appreciative approach to poetry led him to suggest that a love for it could be developed—but only in those who already possessed "the seed"—better by the reading of "fine poets" and the study of concrete examples, than by "any textbook system." To this study might be added some "zestful comment," but for the beginner, at least, there ought to be a minimum of attention given to expositions of poetic "principles" in the abstract.

He offered no set definition of poetry and he never fully identified himself with any other poet's attempt to do so, but it is evident that if all he had to say on the subject is taken into consideration, it was Coleridge's extended definition in Chapter XIV of *Biographia Literaria* which most satisfied Thompson's own conception, as it had so great a part in forming it. There, it will be remembered, Coleridge said that poetry has "for its *immediate* object pleasure, not truth." Truth, in some sense, he recognized as a desirable ultimate end, but poetry must be distinguished from "works of science" of all kinds, and among those kinds of writing which aim at giving pleasure, it must be further distinguished by its aim of giving "such delight from the *whole,* as is compatible with a distinct gratification from each component part." For Thompson, too, no one could begin to understand the real essence of poetry until he had first learned to know and love the meaning of poetic "wholeness" and the delight which a poem in its unique completeness can supply.

If there is a true opposition and a clear distinction between the Romantic and the Classical conceptions of poetry—and Thompson had no doubt that there was—it is evident that he takes a stand with Coleridge and Shelley against the image of Pope as he conceived it:

> The form of classicism is form imposed from without,
> while true form is form evolved from within. . . . Great
> form unfolds like an organism, like a flower under the
> shaping of the inward spirit; the form of classicism is
> external and put upon it with a chisel so to speak.[28]

He did not agree with the idea of some modern Catholic critics
that the classical style—with its prudent cultivation of moder-
ation—is the "connatural expression" of the Christian spirit.[29]

Thompson's direct comments on religion are charged with
his Romanticism:

> Many think in the head; but it is the thinking in the
> heart that is most wanted. Theology and philosophy are
> the soul of truth; but they must be clothed with flesh,
> to create an organism which can come down and live
> among men. Therefore Christ became incarnate, to cre-
> ate Christianity. Be it spoken with reverence, a great
> poet, for example, who is likewise a great thinker, does
> for truth what Christ did for God, the Supreme Truth. . . .
> What of the man who—like the illustrious canon of
> Loreto—should be poet and saint? Ah, 'hard and rarest
> union' indeed! for he is a twofold incarnation of truth.
> He gives to it one body which has the life of man, an-
> other which has the life of humanity and the diuturnal
> hills.[30]

Did Thompson, in his avowed Romanticism, display less of
the Christian spirit than the Catholic Alexander Pope in his
Classicism? Quite the contrary is the case. Nor did Thompson's Romantic attitude lead him to think less of the structural
rigidity of the Church. In fact, his acceptance of Coleridge's
doctrine of organic form in literature gave him an even greater
appreciation of the Church as the Mystical Body of Christ:

> To avoid formalism by destroying form is to remedy
> carnality by committing suicide. You have the spirit
> freed from the letter then, with a vengeance; but the

spirit no longer quickens. . . . The Church is like man's body: which grows to completion altering or adding a little in superficialities and details of figure, but unchanging in line and structure. Each bone, muscle, nerve, and blood-vessel, though it have increase, is in form, position, and constitution immutable. And with the Church, also, which is Christ's body, you may add in nonessentials, you may develop in essentials; but you shall not alter in essentials by so much as a clause of its dogmatic theology.[31]

Most of what Thompson wrote about the nature of poetry and its relation to religion came after the process of his own poetic development was ended, after he had fought through the pain of his conflict between sense and spirit, after he had demonstrated his capacity for organic integrity in certain lasting examples of the perfect fusion of feeling and thought in poetic wholeness. His knowledge and his convictions were derived from many sources, but they were, in the final analysis, the products of an experience of religion and an achievement in poetry which more than earned him the right to be heard.

Thompson's attainments as a poet, a critic, and a human being were gained against the greatest of odds. How great those odds were to be he did not know until he was almost overwhelmed by them. He once compared life to a battle fought in a mist that mercifully hides from us the full extent of the conflict, "which, if we could behold it as it is, would wither away our souls." But, he said,

God . . . opens the eyes of a few who have passed through a special preparation of gradual inurement. And if He lets them behold the odds against them, He also opens their eyes, like the eyes of Elisha's servant, to the chariots of fire which fight on their side.[32]

Francis Thompson was one of those few.

SELECT BIBLIOGRAPHY

I. MANUSCRIPT SOURCES

The manuscripts consulted are in the Thompson-Patmore Collection of the library of Boston College, Chestnut Hill, Massachusetts. This is now the largest assemblage of primary sources for the study of Thompson, as the result of steady growth since its beginnings in the summer of 1937 under the direction of the Rev. Terence L. Connolly.

Over seventy notebooks were examined and the following separate manuscripts were studied:

A Critique of Coventry Patmore's Odes; "An Allegory of Poetic Composition" (verse); *Analogies Between God, Nature, Man, and the Poet; An Enemy Hath Done This; A Threnody of Birth; Essay-Theme, Comments on Titus Andronicus; Infera; Francis Thompson's Reaction to Lewis Hind's "Things Seen"; Internatural for Supernatural; Letter to Father Anselm; Man Proposes, Woman Disposes; Mystery, Mysticism and Allegory; Mysticism; On Obscure Books; Outline of a Projected Poem; Out of the House of Bondage; Rhythm and Metre;* "St. Anthony of Padua" (verse); "Sidereal Musings" (verse); *Simplicity; Symbolism;* "The Democratic Idea" (fragment); "The Trecentisti up to Date"; *Venus' Fly-Trap; Without a Parable Christ Spake Not.*

In addition, I have also been able to read the original draft of "Catholics in Darkest England" through the courtesy of the Very Rev. Kevin Harrison, O.F.M., Cap.

A complete survey of the places in which Thompson manuscripts, notebooks, drafts, and letters may be found is given by Pierre Danchin on pages 526 and 527 of his study *Francis Thompson, La Vie et L'Oeuvre D'Un Poète,* which is listed in Sections II and V. Professor Danchin's work, which has not yet been translated into English, is authoritative in its effective use of primary sources. As he indicates, many of the items which he was able to examine in the library of Wilfrid Meynell at Greatham and elsewhere are now in the Boston College Collection.

II. BIBLIOGRAPHIES

The books and articles listed in Section V are those which have had a particular interest or importance for this study. Fuller bibliographical information may be found by consulting the following:

Connolly, Terence L., *Poems of Francis Thompson*, N.Y. (D. Appleton-Century), 1941, pp. 561-573.

Literary Critisims by Francis Thompson, N.Y. (Dutton), 1948, Appendix: "An essay towards a bibliography of Francis Thompson's uncollected book reviews and literary criticism contributed to periodicals."

The Real Robert Louis Stevenson and Other Critical Essays by Francis Thompson, N.Y. (University Publishers), 1959, pp. 353-398.

Danchin, Pierre, *Francis Thompson, La Vie et L'Oeuvre D'Un Poète*, Paris (A. G. Nizet), 1959, pp. 525-544.

Faverty, Frederic E., ed., *The Victorian Poets, A Guide to Research*, Cambridge (Harvard University Press), 1956.

Pope, Myrtle P., "A Critical Bibliography of Works by and about Francis Thompson," *Bulletin of the New York Public Library*, Vol. 62, No. 11, Nov., 1958; Vol. 63, No. 1, Jan., 1959; Vol. 63, No. 3, Mar., 1959; Vol. 63, No. 4, Apr., 1959.

III. WORKS OF FRANCIS THOMPSON:

Poems, London (Elkin Mathews and John Lane), 1893.

Sister Songs: an Offering to Two Sisters, London (John Lane), 1895.

New Poems, London (Constable), 1897.

Health and Holiness: A Study of the Relations between Brother Ass, the Body, and his Rider, the Soul, London (Burns & Oates), 1908.

St. Ignatius Loyola, London (Burns & Oates), 1909.

Shelley: An Essay, With an introduction by George Wyndham, London (Burns & Oates), 1909.

A Renegade Poet and Other Essays, Boston (Bell Publishing Co.), 1910.

The Life and Labours of St. John Baptist de la Salle, London (Burns & Oates), 1911.

Selected Essays (in the series *Essays of Today and Yesterday*), London (Harrap), 1927.

Literary Criticisms by Francis Thompson, T. L. Connolly, ed., N.Y. (Dutton), 1948.

Minor Poets, Criticisms by Francis Thompson, newly discovered and collected by Terence L. Connolly, S.J., Los Angeles (Anderson & Ritchie), 1949.

The Man Has Wings, new poems and plays by Francis Thompson, edited with preface and notes by Terence L. Connolly, S.J., Garden City, N.Y. (Hanover House), 1957.

The Real Robert Louis Stevenson and Other Critical Essays by Francis Thompson, T. L. Connolly, ed., N.Y. (University Publishers), 1959.

IV. COLLECTIONS OF POETRY:

Selected Poems by Francis Thompson, Wilfrid Meynell, ed., London (Burns, Oates and Methuen), 1908.

The Works of Francis Thompson, Wilfrid Meynell, ed., 3 Vols., London (Burns, Oates), 1913. Volume three is prose.

The Poems of Francis Thompson, edited with notes by Terence L. Connolly, S.J., N.Y. (D. Appleton-Century), 1941. All quotations from the published poems in this study are taken from this edition, unless otherwise noted.

Poems of Francis Thompson: Collected Edition, London (Hollis & Carter), 1946.

V. BOOKS AND ARTICLES BEARING ON THOMPSON AND HIS WORK:

Abercrombie, Lascelles, "Francis Thompson," *The Circle*, XIX, 1930, pp. 5-7.

Alexander, Calvert, *The Catholic Literary Revival*, Milwaukee (Bruce), 1935.

Anon.: "Recent Poetry," *Edinburgh Review*, April, 1896, pp. 493-503.
"Some Minor Poets," *Quarterly Review*, July, 1897, pp. 347-49.
"Francis Thompson's Memory Vindicated," *Universe*, November 17, 1933.

Armstrong, Robert, "The Simplicity of Francis Thompson," *Poetry Review*, January-February, 1921, pp. 13-16.

Beacock, George A., *Francis Thompson. Versuch einer literarischen und metrischen Würdigung seiner poetischen Werke,* Marburg, 1912.

Blunt, Wilfrid S., *My Diaries,* being a personal narrative of events, 1888-1914, London (Martin Secker), 2 Vols., 1919-1920.

"Francis Thompson died at dawn ...", obituary article, *Academy,* November 23, 1907.

Burdett, Osbert, *The Beardsley Period,* London (Lane), 1925.

Bush, Douglas, *Mythology and the Romantic Tradition in English Poetry,* Cambridge (Harvard University Press), 1937.

Champneys, Basil, *Memoirs and Correspondence of Coventry Patmore,* London (Bell) 2 Vols., 1900.

Chesterton, Gilbert K., *The Victorian Age in Literature,* London (Williams & Northgate), 1913.

Cohen, J. M., "Francis Thompson, His Strange Life and Its Effect on His Poetry," *Month,* December, 1949, pp. 390-401.

Connolly, Terence L., *Francis Thompson, In His Paths,* Milwaukee (Bruce), 1944.

"In Defence of Francis Thompson," *America,* February 4, 1950, pp. 525-527.

Danchin, Pierre, *Francis Thompson, La Vie et L'Oeuvre D'Un Poète,* Paris (Nizet), 1959.

De La Gorce, Agnes, *Francis Thompson,* H. F. Kynaston-Snell, trans. from the French, London (Burns, Oates, & Washbourne), 1933.

Delattre, Floris, *De Byron à Francis Thompson, Essais de Littérature Anglaise,* Paris (Payot), 1913.

Figgis, Darrell, "The Poetry of Francis Thompson," *Contemporary Review,* October, 1913, pp. 487-95.

Garvin, Louis, "Living Writers: Francis Thompson," *Bookman,* March, 1897.

Gerrard, Thomas J., "Francis Thompson, Poet," *Catholic World,* February, 1908, pp. 613-28.

Haecker, Theodore, "Über Francis Thompson und Sprachkunst," *Hochland,* October and November, 1924, pp. 68-80; 206-15.

Hamilton, George R., "Wit and Beauty. A Study of Metaphysical Poetry," *London Mercury,* October, 1926, pp. 606-20.

Harrison, Austin, "The Poetry of Francis Thompson," *English Review,* August, 1923, pp. 103-16.

Hennessy, Doyle, "Did Francis Thompson Attempt Suicide?," *Catholic World,* February, 1950, pp. 346-50.

Hodgson, Geraldine E., *A Study in Illumination,* London (Heath-Cranton & Ouseley), 1914.

Hutton, John A., *Guidance from Francis Thompson in Matters of Faith,* London (Hodder & Stoughton), 1926.

Jackson, Holbrook, *The Eighteen Nineties,* a Review of Art and Ideas at the Close of the Nineteenth Century, London (Grant Richards), 1913.

Jarrett, Bede, "The Hound of Heaven as a Retreat Book," *Carmina,* March, 1931, pp. 105-14.

Johnston, Leslie, "Modern Mysticism: Some Prophets and Poets," *Quarterly Review,* January, 1914.

Kehoe, Monica G., *The Influence of Roman Catholicism on Francis Thompson's Poetry.* Ohio State University, Abstracts of Dissertations, No. 19, pp. 65-72, 1936.

Kenealy, Anselm, "Francis Thompson, the Man and His Poetry," *Capuchin Annual* (Dublin) 1933, pp. 39-59.

LeBuffe, Francis P., *The Hound of Heaven: An Interpretation,* N.Y. (Macmillan), 1921.

Le Galliene, Richard, *The Romantic Nineties,* London (Putnam), 1926.

Leslie, Shane, *Studies in Sublime Failures,* London (Benn), 1932.

Lewis, Charlton M., "The Poetry of Francis Thompson," *Yale Review,* October, 1914, pp. 99-114.

Mégroz, Rodolphe L., *Francis Thompson, the Poet of Earth in Heaven,* London (Faber), 1927.

Meynell, Alice, "Some Memories of Francis Thompson," *Dublin Review,* January, 1908, pp. 160-72.

Meynell, Everard, *The Life of Francis Thompson,* rev. ed., London (Burnes & Oates), 1926.

"The Notebooks of Francis Thompson," *Dublin Review,* January, 1917, pp. 109-22.

Meynell, Viola, *Alice Meynell, a Memoir,* London (Burns & Oates), 1929.

Francis Thompson and Wilfrid Meynell, London (Hollis & Carter), 1952.

Moore, Thomas V., "The Hound of Heaven," *Psychoanalytic Review,* October, 1918, pp. 345-63.

More, Paul E., "Francis Thompson," *Nation* (N.Y.), November 19, 1908.

Newman, John H., *Lectures on the Present Position of Catholics in England,* D. M. O'Connell, ed., N.Y. (America Press), 1942.

O'Brien, Joseph, "Francis Thompson, Poet and Mystic," *Catholic World,* August, 1914, pp. 600-8.

O'Donnell, John J., *A Study of the Prose Writings of Francis Thompson*, Dissertation, Catholic University, Washington, D.C., 1910.

Osmond, Percy H., *The Mystical Poets of the English Church*, London (SPCK), 1919.

Patmore, Coventry, "English Metrical Critics," *The North British Review*, August, 1857.

"Mr. Francis Thompson, a New Poet," *Fortnightly Review*, January, 1894, pp. 19-24.

Principle in Art, Religio Poetae, and Other Essays, London (Duckworth), 1913.

Quiller-Couch, Arthur T., "Mr. Thompson's *New Poems*," *Speaker*, May 29, 1897, pp. 602-3; June 5, 1897, 631-2.

Reid, J. C., *Francis Thompson, Man and Poet*, London (Routledge & Kegan Paul), 1959.

Rooker, Kingsley, *Francis Thompson*, London (Herbert & Daniel), 1913, a thesis presented to the Faculty of Letters of the University of Paris.

Shuster, George N., "Thoughts on Francis Thompson," *Commonweal*, February 12, 1937.

Symons, Arthur, "A Word on Francis Thompson," *Saturday Review*, November 23, 1907.

Dramatis Personae, London (Faber & Gwyer), 1925.

Tardivel, Fernande, "L'expérience poétique et l'expérience religieuse de Francis Thompson," *Revue Anglo-Américaine*, December, 1930, pp. 122-35.

Thomson, John, *Francis Thompson, the Preston-Born Poet*, London (Simpkin, Marshall), 1913.

Thomson, Paul van K., *A Study of Certain Notebooks and Manuscripts of Francis Thompson*, University Microfilms, Ann Arbor, Michigan, No. 19,546, 1957.

Turnell, G. M., "Francis Thompson, a Revaluation," *Catholic Herald*, February 7, 1936.

Tynan, Katherine, "Mr. Francis Thompson's Poems," *Bookman*, January, 1894.

"Francis Thompson's Place in Poetry," *Fortnightly Review*, February, 1910, pp. 349-60.

Weyand, Norman T., *Francis Thompson: His Theory of Poetry*, St. Louis University Dissertation, 1934.

Williamson, Claude, "Francis Thompson, a New Study," *Poetry Review*, May, June, September, 1935 and October, 1936.

Wright, Thomas H., *Francis Thompson and His Poetry*, London (Harrap), 1927.

NOTES

Key to Abbreviations:

E.M.: Everard Meynell, *The Life of Francis Thompson,* London, 1926.

L.C.: Terence L. Connolly, *Literary Criticisms by Francis Thompson,* N.Y., 1948.

P.: Volume III, *Prose* of *The Collected Works of Francis Thompson,* Wilfrid Meynell ed., London, 1913.

R.S.: Terence L. Connolly, *The Real Robert Louis Stevenson and Other Critical Essays by Francis Thompson,* N.Y., 1959.

V.M.: Viola Meynell, *Francis Thompson and Wilfrid Meynell,* London, 1952.

CHAPTER ONE

1. T. L. Connolly, *Francis Thompson, In His Paths,* Milwaukee, 1944, pp. 137-38.
2. L.C., p. 546.
3. In an article rejected by the *Tablet:* L.C., pp. 545 ff.
4. *Lectures on the Present Position of Catholics in England,* D. M. O'Connell, S.J., ed., N.Y., 1942, p. 142.
5. P., p. 66.
6. Ibid., pp. 1-37.
7. E.M., p. 17.
8. Notebook 34, p. 12.
9. Notebook of Early Poems, pp. 37-39.
10. Ibid., pp. 13-22.
11. T. V. Moore, *Personal Mental Hygiene,* N.Y., 1949, pp. 283-307.
12. L.C., pp. 297-298.
13. Notebook 34, p. 5.
14. "This Is My Beloved," *In His Paths,* p. 153.

CHAPTER TWO

1. T. L. Connolly, *The Poems of Francis Thompson,* N.Y., 1941, p. xviii.
2. Notebook 117, p. 10.

3. E.M., p. 232.
4. Large Commonplace Book, p. 37.
5. R.S., p. 110. As Thompson's uncle wrote to Wilfrid Meynell, "There was nothing in his home life to lead him to divulge himself, no encouragement and no sympathy with his ambitions." E.M., p. 46.
6. Notebook 14, p. 5.
7. Notebook 3, p. 4.
8. Notebook 35.
9. Ibid., p. 7.
10. P., p. 32.
11. Ibid., p. 35.
12. Ibid., p. 69.
13. E.M., p. 49.
14. J. C. Reid, *Francis Thompson, Man and Poet,* London, p. 49.
15. P., p. 254.
16. E.M., p. 214.
17. Reid, p. 46.
18. T. L. Connolly, *The Man Has Wings,* Garden City, N.Y., 1957, p. 82.
19. Cf. *Atalanta in Calydon,* "Invocation," ll. 42-43.
20. P., pp. 39-41. Parentheses my own.
21. V.M., p. 23.
22. L.C., pp. 448-49.
23. Reid, p. 48.
24. *Sister Songs,* I, ll. 290-98.
25. *Man Has Wings,* p. 143.
26. *Faerie Queene,* Bk. IV, Canto xii, ll. 23-41.
27. P., p. 62.
28. Ibid., pp. 52-53.

CHAPTER THREE

1. Maisie Ward, *The Wilfrid Wards and the Transition,* N.Y., 1934, p. 339.
2. J. J. Dwyer, "The Catholic Press," *The English Catholics, 1850-1950,* G. A. Beck, ed., London, 1950, pp. 475-514.
3. L.C., p. 546.
4. John J. O'Connor, *The Catholic Revival in England,* N.Y., 1942, pp. 73-74.
5. E.M., p. 77.
6. David Mathew, *Catholicism in England, 1535-1935,* London, 1936, pp. 224-25.
7. *Contemporary Review,* XXVIII (1871), pp. 334-50.
8. Holbrook Jackson, *The Eighteen Nineties,* London, 1913, p. 31.
9. *The Correspondence of Gerard Manly Hopkins,* C. C. Abott, ed., 3 Vols., Oxford, 1935-1938, Vol. I, p. 43.
10. Large Commonplace Book, p. 32.
11. Ms. *Rhythm and Metre.*
12. Ms. *Internatural for Supernatural.*

13. Notebook, B.C. 9, p. 13. See *Man Has Wings,* p. 94.
14. John A. Symonds, *Essays Speculative and Suggestive,* London, 1907, p. 336.
15. P., p. 4.
16. Ibid., p. 2.
17. V.M., p. 31. Thompson's manuscripts regularly show the use of *y* for the *th.* This Middle English spelling, which disappeared generally from printing after the sixteenth century, was part of his personal shorthand. Readers of Thompson's poetry are aware of his love of the archaic.
18. Notebook 117, p. 6.
19. P., p. 258.
20. Notebook B.C. 16, p. 15.
21. Ms. *Outline of a Proposed Poem.*
22. P., pp. 263-64.
23. Ms. *Analogies Between God, Nature, Man, and the Poet,* R.S., pp. 342 ff.
24. Large Commonplace Book, pp. 37 ff.
25. Notebook 14, p. 5.
26. "The Notebooks of Francis Thompson," *Dublin Review,* January, 1917, p. 109.
27. Large Commonplace Book, p. 31.
28. L.C., p. 450.
29. Ibid., p. 122.

CHAPTER FOUR

1. The passage is found in Frost's "The Figure a Poem Makes," and is quoted in Harlow O. Waite and Benjamin P. Atkinson, *Poetry from Literature of Our Times,* N.Y., 1958, p. 669.
2. *In His Paths,* p. 99.
3. Reid, pp. 82-83.
4. *Mysticism in English Literature,* Cambridge, 1927, p. 149.
5. *The Eighteen Nineties,* p. 166.
6. *The Beardsley Period,* London, 1925, p. 172.
7. *The Perennial Philosophy,* N.Y., 1945, pp. 96 ff.
8. L.C., p. 443.
9. F. Delattre, *De Byron à Francis Thompson,* Paris, 1913, p. 189. See also Agnes De La Gorce, *Francis Thompson,* London, 1933, pp. 179-80.
10. L.C., p. 33.
11. L.C., p. 330. He made this statement in a discussion of the so-called Irish literary revival.
12. *"Manus Animam Pinxit,"* ll. 3-4.
13. *"Scala Jacobi Portaque Eburnea,"* ll. 1-2.
14. See "A Carrier Song."
15. "Some Memories of Francis Thompson," *Dublin Review,* January, 1908.
16. "A Corymbus for Autumn," ll. 20-21; 68-69.

17. C. F. E. Spurgeon, *Mysticism in English Literature*, p. 31.
18. Basil Champneys, *Memoirs and Correspondence of Coventry Patmore*, 2 Vols., London, 1900, Vol. 2, pp. 84-5.
19. V.M., p. 107.
20. *In His Paths*, p. 96.
21. "The Notebooks of Francis Thompson," pp. 115-116.
22. Notebook B.C. 10, pp. 6-7.

CHAPTER FIVE

1. E.M., p. 106.
2. V.M., pp. 51-53.
3. T. L. Connolly, *Poems of Francis Thompson*, pp. 497-98.
4. *Principle in Art, Religio Poetae, and Other Essays*, London, 1913.
5. Ibid., p. 224.
6. *Academy*, November 24, 1900.
7. Notebook of Early Poems, pp. 86-8.
8. Notebook 24, p. 1.
9. E.M., p. 217.
10. R.S., p. 342.
11. P., p. 84.
12. R.S., p. 352.
13. *Principle in Art*, p. 301.
14. R.S., pp. 334 ff.
15. Notebook 33, pp. 9-10.
16. E.M., p. 133.
17. L.C., pp. 290-1.
18. Notebook B.C. 5, p. 14.
19. Notebook 32, p. 2 and Ms. *Essay-Theme on Titus Andronicus*.
20. L.C., p. 135.
21. P., p. 145.
22. L.C., p. 135.
23. "Penelope," ll. 13-14.
24. E.M., p. 173.
25. Ibid., p. 174.
26. Ms. *On Obscure Books*.

CHAPTER SIX

1. See 1913 edition of E.M., p. 177.
2. R.S., pp. 295-8.
3. "Any Saint," ll. 73-128.
4. William Y. Tindall, for example says: "The literary symbol, an analogue for something not stated, consists of an articulation of verbal elements that, going beyond reference and the limits of discourse, embodies and offers a complex of feeling and thought." *The Literary Symbol*, N.Y., 1955, p. 12.

5. L.C., pp. 328-9 and pp. 368-9.
6. See Helen F. Dunbar, *Symbolism in Medieval Thought,* New Haven, 1929.
7. Ms. *Symbolism.*
8. L.C., p. 21.
9. V.M., pp. 109-12.
10. Genesis 1:2-10.
11. Cf. "The Kingdom of God."
12. E.M., p. 180.
13. Ibid., p. 115.
14. Quoted in T. L. Connolly, *Poems of Francis Thompson,* p. 391.
15. E.M., p. 110.
16. R.S., pp. 126-31. *Academy,* October 3, 1903.
17. Reid, p. 116.
18. E.M., p. 178.
19. V.M., p. 114.
20. The manuscript is in the Boston College Collection.
21. *In His Paths,* p. 97.
22. V.M., pp. 118-19.
23. G. A. Beacock, *Francis Thompson,* Marburg, 1912, pp. 79-86.
24. P., pp. 184-5.
25. Notebook B.C. 14.
26. Notebooks B.C. 12 and 15.

CHAPTER SEVEN

1. E.M., p. 179.
2. "The Cloud's Swan-Song," ll. 17-20.
3. V.M., p. 116.
4. P. Danchin, *Francis Thompson, La Vie et L'Oeuvre D'Un Poète,* Paris, 1959, p. 111.
5. E.M., p. 247.
6. Danchin, p. 124.
7. Ibid., p. 118.
8. Reid, p. 160.
9. "A Prophet of Nietzsche," *Academy,* June 7, 1902, p. 572.
10. "Mr. Housman's Poems: *Spikenard, Devotional Love Poems,*" *Outlook,* February 26, 1898, pp. 245-6.
11. Notebook 23, pp. 1-4.
12. T. L. Connolly, *Minor Poets by Francis Thompson,* Los Angeles, 1949, p. 47.
13. "An Unreticent Poet," *Daily Chronicle,* November 8, 1901.
14. "Some Minor Verse," *Academy,* April 23, 1904, p. 452.
15. P., p. 186.
16. Ibid., p. 208.
17. *Academy,* June 17, 1905, p. 636.
18. *Merry England,* November, 1888, p. 2.

19. L.C., p. 314.
20. L.C., p. 515. Parentheses are my own.
21. *Academy,* June 17, 1905, p. 636.
22. P., pp. 226-7.
23. E.M., p. 126.
24. P., p. 229.
25. R. L. Mégroz, *Francis Thompson, the Poet of Earth in Heaven,* London, 1927, p. 39.
26. L.C., pp. 110 ff.
27. November, 1888, p. 107.
28. Mégroz, p. 43.
29. Reid, p. 181.
30. L.C., pp. 51-2.
31. "The Case Against Omar Khayyám," *Outlook,* April 30, 1898, pp. 405-6.
32. "The Real Stevenson," *Academy,* November 18, 1899.
33. *Academy,* June 25, 1904, pp. 680-1.
34. *Academy,* August 27, 1904, p. 143.
35. P., p. 197.
36. "The Preacher Poet," *Academy,* February 28, 1903, pp. 198-9. See also *Athenaeum,* April 7, 1906, p. 415.
37. *Minor Poets,* pp. 75 ff.
38. P., pp. 213-14.
39. Ibid., p. 204.
40. *Minor Poets,* p. 28.
41. L.C., p. 515.
42. "Mr. Henley's New Poems," *Weekly Register,* May 21, 1892, p. 664.
43. Cf. J. A. Symonds, *Shakespeare's Predecessors in the English Drama,* London, 1884, pp. 1-9.
44. "Some Excluded Poets," *Academy,* December 22, 1900, pp. 619-20.
45. *Academy,* May 26, 1900, p. 400.
46. V.M., p. 85.
47. Notebook B.C. 9.

CHAPTER EIGHT

1. V.M., p. 177.
2. P., p. 281.
3. V.M., p. 166.
4. Ms. "To the English Martyrs," at Ushaw College.
5. *Man Has Wings,* p. 101.
6. V.M., p. 179.
7. Danchin, p. 135.
8. Ms. *An Enemy Hath Done This,* R.S., pp. 299 ff.
9. V.M., p. 180.
10. "The Poppy," ll. 68-72.
11. Danchin, p. 146.
12. "Laus Amara Doloris," l. 90.

13. E.M., p. 41.
14. From "A Faithless Sword," *Man Has Wings*, pp. 57-58. The title is
    Fr. Connolly's and the word *recreant* in line 7 is bracketed to show
    that it is indistinct in the manuscript.
15. See reviews of Reid's book by Father Connolly in Boston *Pilot*, April
    23, 1960, and *America* of the same date.
16. Reid, p. 216.
17. "Francis Thompson's Centenary, the Fashionable Reaction," *Dublin
    Review*, Spring 1960, pp. 74-83.
18. V.M., p. 198.
19. Danchin, p. 511, n. 11.
20. "Francis Thompson: a Revaluation," *Catholic Herald*, February 7, 1936.
21. Ms. *Anima Simplicitas*, R.S., p. 314.
22. Danchin, p. 513.
23. A. C. Baugh, et al., *A Literary History of England*, N.Y., 1948, p. 1534.

CHAPTER NINE

1. Danchin, p. 145, n. 75.
2. E.M., p. 257.
3. Ibid., p. 258.
4. Ibid., pp. 81-5.
5. *Hamlet*, IV, 7. 1. 185, "Too much of water hast thou, poor Ophelia."
6. Notebook B.C. 10.
7. Large Commonplace Book, pp. 12-14.
8. Ibid., p. 5.
9. L.C., pp. 249-54.
10. See Mark Van Doren, *The Poetry of John Dryden*, Cambridge, 1931,
    pp. 275-77.
11. P., p. 220.
12. Notebook B.C. 8, pp. 2-4.
13. R.S., pp. 310-11.
14. Ibid., p. 312.
15. *Man Has Wings*, p. 117.
16. R.S., p. 328.
17. Ibid., p. 326.
18. Notebook 101, pp. 5-6.
19. Large Commonplace Book, p. 11.
20. Notebook 26, pp. 21-3.
21. Notebook 53, p. 4.
22. *Academy*, December 17, 1904, p. 614.
23. L.C., pp. 24-6.
24. *Academy*, June 9, 1900, pp. 485-6.
25. R.S., p. 139.
26. R.S., pp. 226-31.
27. P., p. 36.

28. R.S., p. 261, from a review of George Brandes' *Main Currents in Nineteenth Century Literature,* Vol. I, *The Emigrant Literature, Academy,* June 20, 1901.
29. R.S., pp. 268-9.
30. "The Dread of Height," ll. 92-3.

CHAPTER TEN

1. See Calvert Alexander, S.J., *The Catholic Literary Revival,* Milwaukee, 1935, pp. 150-74.
2. Danchin, p. 510, n. 3.
3. *Selected Essays,* N.Y., 1932, p. 8.
4. L.C., p. 282.
5. Notebook 26, p. 2.
6. R.S., pp. 316-17.
7. *Reactionary Essays on Poetry and Ideas,* N.Y., 1936, p. 112.
8. L.C., p. 157. For Hopkins' views on Browning see *Correspondence* I, p. 137; II, pp. 70; 74; 99.
9. Frederick B. Tolles, "The Praetorian Cohorts: A Study of the Language of Francis Thompson's Poetry," *English Studies,* XXII, 1940, pp. 49-64.
10. Notebook B.C. 11, pp. 3-4.
11. R.S., p. 234.
12. Notebook B.C. 10.
13. R.S., p. 236.
14. Notebook 101.
15. P., pp. 106-7.
16. John A. Symonds, *Essays Speculative and Suggestive,* London, 1907, p. 100.
17. L.C., p. 514.
18. *Principle in Art,* p. 23.
19. L.C., pp. 513-14.
20. R.S., p. 238.
21. Notebook 26, p. 2.
22. Danchin, p. 169, n. 42.
23. "Mr. Lysaght's Poems," *Academy,* June 1, 1901.
24. Jacques and Raissa Maritain, *The Situation of Poetry,* N.Y., 1955, pp. 66-8.
25. *Academy,* December 15, 1900.
26. V.M., p. 186.
27. See the review of Laurie Magnus' *Introduction to Poetry, Academy,* July 19, 1902 in R.S., pp. 278 ff.
28. Quoted by Danchin, p. 171, n. 70.
29. See, for example, Victor M. Hamm, *The Pattern of Criticism,* Milwaukee, 1951, p. 65.
30. P., p. 71.
31. Ibid., p. 75.
32. R.S., p. 299.

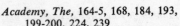

INDEX

CARMELITE MONASTERY
Beckley Hill
Barre, Vt., 05641

DATE BORROWED